THE DAPPER LITTLE BANKER

The Dapper Little Banker

PAUL BANGAY

First published in Great Britain in 2011
by Scotforth Books
www.scotforthbooks.com

Copyright © Paul Bangay 2011

The moral right of the author has been asserted

Printed in Great Britain by Page Bros

ISBN: 978-1-904244-70-7

CONTENTS

LIST OF CHARACTERS

Birnie, Sir Richard – chief Bow Street magistrate.

Brooke, Henry James – secretary to the London Life Assurance after July 1827.

Buchanan, James – His Majesty's Consul in New York.

Burton, Decimus – architect and designer of the extravagant Regent's Park Colosseum.

Burton, Septimus – lawyer who drew up the contracts for the Colosseum.

Cope, William – principal Marshall of the City of London.

Cox, Philip Zachariah – client of Remington's bank.

Croker, John William – secretary to the Admiralty.

Digby, Thomas – clerk at Remington's bank.

Down, Edward – independent stockbroker

Forward, Jonathan – wealthy transporter of convicts, owner of St Katherine's dock and father of Susannah.

Forward, Susannah – daughter of Jonathan Forward, married the cousin of Rowland Stephenson, the elder, to whom the great wealth was left.

Gates, Thomas – solicitor to the Committee of London Bankers.

Good, Christopher – a clerk who worked at the Argyle Rooms.

Goodhue, Jonathan – merchant of New York and agent for the London banks.

Grant, Thomas – collector for H.M. Customs, Bideford.

Grave, William – the coachman, employed by Joseph Hunton and then by Rowland Stephenson.

Greenwood, William – client of Remington's bank.

Hall, Edward – clerk at Remington's bank.

Hankey, William – stockbroker.

Hays, Jacob – high constable of New York.

Heathfield, Richard – Secretary of London Life Association from June 1821 until 11 July 1827.

Helps, Thomas – almoner at St. Bartholomew's hospital.

Hodgkinson, Thomas – almoner at St. Bartholomew's hospital.

Hornor, Thomas – graphic artist and entrepreneur, client and friend of Rowland Stephenson.

Knibbs, Joseph – independent stockbroker.

Lennox, William Pitt – writer who described Rowland as the *Dapper Little Banker.*

Lloyd, James Harman – Rowland's clerk and confidant at Remington's bank.

Mann, Abijar – duplicitous American financial advisor of Joseph Parkins.

Myers, John – sea captain and adventurer.

Murray, Adam – a surveyor ruined by the closure of Remington's bank.

Northesk, Lord – commander in chief of the navy, stationed in Plymouth. In charge of the search in the Atlantic.

Oates, William – deputy jailer of the city of Savannah and chief kidnapper.

Parkins, Joseph Wilfred – the unforgettable ex-sheriff of London.

Parris, Edmund T. – marine artist who created the London panorama from Thomas Hornor's many drawings.

Peel, Robert – home secretary.

Peto, Henry – the builder of the Regent's Park Colosseum.

Remington, David – partner at Remington's bank and son of William Remington.

Remington, William – senior partner in Remington's bank.

Reeve, Ellis – stockbroker at Ellis Reeve & Co.

Serres, Olive – friend of Joseph Parkins, claimed the title of Princess Olive of Cumberland and to be the illegitimate niece of George III.

Stafford, Admiral Robert – coordinator of the search in the English Channel, stationed on HMS Victory in Portsmouth Harbour.

Stanley, Joseph – clerk to Ellis Reeve & Co., stockbrokers.

Stephens, Catherine (Kitty) – soprano, much admired and wooed by Rowland Stephenson.

Stephens, John – the porter at Remington's bank.

Stephenson, Edward (1734–1813) – music loving father of Mary Eliza and partner at the Remington's bank.

Stephenson, Edward (1691–1768) – made a large fortune with the East India Company, the second great inheritance left to Rowland Stephenson, the elder.

Stephenson, Henry – junior partner in Remington's bank and Mary Eliza's younger brother.

Stephenson, John – father of Rowland Stephenson and partner in Remington's bank.

Stephenson, Mary (née Broadley) –mother of Rowland Stephenson.

Stephenson, Mary Eliza (née Stephenson) – cousin, wife and sister-in-law of Rowland Stephenson.

Stephenson, Mary Frances – cousin of Rowland Stephenson and younger sister of Mary Eliza who came to live with them at Marshalls.

Stephenson, Rowland (1782–1856) – the dapper little banker.

Stephenson, Rowland (*the elder*) (1727–1816) – grandfather of Mary Eliza, one time M.P. for Carlisle and the original Stephenson at Messrs Remington, Stephenson, Remington Toulmin and Co. (Remington's)

Stephenson, Rowland (1789–1843) – Mary Eliza's youngest brother who played no part in the story.

Stephenson, Rowland Macdonald – eldest son of Rowland Stephenson and gentleman clerk at Remington's.

Stephenson, William Walter – army officer and brother of Mary Eliza.

Strickland, Mary Cecilia – unhappy wife of Edward Stephenson and mother of Mary Eliza.

Tate, John – clerk at Remington's bank and also a partner at the stockbrokers, Messrs. Williams & Co.

Thornton, Henry – stockbroker and a partner in the brokers, Williams & Co.

Toulmin, Joseph Petty – partner of Remington's bank known for his regular habits.

Welch, Thomas – musician and manager of the Argyle rooms, Rowland's loyal friend.

White, Wright – skipper of the pilot boat Savannah.

Wilby, William – receiver of rents at St. Bartholomew's hospital.

Wilson, John – clerk at Remington's bank who was dispatched to America to help bring Stephenson back to face justice.

Wood, John – solicitor to St. Bartholomew's hospital.

Wright, Robert – client and friend, building contractor of Theobald's Road.

For Rowland Macdonald Stephenson
(1905–1993)

INTRODUCTION &
ACKNOWLEDGEMENTS

T HIS IS THE STORY of a London banker, Rowland Stephenson. The account of his extraordinary life has never been told. In the course of researching his life we have trawled through contemporary accounts of the time, newspapers of the early nineteenth century on both sides of the Atlantic and of course the records at the National Archive at Kew.

To tell this story I received so much help and support from a number of people. Cilla, my wife, spent hours finding, deciphering and transcribing the evidence, much of which is handwritten statements, lying undisturbed for nearly two hundred years. I am very grateful to our daughters, Willow, who also spent hours in the National Archives and it was her brainwave that discovered the boxes of evidence, and Miranda who trawled the newspapers in America; also to Paul Seed and Liz Cassidy who gave me great support and encouragement from start to finish. The writer and educator, John Lane, read the manuscript and gave invaluable guidance. I received expert advice from Alastair Cameron on banking practices and Christopher Elwins on nineteenth century law. Lastly many thanks to Dr. David Wallace of Maryland for all the information about Joseph Parkins and his meticulous proof reading.

Paul Bangay
2011

PROLOGUE

JUST BEFORE ONE O'CLOCK on 26 December 1828 a well-dressed middle aged gentleman walked into a pawnbroker's shop near St Paul's Cathedral in the City of London. He placed on the counter a large parcel which was addressed to a Mr. Robert Wright of Theobald's Road and asked if, for a consideration, it could be delivered to him as soon as possible. The gentleman then purchased a brace of flintlock pistols and requested the shopkeeper to load one of the weapons. He paid the pawnbroker and calmly retired to the back of the shop where he placed the muzzle of the loaded pistol against his right temple, fully cocked the hammer and pulled the trigger.

The gentleman was Rowland Stephenson. He was 46 years old and a well-known banker, a partner of Messrs. Remington, Stephenson, Remington, Toulmin & Co., a respected banking house of 69 Lombard Street in the City of London.

CHAPTER ONE

THE STEPHENSON FAMILY ROOTS

R OWLAND STEPHENSON WAS BORN at sea on 19 May 1782, aboard a ship that had sailed from New York and was bound for the Port of London. He was the second son and third child of the eight children of John and Mary Stephenson. John Stephenson was born in 1741 in Kendal, Westmorland, into a family of landowners whose previous generations had made their mark and fortunes in India, working for the East India Company. Mary was born in 1752 and was the daughter of James Broadley, captain of HMS Terror.

In 1771 John and Mary married and he became a successful merchant in London and Dover. John Stephenson was ambitious and wished to establish himself further by working overseas. Instead of following the family tradition by going to India, he decided to try his luck in the New World. On 14 March 1778 John Stephenson, at the age of 37, and his friend and fellow merchant, John Blackburn, submitted a proposal to the Lords Commissioners of His Majesty's Treasury for the lucrative appointment of supplying food to the ships of the British Navy in Mobile and Pensacola in the province of West Florida.

> The said John Stephenson and John Blackburn do propose to deliver or cause to be delivered at their own costs, charges and risqué as soon as possibly may be into stock houses provided at His Majesty's expense at Pensacola and Mobile in the province of West Florida such quantities of good wholesome and sound provisions as will be necessary to supply fifteen hundred men.[1]

The proposal was accepted and in May 1778 John and Mary set off to West Florida in the hope of making their fortune. Pensacola is a strategic port situated on Pensacola Bay that opens into the Gulf of Mexico. It has been known as the City of Five Flags since it has been ruled by five different nations, France, Spain, Great Britain, Spain again, the Confederate States of America and now the United States of America. It was unfortunate that John and Mary had only been there three years when the union jack was replaced by the Spanish flag.

As part of the Treaty of Paris in 1763, Spain had handed Pensacola over to the British. The town had not proved profitable for the Spanish and remained, while under their control, just a small frontier settlement. Under British rule, however, there was considerable investment in the town, which consequently enlarged and prospered. The most important industry of the town was the British naval dockyard. John Stephenson using his experience in commerce thrived and soon became a well-known citizen of the town, being elected a member of His Majesty's Council in 1779. Their first two children were born, Philadelphia and John Henry, and all was going very well until the American War of Independence intruded on their lives.

The war had started in 1778 and initially had brought the benefit of extra naval work to Pensacola. West Florida remained a long way from any hostilities but in 1781 Spain exploited the weakness of the British and invaded this territory and the Battle of Pensacola was the culmination in the repossession of the Floridas by the Spanish.

The Spanish Governor of Louisiana, Field Marshal Bernardo Galvez, invaded Santa Rosa Island to the south east of Pensacola on 7 March 1781. He had with him a force of 40 ships and 1,400 troops, including 700 French soldiers. He was well prepared and had previously campaigned successfully against the British at New Orleans, Natchez and Baton Rouge. Despite the arrival of a hurricane which forced his ships to put to sea again, Galvez was ready to attack the English forts on the mainland by 24 March.

First he had to find a way to sail his fleet through the narrow channel into Pensacola Bay under the British guns situated high up on the Red Cliffs, which dominated the entry into the bay. Galvez took command of a small ship, sailing it cautiously up the channel; it was not long before he realised that the gunners on the cliffs were unable to tip their canons low enough to hit ships sailing close to the shore beneath the cliffs. With little damage Galvez brought his fleet into Pensacola Bay and began his ground assault on Pensacola.

On 27 March John Stephenson in his capacity as Parliamentary counselor of the city was dispatched to the Spanish camp on behalf of Governor Chester to negotiate for the safety of the civilians in the city. Initial discussions were going well until three Spanish seamen arrived in the camp, recounting how they had escaped from the English who had mistreated them. Galvez was understandably most displeased and John Stephenson was dismissed back to the city.

Major General John Campbell, commander of the British troops and their allies, the Creek Indians, resisted as well as he could under such force but more Spanish reinforcements started arriving on 20 April and by 22 April the Spanish had an overwhelming strength of nearly 8,000 men. Don Galvez blockaded Pensacola and began bombarding the outskirts of the city. He dug a long trench forward so that he could safely bring up his 24 pounder cannons and 13 inch mortars, now close enough to be within range of the English forts. At 9.30 on the morning of 8 May Spanish artillery hit the Queen's Redoubt containing the British powder magazine, which exploded, killing over 100 men. The blast opened the outer defenses and by three in the afternoon the English had surrendered.

As a result of the negotiations that John Stephenson had already had with Don Galvez the British troops and civilians with all their families and possessions were allowed to leave unharmed. Don Galvez provided ships to take them to New York, even permitting the troops to take their personal weapons with them. The surrender of Pensacola was a turning point in the American War of Independence since it prevented English reinforcements coming up the Mississippi and East and West Florida soon fell to the Spanish. England relinquished all claims to the Floridas in return for possession of the Bahamas.

John Stephenson and his family were unharmed in the siege and battle and with the other civilians joined the troops in the ships taking them to New York for repatriation. The Stephenson family finally set sail to England on 18 April 1782 by which time Mary Stephenson was expecting her third child. The ship did not quite make it as far as the Port of London before Mary went into labour and Rowland Stephenson was born on 9 May 1782 as the ship passed through the Straits of Dover.

Rowland Stephenson's return to America, 46 years later, would be no less dramatic, pursued across land and sea by all the powers that the Home Secretary, Robert Peel, had at his disposal and £1000 reward for his capture.

CHAPTER TWO

THE STEPHENSON FAMILY'S TANGLED BRANCHES

O N 11 MAY 1782 John and Mary Stephenson with their now three children arrived back in England where George III was in the 33rd year of his 59 year reign. They returned to Kent where John intended to return to his previous occupation of merchant. However when his cousin, another Rowland Stephenson, invited him to join his bank at 69 Lombard Street, John readily agreed and the family moved to London.

This Rowland Stephenson who was the partner in the bank and who had invited his cousin, John, to join the bank, was born in 1727 and shall be referred to as 'the elder' to avoid confusion. 'Rowland' is a recurring name in the Stephenson family and there has been at least one Rowland in every generation of Stephenson since 1658, until the last Rowland was born in 1969. Rowland Stephenson, the elder, was the original Stephenson in the Lombard Street bank. He was a distinguished patron of the arts and a Member of Parliament for Carlisle from 1787 to 1790. He had recognised the qualities of his young cousin, John, and was keen to bring the younger man's trading and negotiating skills to the banking house. John Stephenson proved his worth and became a partner in the bank almost immediately in 1783. As he prospered he bought a large house at 41, Queen Square, Bloomsbury which was soon filled with his family that grew with the birth of six further children, making nine offspring in all.

Rowland Stephenson, the younger, who had been born at sea, was baptised at Saint Andrew's Church, Holborn on 2 August 1782. He was educated at home until the age of 13 when he was sent to Eton where he was a contemporary of George 'Beau' Brummell and William Lamb, 2nd Viscount Melbourne, now better known as the husband of Lady Caroline Lamb. Eton College at that time had two very different aspects to it. There was the easy going side: 'unhampered by the virtuous discipline of organized games, the boys spent their leisure time rabbit hunting, attending dog fights and getting tipsy on beer.'[2] The other side of the unreformed public school of the late eighteenth century had its drawbacks, fagging and floggings to name two while 'bloody duels of fisticuffs were the approved method of settling schoolboy quarrels.'[3]

Unscathed by his experience, Rowland left Eton in 1799 and he too joined the family bank in Lombard Street where he became a gentleman clerk with a view that he would eventually become a partner.

Living at 41, Queen Square it was inevitable that Rowland would have close contact with his cousin Mary Eliza Stephenson who lived at number 29, Queen Square. She was the daughter of Edward Stephenson who was the son of Rowland Stephenson, the elder. Edward was also a partner in the family bank and there was considerable wealth on this side of the Stephenson family because Mary Eliza's ancestors had been the beneficiary of two great fortunes.

The first fortune was passed down by an Edward Stephenson who was born in 1691 and had left England at the age of eighteen to work as a clerk for the East India Company in Calcutta. Four years later, in 1713, he was promoted to

Rowland Stephenson at Eton

sub-accountant of the Company and in 1714 he was made factor at the town of Hughli, a trading post further up the River. This gave him his first opportunity to embark on a little private enterprise, making deals with the locals and beginning to amass his fortune.

This fortune and the great fortunes of the East India Company were in no small part due to a trading agreement between the Company and the Moghal Empire. Edward Stephenson had helped to secure this agreement, or Firman as it was called, when he accompanied John Surman as his deputy to Delhi to negotiate this commercial treaty with the court of the Moghal, Farrukhsiyar. The long and hazardous journey as well as the long and protracted negotiations were rewarded by an agreement that exempted the East India Company from all duties and tariffs in Bengal. There followed a period of intense bloody rivalry amongst the local inhabitants, which saw the end of Farrukhsiyar, but the agreement held and the company thrived.

Edward Stephenson declared in a letter,

> It is my determined resolution not to interfere with the internal politics of this country, but to carry on the trade quietly, and only to defend the Company's estate.[4]

The obituary of Edward Stephenson described his time in India as being, 'during one of the darkest and most sanguinary periods of its domestic history, when the tyranny of the Seyds, those mighty Omrahs, dethroned and murdered five successive sovereigns of the imperial house of Timur.'[5]

In 1727 Edward Stephenson was appointed factor in Cassimbazar where it was alleged that he supplemented his fortune by extracting one hundred and seventy-five thousand rupees from local merchants during his three year tenure. In September 1728 the governorship of Bengal became vacant. Because of a delay in the arrival of John Deane, the next governor, and the statutory requirement for having a governor in post, on 17 September 1728 Edward Stephenson was appointed Governor of Bengal, but for only one day. When he returned to England in 1730, not only was he very rich but he carried the prestigious reputation of having been the Governor of Bengal, with no mention of for how long. He bought the house at 29, Queen Square and when he went to Cumberland looking for a suitable country estate in which to settle down, he made it known that he had £150,000 to spend, eventually buying Scalesby Castle.

This Edward had no children and died in 1768, aged 73. His estate of over £500,000, worth at least 32 million pounds today,[6] was passed to his brother, John. He was also an East India Company trader, but in the Levant and was

already a very rich man through the second great fortune to befall this side of the Stephenson family. Edward's brother, John, had married Susannah Forward who had been left by her father a vast fortune even more tainted than the first family fortune.

Susannah Forward was one of two daughters of a man named Jonathan Forward. He was a merchant in London with high connections. He dealt in tobacco, which he imported in his two ships from the New World colonies of Virginia and Maryland but it troubled him that his ships, the Jonathan and the Forward, were heavily laden coming back from America but empty going over. The answer came from his friend, the Solicitor General, Sir William Thomson, who was the instigator of the Transportation Act of 1718. Convicts could now be transported to the New World and the Treasury was more than happy to pay Jonathan Forward to carry convicts across the Atlantic in his two frigates.

On 8 August 1718 Forward was appointed to be the first 'Contractor for Transports to the Government', an indecently lucrative situation which he held for 20 years, transporting thousands of convicts to the southern states of America. He purchased St. Katherine's Dock, which he rebuilt to accommodate his expanding fleet.

The ordeal of transportation for the convict began on leaving the prison at Newgate and being marched in chains to a wharf on the Thames. Crowds gathered along the route and threw abuse and missiles. The passage itself was unbelievably cramped and unhealthy, carrying a mortality rate of at least fifteen per cent. Epidemic Typhus, known as jail fever, and smallpox were common causes of death, prompting Jonathan Forward to request a subsidy to cover the inevitable losses from 'death, sickness and injury'.[7] He was not only being paid to transport the convicts but also when they arrived in America he sold as many as he could. He already had connections to the slave trade in the New World and used his expertise to negotiate a price with the plantation owners which was between ten and fifteen pounds per convict. This suited the plantation owners who would have to pay on average £50 for an adult black slave.

The great fortunes of Edward Stephenson and Jonathan Forward were passed down to their cousin Rowland Stephenson, the elder, who in turn bequeathed the prosperity along with Scalesby Castle and 29, Queen Square to his son, the Edward Stephenson who was Mary Eliza's father.

Mary Eliza, by Thomas Horner

Rowland and Eliza Stephenson with their six children and Mary Eliza's sister, Mary Francis (far left)

This Edward Stephenson had married Mary Cecilia Strickland in Kendal on 27 February 1786 and they resided at the family house at 29, Queen Square. As their family enlarged they moved in with Edward's father, Rowland Stephenson, the elder who in 1790 had bought a large and elegant house called Farley Hill, near Swallowfield, in Berkshire which became their country estate while retaining their London house at Queen Square.

Farley Hill was described in the Times in 1790 when it came up for sale as a 'desirable freehold estate consisting of a spacious and elegant mansion ... a most beautiful and admired Situation, elevated, dry, and remarkably healthy'.[8]

The marriage of Edward and Mary Cecilia was not a happy one but did produce eight children. Mary Eliza was born in 1886 and christened at St. Mary's Church, Marylebone. In the family tradition of creating confusion with first names, all the daughters were called Mary, Mary Eliza, Mary Cecilia, Mary Frances and Mary Augusta who was the youngest child. The sons were called Edward Archibald, William Walter and Henry and of course yet another Rowland Stephenson, born 16 December 1789.

Edward Stephenson worked at the Lombard Street bank but his most abiding interest was music. He owned what the oboist William Thomas Parke described as 'perhaps the best and the most valuable collection of Cremona violins in any private collection in England',[9] including three Stradivari violins and the Stradivari Paganini viola. He also collected manuscripts of Handel's music. The marriage of Edward and Mary Cecilia came to an end in 1808. Before they were married, his future mother-in-law, Cecilia Strickland, commented in a letter to her brother, Charles Townley, 'Edward is an exceedingly good musician and delights in how little Mary Cecilia knows about music.'[10]

That delight did not last very long. In a memorandum dated 8 August 1800 Edward Stephenson wrote of his wife, 'Mrs. Stephenson's intractable disposition and ungovernable temper, her disobedient and undutiful conduct to her husband, for several years past, has render'd my home uncomfortable and my mind unquiet.' [11]

They did separate shortly afterwards but reunited after a few months only to part permanently in 1808. After protracted, unpleasant and costly negotiations Edward Stephenson grudgingly agreed to pay a settlement of £1000 per year. On the 12 June 1809 Mary Cecelia was denied access to 29, Queen Square and fled to Paris where she died in 1817.

Rowland Stephenson, the younger, and his future wife, Mary Eliza, did share a common interest in music and when Mary Eliza was twenty-one they were married on 23 April 1807. The marriage was a very happy one and he provided for her lavishly. The young couple moved into a wing of Farley Hill and their first child was a boy, born in 1809 and named of course Rowland Stephenson but with the addition of the middle name of Macdonald. 'Rowland Macdonald Stephenson' became the name of the eldest son of the family in the next four generations. The 'Macdonald' came from a friend of the family, Lord Macdonald who was a very fine musician. His godson, Charles Edward Horn, in his memoirs, recalls how Lord Macdonald fought at the battle of Waterloo with 'a quartetto of Mozart in his greatcoat pocket'.[12] 'His love of music was such that he had a servant at all his campaigns to take care of the music and instruments that he might practice in camp'.[13] On one occasion when Charles Horn visited his godfather for a musical evening, Lord Macdonald was unable to find the bow of his Stradivari violin. After much searching it was discovered in a kitchen drawer with the knives and forks. His excuse was 'this always happens when the children are home from school'.[14]

Rowland and Mary Eliza went on to have seven children, six boys and a girl, Emma Louise, born in 1820. Mary Eliza was never strong and the rapid succession of pregnancies was to take its toll on her health.

Rowland had worked very hard over the years since entering the bank and in 1816 bought the estate of Marshalls near Romford in Essex. The house was situated on the northeastern side of Romford, close to the road to Southend.

A full and lavish description of the elegance of the house was published in the Times when it was sold in 1829 but Nikolaus Pevsner had little to say about the house except 'Stuccoed Georgian five-bay front and earlier gabled back parts'.[15]

To get some idea of the life at Marshalls and the personal and professional life of Rowland Stephenson there is a long account written by William Pitt Lennox in his book *Fifty Years of Biographical Reminiscences*, published in 1863. He was an army officer who became aide-de-camp to the Duke of Wellington and was present at the Battle of Waterloo. After leaving the army he mixed in the society of writers, musicians and sportsmen. He wrote novels, which were described by a critic as 'feeble'[16] but did enjoy some brief success.

Here is his ornate description of weekend life at Marshalls,

At this period of my life I became acquainted with a celebrated man of his time, Rowland Stephenson. He was a banker in Lombard Street, held a high reputation in the city of London, was extremely attentive to business and from all that was known of him stood very conspicuously forth as a hard working, moral and religious character. He had a remarkably pretty villa near Romford, Marshalls, where from Saturday afternoon until Monday morning he was in the habit of entertaining his friends. Being passionately fond of music his parties were occasionally enlivened by the presence of the fascinating Misses Foote and Stevens. Stephenson's wife was an invalid, but she was always present to do honour to her guests.

On Saturday evening about 5 o'clock, for the early closing hours of Saturday had not then been introduced, Mr. Stephenson's neat, plain yellow travelling chariot was at the door of the bank and the head of the firm having given his instructions took his departure for his country residence. Often upon such occasions I attended him and was struck at the extreme method of punctuality with which his affairs were conducted, whether financial or social. As I had been brought up in the school of punctuality – the army – I was always ready at my post 10 minutes before the appointed time with my small portmanteau. This seemed to delight my host, who upon my arrival in Lombard Street always dispatched a messenger to apologise for his not being able to receive me as he was prevented by unforeseen business and to say that there was a biscuit and a glass of sherry in the dining room.

Precisely as the clock struck five the dapper little banker would make his appearance, shake me by the hand and conduct me to the carriage. He bowed consequentially to the head clerk, gave him some parting instructions and off we started through the eastern most part of the city to Romford.

With Rowland Stephenson everything seemed to be regulated by machinery and to go by clockwork. The carriage started at the moment, the post boy never varied two minutes in the journey; the turnpike gatekeeper seemed

Marshalls in its heyday, drawing by A. B. Bamford, 1899

to be looking out for the toll. The keeper at the small lodge was in readiness and threw open the iron gates to us. Mrs. Stephenson was watching our arrival from her sofa in the library and the old butler as he passed the handsome Louise XV ormolu clock in the hall looked up to it in as much as to say 'master and you keep pretty good time, I could set you any day by his movements.

Upon arriving for the first time I was shown over the villa and a more comfortable residence could not be imagined .... An officer or two from the cavalry barracks at Romford generally formed part of the eight which Stephenson never exceeded, although a friend or two might drop in during the course of the evening to listen to the siren of the day or take part in a quiet rubber of whist – long game six penny points and a shilling on the rubber'.[17]

This extract gives one an idea of Rowland Stephenson's disciplined professional life, as well as a description of a pleasant weekend at Marshalls. He also points out that Mary Eliza was an invalid, the exact cause of which is unknown. A family portrait painted in about 1820 shows not only his children and Mary Eliza, clearly pregnant, but there is also a young lady to the left of the picture who was probably Mary Eliza's sister, Mary Frances, who had come with them from Farley Hill to help look after the enlarging family and the running of the house.

Rowland did not associate with the local gentry but was said to have frequent visitors from London. Most of his close friends were actors and musicians.

Mary Eliza was also an accomplished singer and became a private scholar of Sir George Smart who visited Marshalls and often seen sharing Rowland's pew in church. Smart had risen from being a choirboy at the Chapel Royal to become one of the most influential musicians in England. To be a pupil of his was no small privilege.

Mary Eliza who had been well liked in the area as a 'liberal and generous benefactress',[18] died at Marshalls on 21 October 1821 at the age of thirty-five. Rowland was left with seven children of whom the oldest, Rowland Macdonald, was now thirteen and the youngest, Emma Louise was just over a year. Rowland Macdonald was sent to school at Harrow and Rowland's sister-in-law, Mary Frances, remained with the family to care for the younger children.

The year after Mary Eliza died, Rowland's father, John Stephenson, also died at the age of 81 and Rowland became a full partner and the 'Stephenson' in the Lombard Street Bank, Messrs. Remington, Stephenson, Remington, Toulmin and Co., commonly known as Remington's.

CHAPTER THREE

STEPHENSON FOREVER

B Y 1816, FIVE YEARS before the death of his beloved wife, Rowland was well established in the bank, owned a true Gentleman's residence at Marshalls and enjoyed a flourishing family and social life. Now he felt it was time to enter public life and stand for Parliament.

The original banker, Rowland Stephenson, the elder, had been elected M.P. for Carlisle in 1786. He remained a Member of Parliament for three years but his contribution was unremarkable. His involvement in public life is summarised, 'Rowland Stephenson: never spoke in the House and only voted once, in opposition to the Regency in 1788'.[19]

The first attempt by Rowland Stephenson, the younger, to enter parliament was in Hull in 1816 but his ambitions were thwarted by lack of money. In the same year he tried to stand for the old family seat in Carlisle but withdrew before the election.

After this disappointing start Rowland let things be for a while but the death of his wife in 1821 and that of his father in 1822 brought about a change of circumstances. He was now ready to try again particularly since his financial circumstances had radically improved. He certainly spent a large amount of money, first in February 1822, unsuccessfully opposing the re-election of Henry Goulburn at West Looe, then in March 1823, attempting to replace Jonathan Raine for the borough of Newport, again in Cornwall.

Neither of these elections were examples of great British democracy. The election in West Looe, held on 13 February 1822, was won by Henry Goulbourn after many of the votes cast for Rowland Stephenson were disallowed. The second election was at Newport, near Launceston and was a notorious rotten borough. In 1823 the sitting member was Jonathan Raine who was the candidate for The Duke of Northumberland. The Duke was known locally, not out of any great fondness, as 'Uncle Hugh'. Many of the electorate were dependent upon him not only for their livelihoods but also for their homes, from which they could be evicted at any time. The description of the Newport election in the Royal Cornwall Gazette deserves reprinting in full:

Newport election Friday March 23rd 1823

Jonathan Raine Esq., was the late member of this Borough and the utmost secrecy was observed with regard to the new election until the arrival of Mr. William Wilson, the Duke of Northumberland's agent on the preceding Sunday night with the writ appointing the election to take place on Friday. Early on Monday morning Mr. Raine also arrived and immediately began a canvas on the Duke's interest. Many of the electors thus taken by surprise promised their votes believing that no other candidate would offer.

About 2 o'clock Rowland Stephenson Esq., a gentleman of amiable and unassuming manners, appeared and declared himself a candidate. He was warmly received on his canvas by all electors who had not promised their votes and the general wish appeared to be for his success. All was now hustle, anxiety and expectation until the day of election. When Mr. Stephenson and his friends, preceded by music and banners, approached the hustings he was greeted with loud acclamations by the multitude and the waving of handkerchiefs etc. from the windows of the adjoining houses, which were crowded with females. The agents and friends of Mr. Raine approached in silence, that gentleman having left the town on closing his canvas.

John Roe Esq., in a short speech then proposed Mr. Raine as a fit and proper person to represent the ancient Borough of Newport in Parliament and he hoped the electors would express their approbation of his former conduct by supporting him on this occasion with their votes and interest – this nomination was seconded by Mr. George Pierce.

T.J. Phillips Esq., an elector, desired Mr. Raine's qualification to be produced which not being complied with asked the electorate if after the non-production of the qualifications and Mr. Raine's not appearing to be sworn they would permit him to be put in nomination.– Raine was however nominated on which Mr. Phillips said he did most certainly consider that Mr. Raine was not at all qualified to represent them. Where was Mr. Raine? Why did he not appear himself before them to state his claims and produce his qualification, or have sent home one to do it for him?

Perhaps by and by they should be called upon to elect the stick which he held in his hand to represent them, which they might do with as much propriety as to elect a person who was not present, who had not produced qualifications and of whom they knew nothing, but that they had before elected him through the influence of the Duke of Northumberland.

He would nominate a gentleman much better qualified to represent them, one he hoped who would meet with the support of every friend to independence and he had great pleasure in proposing to them Rowland Stephenson Esq., to be their representative – (here the air was rent with acclamations of STEPHENSON FOREVER) a gentleman he felt confident who would, when he came amongst them, prove himself to be the friend of the rich and father to the poor. He called upon the electors to assert their right and maintain their independence by giving their suffrages to Mr. Stephenson. (LOUD APPLAUSE).

Thomas Pierce Esq., solicitor of Launceston warmly seconded the nomination.[20]

At this point Rowland gave his nomination speech reproduced in full in the West Britain newspaper,

Worthy and Independent Electors of the Borough of Newport.

Having, on the invitation of several of your respectable body, been persuaded to offer myself as a CANDIDATE for the honour of Representing your Ancient Borough in Parliament, on the vacancy occasioned by the elevation of your late respectable Member, Mr. Raine; it becomes now, no less my duty than my inclination, to return you my most sincere thanks for the very flattering reception I have experience on my Canvas; a circumstance, which while it will determine me to persevere to the utmost in maintaining your rights, will afford you the opportunity of asserting your independence, and of demonstrating to our opponents, the impossibility of their successfully resisting the exertion of men, determined to be Free!!

I am aware, that on occasions like the present, it is customary for the Candidate to repeat his Political Creed, and to make many professions; but, Gentlemen, to you whose Ears have been so often entertained with promises, ('made but to the Ear, and broken to the Heart') and so woefully disappointed, by the non-performance of them, I have only to beg, that, on this point, I may be permitted to trespass on your patience, and my future conduct shall testify my sense of the honour you have offered on me.

You will ever find me a steady friend to the true principles of our Glorious Constitution, ever ready to uphold the Throne, and to advocate the Rights and Liberties of my fellow Countrymen.

I have the honour to be,
Gentlemen
Your obliged and faithful humble servant,
Rowland Stephenson.[21]

The Cornwall Gazette continued,

His qualifications produced and the show of hands appearing to be in his favour
a poll was demanded by the opposite party. The electorate then adjourned to
the White Horse. None but electors were first admitted into the room, until
the interference of Mr. Wilde procured the admission of the public.

On our admission we found one of the Duke's voters unwilling to digest
the bribery oath, but on being satisfied he had only to swear that he had not
taken any bribe to vote on this election he complied. The number of votes
was so nearly equal that until the state of the poll was actually declared it was
doubtful which of the candidates would be returned. At length, however, the
numbers were announced when they appeared to be for Mr. Raine 40, Mr.
Stephenson 36. Mr. Raine was therefore declared duly elected.

Mr. Stephenson was certainly the popular candidate having by the urbanity
of his manners and gentlemanly conduct won the hearts and good wishes of the
Borough and run the Northumberland interest so hard on a short canvas of only
three days and after the canvas of his opponent had been finished. After the election Mr. Raine's party dined at the White Horse, Newport and Northumberland
Arms, St. Stephens. Mr. Stephenson's friends dined with him on Saturday at
the Kings Arms, Launceston, to which place they walked in procession from
Newport and 60 sat down to a sumptuous entertainment provided with every
delicacy of the season by the excellent arrangement of Mr. Smith.

Mr. Stephenson presided at table and was particularly attentive to the
comfort of his guests. On his health being given he returned thanks in a neat
speech, which the great length of our own assize news would not permit us
to give. In the evening there was a dance with refreshments for the ladies at
half past eleven the company retired highly delighted with the attention and
hospitality of their entertainer.'

This election, in a rotten borough and in a far corner of England, did attract
some comment in the London newspapers. The Times of 26 March 1823 saw
the election as less of a circus and more of a demonstration of the influence of
aristocracy, adding that 10 of Rowland Stephenson's votes had been disallowed
by the returning officer who just happened to be the agent and solicitor for the
Duke of Northumberland. John Bull of 31 March 1823 stated that Rowland
Stephenson never had a chance of winning the seat because of the influence of
the Duke of Northumberland. 'Of one thing we can assure Mr. Stephenson,
that whoever made him believe that he has a chance of ever sitting for the
borough of Newport was just humbugging him'.[22]

Alfred Farthing Robbins, journalist and author, was a native of Launceston.
In his book 'Launceston, Past and Present' he compared the 1823 election

with that held at Eatanswill in Charles Dickens' The Pickwick Papers where there was 'a picture of bribery, treating, and general corruption which characterized contests in the very small and often venal boroughs'.[23] He added in his book that his father, Richard Robbins, as a small boy, had taken part in the procession to welcome Rowland Stephenson to the borough of Newport. His father remembered how they greeted the candidate with 'bands, banners and beer, in accordance with the fashion of the time, which dictated also the scattering of red-hot coins from a frying pan among the crowd waiting outside the hotel at which the candidate and his friends were dining freely'.[24]

Rowland may have lost this election but he had shown himself to be popular with the electorate and to have plenty of resources to spend freely on entertaining. What he required now was a borough without the overbearing influence of someone like Duke of Northumberland.

There was one compensation for Rowland Stephenson in Cornwall. In expectation of winning the seat of Newport he had purchased the manor house at St. Stephens near Launceston. After his defeat he sold the property to his adversary, the Duke of Northumberland, 'for a tidy profit'.[25]

In May 1823 he cast his eye on the Borough of Bossiney covering the area around the town of Tintagel but when Rowland Stephenson withdrew the Times pointed out that 'it is generally understood that matters are too snugly managed there to admit any chance of success'.[26]

Rowland had to wait until 1826 when the seat at Leominster came available. The election was held on 16 June and he appeared as candidate for Lord Holtham. The result was as follows:

Rowland Stephenson 254 votes, Thomas Bish 445 votes.

All was not lost as Rowland Stephenson contended that Mr. Bish was a lottery contractor to the Treasury and therefore ineligible to stand. The case of 'double return' duly came up to a select committee in the House of Commons in February 1827 and the committee declared that Thomas Bish was not duly declared and that Rowland Stephenson Esq. be elected.

It is unclear quite why Rowland wished to be an MP since he never spoke or voted in Parliament and there is no evidence that he did anything for the well being of the people of Leominster.

An acquaintance asked him why he had stood for Parliament since he was 'no orator and cared little for politics'.[27] Rowland readily agreed but said he wished to take advantage of the free postal service available to Members of Parliament.

That acquaintance was a man named Joseph Wilfred Parkins.

CHAPTER FOUR

HIGH LIFE & HANGINGS

ROWLAND STEPHENSON CONTINUED TO busy himself at the bank as he built up a reputation for being a man about town and someone of increasing influence and resource.

In January 1823 the Treasurer of St Bartholomew's Hospital, Thomas Courtney Warner, died. The appointment of Treasurer was very attractive to Rowland since the post included the use of a house attached to the hospital and this was just a short walk to Lombard Street. Rowland already had contacts at the hospital because Remington's was their bankers. He immediately donated some money to the hospital and put his name forward for the post of successor to Thomas Warner. The proposal was accepted and he was elected Treasurer of the hospital on 26 November and the Treasurer's House became his opulent London residence.

The ever affable Rowland was popular with the hospital governors and set about the task of Treasurer with his usual enthusiasm. In his first year he collaborated with the architect Thomas Hardwick to rebuild the interior of the small church of Saint Bartholomew the Less, which is situated just inside the main gate of the hospital, known as the Henry VIII gate. Rowland was re-elected Treasurer on 28 July 1824, 27 July 1825 and 25 July 1827 'with the warm thanks of the Governors'.[28] The last reference to Rowland in the St. Bartholomew's archives is less warm, '29th December 1828. The office of Treasurer to St Bartholomew's Hospital is vacant in consequence of the sudden absence of the treasurer and the extraordinary circumstances attending the same'.[29]

For now however he could spend the weekdays in London at the Treasurer's House and the weekends with his family and friends at Marshalls. He was well known in theatrical circles and had permanent boxes at the Theatre Royal, Drury Lane and at the Theatre Royal, Covent Garden. Many actors were not just his friends but were also only too pleased to use the banking house of Remington's where Rowland Stephenson was offering better interest than most other banks.

Rowland's greatest love was music and he frequented all the concert halls of London. He particularly liked the Argyle Rooms in Regent Street, which were owned and managed by his good friend, the well known musician and impresario Thomas Welch. It was here after his wife's death that he met a young singer by the name of Kitty Stephens. The Argyle Rooms had a chequered history. They were situated at the corner of Oxford Street and Argyll Street and had been converted from a private house to a concert hall at the end of the eighteenth century. The old concert hall was demolished in 1818 and rebuilt, using a lavish design by John Nash. Applications were invited to take up the lease and Thomas Welch and William Hawes gathered together a consortium of twenty-one music lovers to apply for a crown lease of the property. When this was granted the syndicate formed itself into a society with the purpose of entertaining the public and the hope of making money.

The Argyle rooms were opened on 28 February 1820. On the ground floor there was a shop, Welch and Hawes, selling original music and on the upper storey there was an eight hundred seat concert hall for music and entertainments, such as grand balls and masquerades.

Thomas Welch engaged famous musicians and singers from all over the world; Mendelssohn, Weber and Liszt, then aged twelve, performed to the packed auditorium. Despite entertaining the public lavishly the rooms failed to make any money. Thomas Welch and William Hawes had been the prime movers and when all the other members withdrew, an agreement was drawn up between these two men; the contract gave Welch a bigger share of the proceeds at three-fifths to Hawes two-fifths. The rooms were mortgaged for £7,000 and the partnership commenced in 1824. Mr. Welch promptly went to Italy for a long holiday and by the end of 1825 there was a growing hostility between the two partners. In 1826 open warfare was being waged and Hawes wished to withdraw from the contract. He decided the only way out was to declare himself bankrupt in the hope that, by doing so, Welch would release him from the contract. Instead Welch took Hawes to court but lost the case. The damages would have ruined him if it were not for the unstinting support of his banker and friend, Rowland Stephenson. Thomas Welch did not forget the favour that he owed his banker friend nor did he fail him when the time came.

The young singer who had particularly caught Rowland's eye at the Argyle Rooms, Catherine, known as Kitty, Stephens, was 29 years old when she met Rowland who was then 41. She was a 'highly-gifted vocalist'[30] who had been a pupil and protégé of Gesualdo Lanza, a greatly respected singing master. In 1812 she came under the influence of Thomas Welch who launched her singing career in Manchester. She was described as 'being of medium height with a figure more pleasing than excellent, dark hair and eyes and a fascinating countenance but not strictly speaking handsome'.[31] She was said to have the sweetest soprano voice of the time both in opera and as a concert singer; she also had a reputation 'as unblemished as the new fallen snow'.[32]

Like Mary Eliza she caught the musical eye of Sir George Smart who advanced her interests and in 1821 took her to Brighton to perform in front of George IV. Perhaps the king was discouraged by her purity since George Smart later noted, 'her voice did not please the King'.[33]

However her voice certainly did please Rowland Stephenson and he became an ardent admirer and soon proposed marriage to her. Encouraged by her reputation for innocence and hearing rumours of an engagement, the Edinburgh Advertiser announced in February 1824 'Miss Kitty Stephens is to be led to the hymeneal altar at the close of the present season by Mr. Rowland Stephenson, the banker'.[34]

Kitty Stephens had in fact declined the offer and the newspaper printed a retraction the following week: 'The paragraph stating that Miss Kitty Stephens is shortly to be married to Mr. Rowland Stephenson is without foundation'.[35] This was hidden at the bottom of the page and swiftly followed by the announcement: 'No less than 17 people have died of the smallpox in Trowbridge, Wilts'.[36]

Kitty Stephens later said that she had declined Rowland for three reasons; firstly the disparity of their ages, secondly the large family Rowland Stephenson by his first wife and thirdly her great attachment to her father, her sisters and her brother.[37] Rowland and Kitty remained good friends and Kitty regularly sang at the concert parties at Marshalls. She was a valued client of the bank since she was very wealthy in her own right; on a single singing tour of Ireland she earned £5,000.

Rowland may have failed to win the chaste heart of Kitty Stephens but he continued to enjoy life and spent much of the 1820s living and spending lavishly. Marshalls was full of beautiful objet d'art, the paintings of famous artists lined his residence at St Bartholomew's and his lifestyle generally reflected that of a city banker, a country gentleman and a Member of Parliament.

To complete his acceptance as the man about town he was invited to become a member of the Beef Steak Club. This exclusive gentleman's club was founded in 1709 and was also known as 'The Sublime Society of Beefsteaks'.

The members never exceeded twenty-four in number and met every Saturday night at the Theatre Royal, Covent Garden to eat beefsteaks and drink port wine. The members of the Club were strongly Whig and proud to call themselves, 'The Steaks'. Over the years members included William Hogarth, David Garrick, John Wilkes and many others, described as, 'Chief Wits and Great Men of the Nation'.[38] In 1785 the Prince of Wales was invited to join, as were two of his brothers.

The members of the club were very pleased to have a banker like Rowland Stephenson join their ranks. In the book, 'The Clubs of London', published in 1826, he was described as 'the most respectable of bankers. Never did a clearer head, and a better heart meet together; nor does the heart wait, as it does, in ordinary cases, a cold and calculating lesson from the head; but the most spontaneous and generous impulses of the one, are ratified by the cool decisions of the other. 'Never,' as Hamlet says, 'were the blood and judgment so well commingled'.[39]

Rowland Stephenson also continued to invest in property. He already owned the large estate of Marshalls in Romford and the family spent holidays in a house in Clarence Place, Dover that had been left to him by his father. He was insatiable in his desire to acquire property. In Romford he bought five dwellings called Brook Cottages along with twenty acres. Not far from Marshalls, opposite the workhouse in Collier Row Lane, he bought a row of twelve cottages and at the entrance of the town of Romford he acquired two 'genteel residences' called The Gothic Lodge and a house called Watkins. At the top of town he bought the Romford windmill, which ground the local grain and in the parish of Dagenham he owned the Manor of Cockermouth, which was a right to rents and royalties rather than a baronial pile.

In Harold Wood he bought Harold Wood Farm with 52 acres, near Epsom he bought a house called Pitt Place and in South Weald he purchased a house called Howe Hatch. He acquired twenty-four houses in total and the tenants provided a steady income. He could also raise money on the deeds of his houses, many of which became heavily mortgaged.

Before 1828, apart from his standing for Parliament, the life of Rowland Stephenson was relatively private. His name was rarely seen in the newspapers unless associated with his charitable work on behalf of the bank. He was however a witness in a case of fraud at the Old Bailey on 1 April 1818 that was widely reported in the newspapers. This was the case of Joseph Davey who was indicted 'that he, on the 5th March 1818, at St Mary Woolnorth, feloniously did falsely make, forge, and counterfeit a certain order for the payment of money ... with intent to defraud Edward Stephenson, John Stephenson, William Remington, Rowland Stephenson, David Robert Remington, and Joseph Petit Toulmin, partners of the said Bank'.[40]

Joseph Davey was aged 32 and on 5 March 1818 at half past four in the afternoon he entered the bank and presented a cheque for £124 10s. to be cashed. The cheque appeared to be signed by a Mr. James Fairlie but the pay clerk on the desk, Edward Hall, became suspicious and asked Davey from where he had acquired the cheque. Davey replied that Messrs. Smith and Co, who were distillers at Bow in East London, had given it to him. Hall thought the signature was forged and asked Davey to wait while he consulted one of the partners.

Davey was either brazen, naïve or desperate but wait he did and one of the partners, Joseph Toulmin, came out of his office and asked Davey for the name of the person for whom he was cashing the cheque. Davy again said Smith and Co. but Mr. Toulmin thought this was unlikely since their cheques usually came directly to the bank. Davey then embellished his story by saying that someone called Mr. Thompson, who was a clerk at Smiths', gave him the cheque. He had been drinking in the Bird in Hand public house in Bow when he met Mr. Thompson who, hearing that Davey was coming to the City, asked him to cash the cheque and he would give him five pounds for his trouble. Joseph Toulmin thought this was highly improbable and summoned the bank's burly porter, John Stephens, to take Davey to find Mr. Thompson whom Davey said was waiting in the pub for the money.

When they arrived outside the Bird in Hand public house Davey changed his mind and said it was the Kings Arms across the road. John Stephens took Davey into the Kings Arms to find Mr. Thompson whom Davey described as 'tall and wearing a brown coat and a black waistcoat'. Unable to find him Stephens asked the landlord if he had seen Davey or the mysterious man with the black waistcoat.

'No I haven't', was the reply.

John Stephens brought Davey back to the banking house where he searched the unfortunate man and found a genuine bill written by Mr. Fairlie with his signature at the bottom, which Davey had clearly tried to copy. Rowland Stephenson was summoned and asked Davey if he had received the cheque from Mr. Fairlie.

'No.'

'Did you find it?'

'No'

'Did you write on it?'

'No'

Davey broke down and said that he was in a very distressed state and had written it all himself.

When asked by the judge what he had to say in his defense William Davey said 'I leave my case to my counsel.'

What his counsel said is not recorded but it had little effect and Davey was found guilty and sentenced to death. He was hanged ten days later.

At that time retribution for forgery was certainly harsh and not reserved for the poor and desperate.

In 1824 a partner in another well respected banking house in the City was accused of forgery and his trial took place at the Old Bailey on 30 October 1824. Henry Fauntleroy was a partner in his father's firm, Marsh, Stracey, Fauntleroy and Graham, situated in Berners Street, Westminster.

In many ways his professional life paralleled Rowland's. He was taken on as a clerk in 1800 and became a partner in 1807. He was the most active partner in the firm taking over the day-to-day management of the bank. It was alleged at his trial that his lavish lifestyle could not be supported by his income and around 1814 he began forging the signatures on securities belonging to his customers. On 10 September 1824 Henry Fauntleroy, aged thirty-nine, was arrested when it had been discovered that stock valued at £10,000 had been sold, the co-trustees signatures having been forged. He was eventually accused of forging securities to the value of £170,000. He admitted his guilt but said he had used the money to pay the debts of the firm.

Seventeen gentlemen of the highest respectability were called to his trial, and they all attested their opinion of his 'honour, integrity and goodness of disposition'.[41] The jury however took 20 minutes to return a verdict of guilty of the crime of uttering (passing a document known to be forged to the detriment of another) and he was sentenced to death and was executed on the 30 November at Newgate in front of a crowd estimated to be close to 100,000.

Executions for forgery were coming to an end but before the Home Secretary, Robert Peel, changed the law there was one more case that ended in the death sentence.

Joseph Hunton, a Quaker, had started business as a slop seller in Yarmouth and having prospered he came to London where he became a partner with Dickson and Co., a firm of warehousemen. Unfortunately he began to trade on the stock market, 'particularly unsuccessfully'.[42]

In 1828 bills of exchange in the name of Edward Wilkins of Abingdon had been circulated by the firm of Dickson and Co. and when it emerged that Edward Wilkins had been dead for some years, Joseph Hunton absconded. He was traced to Plymouth and Mr. Forrester, a City of London constable, was dispatched in pursuit. When the constable arrived in Plymouth he discovered that a man fitting Hunton's description, now calling himself Wilkinson and dressed in Quaker clothes, had boarded a ship which was about to depart for New York. The intrepid Forrester rowed out to the ship and surprised Hunton who was by now relaxing in the saloon, wearing a 'light green frock, a pair of light grey pantaloons, black stockings and a foraging cap'.

At the Old Bailey sessions on 28 October 1828 Hunton was found guilty on a charge of forging a bill for £162 9s 11d and sentenced to death. The sentence was delayed but took place nonetheless on 8 December 1828.

Joseph Hunton's coachman was a man called William Grave. He had driven the coach that had taken his master to Plymouth and having lost his employment went looking for work in the City of London. He was eventually taken on at St. Bartholomew's Hospital to look after the horses and to be the coachman for the Treasurer, Rowland Stephenson.

Chapter Five

... A Stately
Pleasure-Dome Decree

M ORE PEOPLE TODAY WILL have heard of the fictional pleasure dome built by Kubla Khan than will have heard of the London Colosseum but for nearly fifty years this enormous building stood in Regents Park. Modelled on the Pantheon in Rome, it was described by the Times as 'without hyperbole, a wonder of the modern world'[43] while others looked upon it as a vulgar white elephant.

The driving force behind the building of the Colosseum was a graphic artist by the name of Thomas Hornor, supported financially by Rowland Stephenson. Hornor was a superb draughtsman, blessed with artistic talent, vision and showmanship but he lacked judgement and restraint and this would eventually be his downfall. He was born in 1785 in Kingston upon Hull into a family of Quakers. At the age of 22 he came to London and rapidly gained a reputation not only for his building designs but also for the unusual presentation of his work.

His first commission, in 1808, was to produce a complete survey of the parish of Clerkenwell which he completed in less than eight months. The plans were outstanding, not just the content, but also the techniques used to delineate the area. The map was 42 square feet in area with intricate detail.

Because of this and other impressive work his reputation grew and he was given commissions all over London. He created elaborate designs of buildings for valuation, and elaborate drawings for decoration. His technique was to use his artistic talent to enhance a perfect facsimile that he could create by using a camera lucida. The camera lucida is a simple device enabling the artist to see the image of the subject, be it person or landscape, projected onto his canvas by the use of prisms. He can then draw a precise outline. The result, in the hands of Thomas Hornor, was an exact and pleasing reproduction.

In late 1817 he advertised himself in Wales as a 'pictorial delineator' and received various commissions, which he carried out over the next two years. Financially secure he returned to London in the spring of 1820 and decided to indulge his desire to record the complete 360 degree sky-line of London as seen from the top of St Paul's Cathedral.

He began by drawing from the highest windows of the dome but, by chance, in 1821 the authorities of the Cathedral had decided to replace the ball and cross which are positioned on the very top of the dome. The scaffolding required for this would give Hornor a unique opportunity to create an even better record of London. The work on the dome was organised by the Surveyor of St Paul's, Charles Robert Cockerell, who was very obliging. The scaffolding was erected all the way up to the pinnacle and a small cabin winched up and precariously attached. From it Hornor would have uninterrupted views of London for 30 or 40 miles.

Throughout the summer of 1821, Thomas Hornor worked on his project. In the very early hours of the morning, he would climb the six hundred and sixteen steps to the dome and then by various unsteady scaffolding ladders reach his eyrie. By first light of dawn he was ready to start work. His objective was to produce a record of London that could only be seen at dawn, before all the domestic fires were lit causing such dense pollution that the view was obliterated for the rest of the day. With the aid of his camera lucida and powerful telescopes he made detailed sketches of every landmark, house, barn and bridge from just below St Paul's to as far as his eye could see. The summer of 1821 was unfortunately not a good one with high winds and heavy rain that battered the small cabin. 'The creaking and whistling of the timbers of the observatory cabin resembled those of a ship labouring in a storm with Hornor's situation not unlike that of a mariner at the masthead'.[44] The tenacious Hornor continued to sketch despite his cabin occasionally shaking loose. His sketches covered seventeen hundred square feet of drawing paper, all meticulously labeled so that they could be put together again at ground level. By 1822 the task was complete.

Thomas Hornor then set about turning this astonishing undertaking into some sort of remuneration. His plan was to create lithographs and produce highly detailed drawings of sections of London as never seen before. To pay for their production he sought commissions for line drawings that would cost £5 and coloured drawings which would cost £10. The plan did not however succeed. Not only was the demand for the drawings less than expected but there were also production difficulties, which postponed their appearance, and in the end none were ever made.

The problem now was that the impulsive showman in Hornor came to the fore. He had the idea of creating from his drawings a huge circular panorama

Regents Park Colosseum

and opening this to the paying public. This could have been a simple enough plan but the idea soon got out of control. He sought financial backing from Rowland Stephenson who had engaged Hornor to undertake a pictorial survey of Marshalls in 1818 and they had become close friends. On behalf of the bank, Rowland would guarantee an initial £20,000. In 1824 John Nash, the personal architect to the King, was designing buildings along Regent Street and was developing Regent's Park. Thomas Hornor acquired land on a 99 year lease on which to build his dream.

In 1824 John Nash recommended to Thomas Hornor a young architect named Decimus Burton to design a building which could accommodate his panorama of London. Decimus, the tenth child of the architect James Burton, was only aged 24 and favoured the classical style. He went on to acquire fame designing buildings all over central London and the south coast. He liked to design buildings on a large scale and this building was his first major project, and it turned out to be his largest. He planned the structure to be, in size, second only to St Paul's Cathedral and it might have been even bigger had John Nash not reined in his ambitions but even so the dome alone was going to be 115 feet high.

A builder from Cobham in Surrey was contracted to do the construction work. He was Henry Peto and had been involved in large projects before. He might not have been chosen had they known that recently he had been accused of using very poor building standards by cutting corners and failing to build proper foundations after the roof of the Long Room in the centre of the new Custom House in the City of London fell in.

Not only was the extravagance of the building a key to the downfall of Rowland Stephenson but so was the financial arrangements made to pay for it. On 1 February 1824, Septimus Burton, Decimus' older brother, drew up a contract between Thomas Hornor and Henry Peto who was to construct the building that was described in the contract as 'a certain brick tenement intended for the exhibition of a Panorama painting, together also with two lodges'.[45] The agreement stated that 'the payment to the said Henry Peto for the several works to be performed by him should be made at the expiration of three years from the completion of the roofs, gutters, skylights, drains and watercourses and interval stages and galleries together with interest thereon at five per cent per annum from the completion of such works'.[46]

Henry Peto did not waste time and the outside of the building was completed in September 1825. Repayment was therefore due by Thomas Hornor on 29 September 1828. The agreement also stated that if Thomas Hornor should default on the payment then his banker, Rowland Stephenson would be liable.

The construction of the building may have been progressing well but by 1825 Thomas Hornor was becoming desperate; the task of turning his drawings into a panorama was far greater than he imagined. He therefore elicited the help of a marine artist by the name of Edmund T. Parris. At that moment Parris should have been employed restoring some paintings on the ceiling of the dome of St Paul's but lack of funds had cancelled the project. Parris was particularly well suited to the Colosseum project since not only was he an excellent artist but he had also studied mechanics and had invented an apparatus to ascend into the dome of St Paul's; this would be perfect for the work in the dome of the Colosseum. Parris then began the mammoth task. There were hundreds of numbered flat sheets of drawing paper, covered in Hornor's sketches and each had to be transferred on to 42,000 square feet of curved canvas. This was due for completion by 1827 but the work was laborious and far from finished by the end of 1828. The area to paint was not only massive but the curve of the walls of the Colosseum had to be taken into consideration on the canvas and straight lines had to be slightly bowed, adding to the Herculean task. Some said it was impossible but Thomas Hornor wrote a letter to the press on 23 September 1828 disputing all the rumours and confirming that the building would soon be opened.[47]

In September 1828 Henry Peto had fulfilled his side of the bargain so the payment was coming due. The building costs had risen to £27,000 and Thomas Hornor had applied to Henry Peto to have the time for payment extended. It had therefore been agreed that installments could be paid and Rowland Stephenson would stand surety against this increasing debt. Rowland had pushed the solvency of the bank to the limits and this was to be one venture too many but Thomas Hornor still wanted more; he wanted to create the most fashionable building in London and no expense was to be spared to do this. There were to be conservatories, grottos and a Swiss cottage, cascades, waterfalls and exotic plants, new mechanical contraptions and recently invented musical instruments.

> That with music loud and long,
> I would build that dome in air,
> That sunny dome! Those caves of ice!
> And all who heard should see them there,
> And all should cry, Beware! Beware!
> His flashing eyes, his floating hair!
> Weave a circle round him thrice,
> And close your eyes with holy dread,
> For he on honeydew hath fed,
> And drunk the milk of Paradise.

Kubla Khan
Samuel Taylor Coleridge

CHAPTER SIX

THEN WE SHALL BOTH GO

A man who mixed very much in a gay life and cut a splendid figure at the west end of the town. His expenses were, it is declared, much increased by his patronage of theatrical, operatic and scenic matters of other kinds, and he embarked largely in the mining speculations, at the destructive period of the bubbles.[48]

TOWARDS THE END OF 1828 financial problems within and beyond Rowland's control were increasing. He was by now the most active and the most popular of the partners at the bank. His enthusiasm for the arts was matched by his great enthusiasm with which he juggled his client's money around the markets, using bills of exchange, accommodation notes, promissory notes, and exchequer bills.

In simplest terms a bill of exchange was a written order binding a debtor to pay a creditor who had lent him money a fixed sum without interest on a predetermined day or on demand. They could be transferred from one creditor to another by changing the names so that the debt could be sold and passed on to a third party to collect.

An accommodation note or bill was the same but was used by a guarantor to oblige a friend with a loan but no goods or money actually changed hands. It was used as a proof of a potential loan and might give someone who was short of money a security with which to barter. The guarantor remained liable until the bill was paid. The bill was negotiable for cash and may, like the bill of exchange, change hands several times before it was finally paid.

A promissory note, otherwise known as a note of hand, was a written promise to pay a specified amount on demand, or at a set future date. This was more robust than a simple I.O.U. which is just an acknowledgement of a debt. A very important feature of a promissory note was that if the date when payment was due was allowed to pass, without it being renewed, the note became valueless. Money may or may not have changed hands at the time the note was written.

Large quantities of money could always be borrowed on the security of an exchequer bill. These featured in the shadier dealings of Rowland Stephenson. Exchequer bills are interest bearing promissory notes generated by the British government. They were introduced into this country in 1696 as a form of public borrowing, issued from the Exchequer by authority of Parliament. They could be used as security or accepted in payment. Stockbrokers bought and sold the bills which could be redeemed at the Bank of England. To obtain the interest on the exchequer bill it had to be presented to the Bank of England annually on specific days and for this reason they were usually kept at a bank where they could be stored safely. The duty of obtaining the interest would be undertaken by the bank staff. The bills were numbered and marked on the back with the name of the holder. The name may change but the number remained the same and the exchequer bills were therefore traceable.

All these bits of paper featured highly in the investigations of Rowland's financial dealings that followed the events of the end of 1828.

So as 1828 drew to a close Rowland Stephenson had been living very much beyond his means for some years and now even greater demands were looming on the precarious financial state of the bank as well as his own resources.

The Colosseum, inspired by Thomas Hornor, was costing far more money than expected and payment to the builder, Henry Peto, had come due in November 1828. Not only was Thomas Hornor unable to repay Henry Peto but the likely final cost had nearly doubled. Rowland Stephenson had gone out on a limb to guarantee this money on behalf of Remington's bank and the funds were going to be severely stretched to cover it. Despite this, just before Christmas 1828 Rowland Stephenson had a meeting with Thomas Hornor and the lawyer, Septimus Burton and had agreed to guarantee a further £20,000 to finish vital work before the Colosseum could open. Septimus drew up another agreement between Hornor and Stephenson to cover this extra expenditure.

To add to the problems the banking house of Remington's earlier in the year had been rumoured to be in some financial difficulties. As a result of this some of the best accounts including the Canterbury Bank, the Winchester Bank and the Ashford Bank had decided to take their business elsewhere. By December 1828 the Committee of City of London Bankers was so concerned about the solvency of Remington's that they decided to examine the financial status of the banking house themselves. On Monday, 22 December 1828 five eminent bankers, partners in well-known banks of the City, spent the morning at the bank inspecting the books and assets.

Having interviewed the partners and clerks, and examined all the books, not only did they declare the bank solvent and above reproach, but also, to demonstrate how confident they were, they each deposited £20,000 of their own money into the bank. This might have seemed foolish under the circumstance but they did receive in return promissory notes to the value of over £40,000 each, double the amount they had invested.

The dramatic events before and after Boxing Day 1828 can be pieced together from the extensive and well documented evidence given under oath to the Commission for Bankruptcy during 1829 by those people who were involved with the bank and with Rowland Stephenson. The Commission at the Court of Bankruptcy began taking evidence on Friday 2 January 1829. The Commissioners were Sir G. F. Hampton, John Turner, H. G. Shepherd and J. B. Macauley. They sat at the Court in Basinghall Street and at the Guildhall. Each interview was documented fully in long hand and is stored at the National Archives at Kew along with lists of creditors and personal claims against the bank itself and the partners personally.

To clarify the other large debts incurred by Rowland Stephenson and the bank, the Commission of Bankruptcy summoned Joseph Stanley to give evidence. He was the clerk to Ellis Reeve & Co., stockbrokers, and he described another pressing matter for Rowland Stephenson that had come to light on Wednesday, 17 December 1828. He testified that a meeting took place at the Treasurer's House at St Bartholomew's Hospital at 8 o'clock on the morning of that Wednesday. Present at the meeting were Rowland Stephenson, his clerk, James Harman Lloyd, his son, Rowland Macdonald Stephenson and a broker named Charles Nicholas. The subject of the meeting was a loan of £60,000, owed by Rowland Stephenson to Ellis Reeves, on the security of £60,000 worth of exchequer bills. Mr. Reeves wanted this loan paid off immediately. Rowland Stephenson appeared unaffected by this demand and said '*Very well*'. He proposed that his clerk, James Lloyd, would bring £60,000 around to Mr. Reeves at 11 o'clock the same day. Lloyd duly arrived at 11 but only brought £10,000 and in return received £10,000 of exchequer bills. Somehow money was found every day for the next five working days and the full value of the loan was paid off but Rowland became even more desperate to raise additional funds to keep himself and the bank afloat. He spent most of Sunday 21 December at the bank. He had a meeting with Mr. Edward Down, a freelance stockbroker and Mr. Henry

Thornton, a partner in the stockbrokers, Williams & Co. A transaction was planned for the Monday morning to raise £30,000 in exchange for the security of exchequer bills to bolster the finances of Remington's.

To make matters worse another large bill required immediate payment. When Robert Wright gave evidence to the Commission on 3 January 1829 he described his dealings with Rowland Stephenson and all the events over the Christmas of 1828. He told the court that he was a builder of Theobald's Road, London and had known Rowland Stephenson for twenty years. In that time he had done building work and acted as agent for him, subcontracting work for which he would settle the account and then be reimbursed by Rowland Stephenson. 'If I wanted money, I might say I wanted so much, he might say "Very well" and I had it.'

The court asked Wright if he had had any conversation with Rowland Stephenson between 8 December and 20 December 1828. He replied, 'Yes. There was a large bill that had become due from Mr. Mitchell for work, which I had done in the building of a house near Pinner, which Mr. Stephenson said he could not renew. It was for £2,900 and upwards'.

Wright said Rowland told him he was unable to pay at that time due to a 'the scarcity of money'.

Q   Did you before the 20th December know or suspect that Mr. Stephenson was in any difficulty?
A   I had not the least idea.

Robert Wright said they agreed to meet again and their paths next crossed at breakfast time on Wednesday, 24 December at the Treasurer's House. Mr. Wright said this was not unusual as he had the habit of dropping in to see Rowland Stephenson and join him for breakfast at the hospital when he needed to discuss business. On this particular morning he again asked Rowland for money; £300 was requested but Stephenson could not give him any. Wright said he would call again the following week to which Rowland Stephenson made his usual enigmatic reply, 'Very well'. Robert Wright then told the court that the next time he saw Rowland Stephenson was on Friday, 26 December.

The movements of Rowland Stephenson on Boxing Day 1828 were described in evidence by his partners in the bank, by the artist, Thomas Hornor, by the musician, Thomas Welch, the builder, Robert Wright and by some of their employees.

Rowland Stephenson must have walked to the bank on the morning of Friday 26 December 1828 with a heavy heart. What exactly was in his mind will never be known. Had he decided to take his life or had he made plans to make a spectacular escape?

By 9 o'clock all the senior partners were present at the bank, William Remington and his son David, Mr. Joseph Toulmin and of course Rowland Stephenson. At 11 o'clock they gathered for a meeting that became very acrimonious. William Remington and Joseph Toulmin were becoming increasingly unhappy about the banking practices that Rowland Stephenson was undertaking in the name of their bank and David Remington was particularly unhappy about the involvement of the bank in the financing of the Colosseum. This venture had cost a huge amount of money and was soon to open unfinished, even with the extra money that Rowland had now promised to Thomas Hornor. All the partners considered the Colosseum to be a financial liability they could ill afford at this difficult time and feared losing all their investment and perhaps more. The meeting came to an abrupt end with Rowland leaving on bad terms with his partners. Around midday he walked out of the banking house for the last time, carrying a large brown paper parcel under his arm.

Rowland walked along Lombard Street towards the Bank of England where he turned left along the Poultry and Cheapside towards St Paul's, turning left again into Queen Street. There he walked into the pawnbroker's shop where he arranged for the delivery of the parcel and purchased the two pistols.

Placing one of the pistols to his right temple and pulling the trigger did not have the expected fatal outcome. It certainly gave the pawnbroker and his staff a shock but there was merely a blinding flash. This was a flash in the pan since the gunpowder in the barrel had failed to ignite. Rowland Stephenson emerged uninjured from the back of the shop and calmly walked out into the street where he climbed into a coach which immediately drove west towards St Paul's.

His survival from the pistol shot was considered by most people as not so much good fortune but more likely to have been the good sense of the shopkeeper who had the foresight not to give this distraught man a fully loaded firearm. Survive he did and spent the rest of the day trying to sort out his convoluted financial dealings.

The coach was taking him towards the house of the lawyer Septimus Burton but first he summoned a messenger and instructed him to go to Burton's house at York Terrace, Marylebone and tell him he wished to see him and Thomas Hornor as soon as possible.

Mr. Thomas Hornor gave a detailed witness account of the movements of Rowland Stephenson after the incident at Queen Street. Hornor was busy that afternoon at the Colosseum. With the extra investment from the bank he hoped to open the building in the New Year and there was plenty to do. To his surprise a very worried Septimus Burton appeared and told him he had received a message from Rowland Stephenson to say that he had to see them urgently and asked him and Hornor to be at Burton's house at three o'clock. The two men walked the short distance from the Colosseum around the south side of Regent's Park to the house in York Terrace where they found Rowland Stephenson in a coach waiting for them. Septimus ushered Rowland Stephenson and Thomas Hornor into his house. As soon as they sat down in the drawing room Rowland announced that he was unable to fulfill the agreement that he had made a few days earlier to lend a further £20,000 to the Colosseum project and that he wished to cancel it immediately. A very disappointed Thomas Hornor had little option but to agree and Rowland Stephenson sat down and wrote a memorandum cancelling the agreement which the three men duly signed.

Hornor later testified, 'Mr. Stephenson then appeared quite calm and collected but in the course of our conversation he said that he had been so worried he now planned go to his house in Dover for a few days.'

At 5 o'clock Rowland Stephenson called for a coach and he and Thomas Hornor set off to the house in Duchess Street where his friend, Thomas Welch, the owner of Rowland's beloved Argyle Rooms lived. The coach turned into Marylebone Road and then turned right down the wide fashionable Portland Place where Rowland asked the coachman to stop for a while. He was calm at first and asked Thomas Hornor to join him that evening for supper at the Treasurer's House but he then began to become very agitated and exclaimed, 'I attempted to shoot myself this morning.'

The two men stayed in the coach for ten minutes while Stephenson gathered himself. 'As we sat in the coach Rowland said to me,' I have done something which I ought not to have done'. I said, "What have you done, Mr. Stephenson", and he replied, "I have done something. I am half mad".'

The coach then continued its journey down Portland Place and turned left into Duchess Street. Leaving Rowland alone in the coach Thomas Hornor walked to Thomas Welch's house and knocked on the front door. The maid answered and he asked if he could speak to Mr. Welch urgently. When Thomas Welch appeared Hornor asked him if he was alone.'Yes, I am.'

Hornor then told him of the events that had occurred and that Rowland would like to see him. Thomas Welch told the Commission how deeply saddened he was to hear of the distress of his good friend and asked Hornor to bring him to the house immediately.

Thomas Welch in his evidence given on 6 January recalled, 'Hornor requested me to give Mr. Stephenson some refreshment for he had had none. Mr. Stephenson told me he had selected me for his confidence and begged shelter under my roof'.

Thomas Welch could not refuse, as he soon stated in a letter to *The Times*, justifying his role in the affair,

> I am most anxious to show that a long intimacy and friendship have subsisted between Mr. Stephenson and myself and to instance some of the proofs of friendship, which he has given me. In consequence of partnership differences, I apprehended a run of my creditors upon my establishment, and communicated my anxiety to Mr. Stephenson who immediately removed my uneasiness by desiring me if necessary to draw upon him to the amount of £10,000.
>
> In another emergency he became guarantee for me and remains so for the payment of no less sum than £9,000. Many other proofs of the most disinterested friendship I could produce, but the two I have mentioned will be quite sufficient to show the debt of gratitude I owe him. Such a benefactor was Mr. Stephenson who on a sudden solicited my protection on Friday the 26th December at half past 5 in the afternoon. He told me that a circumstance had occurred which rendered it impossible for him to return to Lombard-street for he had used some property of the house during the late run which in one fortnight after the payment of the dividends he could have replaced but the discovery of his having so used it having taken place at the banking house at 11 o'clock that morning he had not the fortitude to bear the interrogation to which he should be subjected. I endeavoured to persuade him to allow me to send for the partners, saying it would be to their own advantage to replace the property so used, and I made no doubt but that they might be friends again. He said, rather than see them he would blow his brains out in my parlour and immediately drew from his pocket a brace of pistols. I used every effort to divert him from so horrible a purpose, and to calm his mind, in which I at length succeeded.[49]

Concerned for his old friend, Thomas Welch continued to urge Rowland to stay with him at Duchess Street and offered to summon his partners so that the problems could at least be discussed and hopefully settled. One minute Rowland would agree but the next he would say that he was ruined and must leave immediately. Rowland was also now becoming increasingly concerned about the contents of the parcel that he had left at the pawnshop in Queen Street. He asked Thomas Hornor to fetch Robert Wright from Theobald's Road and to bring the mysterious parcel with him, hoping the pawnbroker had arranged the delivery.

The brown paper parcel that had been addressed to Robert Wright had indeed been delivered by the pawnbroker, even after the dramatic events in his shop. It had arrived at Theobald's Road at 2 o'clock. The courier gave the parcel at the gate to Mr. Davies, clerk to Robert Wright, saying, 'This packet, I fear, contains unpleasant intelligence'.

Wright had immediately opened the parcel and found four packets, one addressed to Mr. Barker, a lawyer of Gray's Inn, one directed to Miss Mary Frances Stephenson at Marshalls, one directed to Mr. Hornor and lastly one for himself. He did not have time to take Mary Frances' packet to Romford himself so he took it around to the Stephenson household at 41 Queen Square where he asked the manservant to have the package delivered at once to Marshalls. The coachman was summoned and dispatched to Romford on horseback.

Wright then returned to Theobald's Road where, in the presence of his clerk, Mr. Davies, he opened the package that was addressed to him. The two men saw that it contained a number of promissory notes and bills but at that moment a junior partner at the bank arrived, desperately searching for Rowland Stephenson.

That junior partner was Henry Stephenson. He was Rowland's cousin, and Mary Eliza's brother, and to complicate the relationship further he was married to Rowland's younger sister, Eliza Margaret. He was now aged a twenty-nine and lived with his wife in an apartment above the bank. He had been working at the counter of the bank when at 2 o'clock news had come that Rowland Stephenson had tried to shoot himself at a pawnbroker's shop in the City. He immediately informed the other partners who instructed him to go and find Rowland. His search was frantic, going around the places where Rowland Stephenson could usually be found. He went first to the Treasurer's House and from there to the Colosseum. He then went to Theobald's Road and it was there he found Mr. Wright and Mr. Davies opening the package. Examining the contents they saw that it contained various loan notes, which they counted and amounted to £74,800, some signed by Henry Peto and some signed by Thomas Hornor. Robert Wright told Henry that he had two more packets, one addressed to a lawyer and the other for Thomas Hornor.

Henry Stephenson strongly advised Robert Wright to hold on to the parcels addressed to Mr. Hornor and the lawyer, Mr. Barker and he set off again to continue his search. He went back to Saint Bartholomew's twice without any sign of Rowland but at 6 o'clock he heard that Thomas Hornor and Rowland Stephenson had been seen in a coach together in Portland Place. He decided that their likeliest destination was Marshalls so he set off in a coach to Romford. When he arrived Mary Frances said she had not seen her brother-in-law but the coachman from Queen Square had come on horseback and had delivered a packet of deeds. Henry told her what had been happening but only stayed there long enough to change the horses and returned to town and to his apartment in Lombard Street to await developments.

Henry was not the only Stephenson searching London. Rowland Macdonald Stephenson, Rowland's eldest son, had also heard of the day's events. He was aged twenty and he too worked at the bank. He was at his desk in the bank when he heard that his father had tried to shoot himself and that Henry had gone to try to find him. He was unsure what to do so waited for news of his father but then James Harman Lloyd, his father's clerk, told him to go to Marshalls to speak to his aunt and the family. He also instructed Rowland Macdonald to take with him a parcel that Lloyd was in the process of wrapping. Lloyd, whom Rowland Macdonald later described as 'much agitated', told him that the parcel, which was large and heavy, contained securities for Miss Stephenson and must be given to her personally. He told Rowland Macdonald that he must stay the night at Marshalls and he would send a gig in the morning to collect him and bring him back to Lombard Street.

The porter, John Stephens, ordered a chaise and Rowland Macdonald set off for Marshalls, clutching the heavy parcel and wondering what was happening to his world that seemed to have been suddenly turned upside down.

Henry Stephenson had already left Marshalls by the time Rowland Macdonald arrived. He found his aunt extremely worried about the day's events as had been related to her by Henry. Not only did she fear for the welfare of her brother-in-law but she had his six other children to look after. She opened the parcels but they only contained deeds and other securities with two old life insurances.

Rowland Macdonald could not understand why James Harman Lloyd had been so insistent that he stay out of the way at Marshalls for the night. He later told the Commission he 'had some suspicions as to Lloyd's having some object of his own in view', and having stayed at Marshalls for about an hour and a half he made his way back to London to try to find his father, himself.

Back at the house of Thomas Welch in Duchess Street, Rowland was waiting for word that Thomas Hornor had found Robert Wright. He had asked Thomas Hornor not to bring Robert Wright to Thomas Welch's house but to meet in a carriage on the corner of Goodge Street and Tottenham Court Road. At about 6 o'clock Thomas Hornor and Robert Wright walked to the corner as arranged and climbed into a coach where they found Rowland Stephenson sitting, looking through some papers. The three men sat in the coach and Rowland Stephenson asked Robert Wright about the parcel. He was pleased to hear that it had arrived and the packet for Mary Frances had been dispatched to Marshalls. He asked for the packets addressed to Mr. Hornor and to Mr. Barker to be returned to him. When Robert Wright gave him the packages, Rowland responded with his usual, 'Very well'.

Robert Wright climbed out of the coach and returned home while Thomas Hornor and Rowland went back to Mr. Welch's house. It was 7 o'clock by now and Rowland Stephenson asked Thomas Hornor to go the Treasurer's House at Saint Bartholomew's where he hoped Rowland Macdonald would be waiting for him. Exhausted he lay down and slept.

When Thomas Hornor arrived at the Treasurer's House he found that Rowland Macdonald was not there, so he left a message with the porter at the Henry VIII gate instructing him to come to Thomas Welch's house as soon as possible. He then returned to Duchess Street, arriving at about 9 o'clock. He was relieved to hear from Thomas Welch that Rowland was resting in the bedroom and had been persuaded to return to St. Bartholomew's; it was hoped he might stay and sort out his affairs with his partners. At 11 o'clock when a much relieved Rowland Macdonald arrived his father asked to speak to him alone in the drawing room.

On 5 January 1829 the Commission interviewed Rowland Macdonald. For some reason he was not at first very forthcoming,

Q   At what time on Friday 26th December after one o'clock did you first see your father?
A   I think about 11 at night.
Q   Where did you first see him?
A   I decline to answer the question; I shall certainly not answer the question.
Q   Question repeated.
A   At Mr. Welch's.

Rowland Macdonald further testified that his father said to him, 'I am ruined'. Rowland Macdonald continued, 'I endeavoured to discover what he meant but he would give no answer. I was with him I should think about half an hour'.

Mr. Welch continued the story. When the father and son came out of the drawing room Rowland Macdonald left the house to walk to the Treasurer's House and Rowland Stephenson said he would follow with Mr. Hornor and Mr. Welch in a hired chaise. As they waited for the chaise on the pavement Rowland Stephenson put his hand in his pocket and said, 'I cannot pay for one as I have but sixpence in the world.'[50] Thomas Welch went back into the house and returned with his wife's purse.

Rowland Macdonald had already arrived when the chaise drew up at the hospital gate. It was now half past eleven and Rowland was calm and they ordered the servant to make tea. The parcel that was addressed to Hornor was opened and Rowland returned to Thomas Hornor three promissory notes for £20,000 each. Thomas Hornor also pressed Rowland for the return of the mortgage papers on his house which he had given to Rowland as a security against some of the money he had received for the Colosseum.

Mr. Hornor testified,

> I asked Stephenson for the mortgage, he told me it was on the mantle piece in his room at the bank in Lombard-street and I might go for it. This might be about 11 at night. I wish to add that for about 3 weeks before the 26th I had intimated to Stephenson that I had some anxiety about the securities he held. He said as to the bills and notes I had given him they were all destroyed and that the mortgage was on the mantle piece and I might go for it and put it in the fire, it was of no use to him.

He also gave Thomas Hornor a note to pay Henry Peto £20,000 for his work on the Colosseum. Rowland seemed happier now that some of his affairs were in order. He sat quietly sipping his tea and perhaps contemplating that the crisis of the day was over. He felt he could 'abide the consequences of the discovery'.[51]

'It cannot be that bad' said Thomas Welch.

But it was. At that moment James Harman Lloyd arrived and brought with him grave news. The partners had heard of the events at the pawnbroker's shop, 'and they had opened his desk and drawers. This communication led Mr. Stephenson to abandon at once his former resolution, and to determine upon immediate flight.

But he exclaimed that he had no money. His eldest son immediately emptied his pockets for his father's service. Mr. Stephenson burst into tears and rejected the offer saying he could not use his son's pittance.

Mr. Lloyd then said, 'I have money, Sir; I have £800'.

Rowland Stephenson replied, 'Then we shall both go'.[52]

CHAPTER SEVEN

SATURDAY MORNING

No event ever excited so painful a sensation in the city as the case of Rowland Stephenson; it seemed to dissolve the ties which bond men together in a business where honour is held almost universally as the governing power. The bankers felt it as a stain upon them; and they exhibited a dejected and downcast appearance; and it was long before they recovered from the shock.[53]

M R. HORNOR LATER RELATED his account of the events of that Friday evening to the Commissioners. He described how Rowland Stephenson was determined to leave London as soon as possible and had asked his son to go to the bedroom to pack a bag for him. William Grave, the recently employed coachman, was summoned and ordered to bring the coach to the front door in preparation for a long journey. While they waited for the carriage Rowland asked Thomas Welch if he would accompany him for the first mile or two of the journey. Thomas Welch readily agreed.

Thomas Hornor described how father and son shook hands in the drawing room and then Rowland hurried out to the carriage where the servants were loading two carpetbags and some parcels,

the carriage door was open, and his servants, I think men only, were assisting in putting in parcels in a hurried manner. I had not an opportunity to speak to him except to say, 'let me hear how you are.' The son I think ran to the other side of the carriage and spoke to his father, but it was all done in an instant and it was dark. I am sure the horses were grey, his horses are grey and I have no doubt they were his. Mr. Thomas Welch and Mr. Lloyd got into the carriage, as it appeared to me and off they went. The son and I returned into the house with heavy hearts.

There is no record of where the carriage went at midnight but someone saw Rowland's coach, distinctive by his crest displayed on the door, leave through the Henry VIII gate of Saint Bartholomew's Hospital again at 4 o'clock in the morning so at some time in the night the carriage must have returned to the Treasurer's House. Where did they go between midnight and 4 o'clock? Perhaps he delivered those brown paper parcels that Thomas Hornor had seen being loaded by the servants into the carriage. To whom he delivered these parcels is not known but it is probable that they contained more loan notes and bills that he wanted to return to their owners to avoid claims on them later. Before he took flight he seemed to wish to avoid any financial embarrassment for his friends. They definitely did returned to Welch's house in Duchess Street since a letter that was addressed to Mr. Christopher Good, a clerk who worked at the Argyle Rooms, was left there sometime in the night. Fearing his wife's wrath perhaps Thomas Welch may also have wished to return her purse.

Christopher Good gave evidence to the Bankruptcy Commission on 9 February 1829. He worked at the Argyle rooms for Thomas Welch and had called at the house in Duchess Street early on Saturday morning to receive his orders for the day. He was very surprised to discover that his employer had been called away so suddenly but there was a letter waiting, addressed to him:

Q   When did you receive that letter?

A   On the morning of the 27th.

Q   From what place was it dated?

A   It was not dated from any place, Friday night was put upon the letter.

Q   How did it come to you?

A   I called at Mr. Welch's house on Saturday morning. Mr. Welch was not there but I found the letter, addressed to me.

Q   Do you remember the contents of that letter?

A   The substance of it was for me to proceed to Romford and then to Dover to present the accompanying cheques, the letter contained three orders for payment of money, one on the Romford bank to the best of my belief for the balance of the account and was signed by Rowland Stephenson. The other was a similar one directed to Fector's Bank of Dover for the balance of amount signed by Rowland Stephenson and the other on Messrs. Latham and Co. Bankers at Dover for balance of amount. The letter directed me to proceed and get payment of those orders and said that Mr. Welch should be back within three days.

Following these instructions, Christopher Good went straight to Romford High Street on Saturday morning and arrived at Johnson's bank at half past ten. He had no difficulty cashing the cheque for £199 and returned to the Argyle Rooms with the money.

On Sunday morning he set out by coach to Dover, arriving in the evening. At 9 o'clock Monday morning he was waiting on the doorstep of Latham's Bank in Dover High Street to present the cheque but by now the game was up. Reports had already reached Dover that Rowland Stephenson had absconded and the payment was refused. The same occurred at the second bank in Dover, Messrs Minet and Fector, and so he returned to London empty handed. Christopher Good told the Commissioners that Rowland Stephenson wanted this money to be given to Thomas Welch, wishing to repay Welch an outstanding debt before he fled.

Having watched the carriage leave Saint Bartholomew's at midnight, Rowland Macdonald Stephenson and Thomas Hornor re-entered the Treasurer's House. Thomas Hornor continued his evidence, 'the son and I returned into the house. The son was violently agitated, he told me there was a mortgage left for me in Lombard-street and he wished to go there for some private papers for his father. We went together to Lombard-street to the banking house. This must have been past 12 o'clock but I cannot speak to time.'

Rowland Macdonald described the events of the early hours of Saturday morning in his testimony on 20 January 1829. The two men arrived at the bank some time after midnight and found Henry Stephenson and his wife awake in their rooms, anxiously waiting for news of Rowland. Henry Stephenson was very uneasy, not least for his own future. When Rowland Macdonald explained to the couple what had happened, Henry replied that he had a confession to make. He admitted that he knew Rowland Stephenson had abstracted £58,000 from the bank and that before he left he had placed a signed cheque for that amount in the bank copybook. This was very bad news for Rowland Macdonald, putting his father way beyond the law. For the moment, however, he had to sort out the bills and notes for Thomas Hornor who continued in evidence,

Q   Respecting you having obtained a mortgage deed from the house in Lombard-street, did not Rowland Macdonald Stephenson accompany you to the house in Lombard-street?

A   We went together.

Q   About what time was this?

A   I have rather a confused idea. I think about after midnight.

Q   Did you obtain any papers except the mortgage?

A   I obtained some old letters and two or three old bills at 3 or 4 years date.

Q   Where were the bills when you arrived in Lombard-street?

A   Several papers were lying about and Mr. Macdonald went to Mr. Stephenson's private box to look for the bills, which I have described, he found two. I burnt them with the others.

Q   Did Macdonald Stephenson get any papers of any sort?

A   Yes he did, he put some papers into a box, some of them he took from a box on which was Mr. Stephenson's name and some from a drawer in the room … The impression on my mind was that he was taking some of his father's private papers.

Q   What was the size of the bag, which he put the papers into?

A   The bag might be about two thirds filled and as one the size of what is called a lawyers bag. Upon recollection I do think there were two bags.

Q   Was the second bag full?

A   Before I answer I wish to explain by saying that my solicitude in accompanying Mr. Stephenson from Duchess Street to the hospital was that he hesitated in Duchess Street to give up the two £20,000 promissory note. I think the second bag was full.

Q   How long were you at Lombard-street?

A   I was at Lombard-street no more than 20 minutes to half an hour.

Q   Did Macdonald come away with you?

A   Yes, and with the bags. We went away together.

Rowland Macdonald supported Thomas Hornor's testimony and when asked why he thought they could remove or burn the papers, Rowland Macdonald replied:

A   They were given for my father's accommodation and they belonged to him by rights.

Q   Who was in Lombard-street when you got there?

A   Mr. and Mrs. Henry Stephenson were up. It was late, we thought it would be better to remove them. We took them out of the boxes and cases. There was a great number of letters and bills and I think two leather cases and we put them into one carpetbag and a little tin box.

Q   Did you take away anything at that time inside the carpetbag and the tin box?

A   I took nothing but what was in the bag and tin box except a great coat.

Gathering these things together, and one of them no doubt wearing the great coat against the cold December night, they set off back to the hospital. The distance is not great but what they carried must have been heavy since they found a coach to take them.

A   We walked to the coach and went in it to the hospital. When we got to the hospital Mr. Hornor and I looked over them all. We found nothing but letters and bills as I recollect. I gave Mr. Hornor bills on which I saw his name and which he said he had given for my father's accommodation. That was three or four only. There was a very large quantity of bills of exchange

Under more hostile questioning Rowland Macdonald denied that there was any cash found in the boxes at Lombard Street. The Commissioners went on to question vigorously all those concerned in the events of Boxing Day, especially those who received Rowland's brown paper parcels. The Commissioners were particularly interested as to whether any witness had received cash from Rowland Stephenson before he absconded, in the vain attempt to discover where the £58,000 had gone.

Poor Henry Stephenson cannot have slept for the little time that was left of the Friday night. Unlike everyone else he knew exactly where the £58,000 had gone and he knew no one was going to find it. At 9 o'clock on Saturday morning he opened the front door of the banking house for trading and set about his usual task of calling over the business of the day before, knowing too well that there was going to be a shortage of £58,000. Despite James Lloyd informing Rowland the night before that the partners had searched his desk, at this stage the partners were unaware that money was missing.

David Remington was the first to arrive and his face must have turned ashen when Henry showed him Rowland's cheque. David Remington described his reaction, 'I confess that my mind was so agitated and the excitement upon such a discovery confused me altogether that probably I was not a judge of what was best to do in such an arduous situation.'

This was a felony, a capital felony no less, and the bank had to take immediate steps to cover the loss. Pulling himself together and knowing that they had on deposit at the Bank of England about £92,000 he decided 'to draw instantly upon the Bank of England the sum of £90,000.' At a quarter past nine he dispatched Rowland Macdonald to the Bank of England with a note to withdraw £90,000 from Remington's account. The young gentleman clerk however soon returned to say that it had been refused as there were not sufficient funds in the account. This puzzled as much as it alarmed David Remington. There was just enough money in the account at the Bank of England to draw £40,000 and this was done immediately but he wanted to know what had happened to the rest of the balance.

At half past nine David Remington's father, William, arrived as did the other partner, Joseph Toulmin. They were informed of the disastrous situation. David Remington continued:

A   I presented Rowland Stephenson's cheque to my father and he sent for Henry Stephenson into his presence for being a party or rather having a knowledge of their abstraction. He asked him whether he did not think himself a very great rascal or scoundrel, I forget which, and ordered him to get out of the house instantly.

What was to be done now? The remaining partners felt the bank was under pressure but could survive. They also knew however that the extraordinary events of the day before and the disappearance of their most active partner would be widely broadcast and may cause a run on the bank. The next day was Sunday and the bank would be closed but they had to keep going until half past four that day and they thought that, with luck, they could.

Surprisingly the first action the partners took was to repay the five eminent bankers £20,000 each that the bankers had so confidently invested on the previous Monday. David Remington explained why:

A   We had many conversations among ourselves respecting this £100,000 and we, my father, myself and Mr. Toulmin, were very desirous on the Tuesday and on the Wednesday previous to return this money to the bankers and there is one particular fact respecting our desire so to do. We felt ourselves strong enough to return it as far back as Tuesday 23rd. On the 27th we resolved to repay the bankers and take back our security which was more than double the amount – we paid back at about eleven o'clock.. The payment of £100,000 was made by Mr. Toulmin to Mr. Martin, I cannot say how.

The bank continued to trade while David Remington set about trying to find out why the credit of the Remington's account at the bank at the Bank of England was much lower than expected.

Q   As you drew upon the Bank of England with the supposition that there was £92,000 and discovered that you were mistaken in your supposition did you initiate any, and what, enquiry to discover the cause?

A   I immediately sent our passbook over to the Bank of England to have it settled and thereby to enable me to discover what the error was.

Q   What did you discover?

A   About one o'clock in the day as near as I can remember Mr. Derby of the Drawing Office in the Bank of England came to our banking house with the request that one of the firm would accompany him to his office at the bank to inspect the banking book. He showed me an erasure which he informed me had caused drafts to be paid out for the sum of £30,000 and £10,000, and the balance previously made in that book had been fraudulently altered by placing a figure of four in the column of ten thousands, making the balance of £44,000 instead of £4,000. The sum of £30,000 and £10,000 on the Monday previous caused a false entry to be entered in the cash book.

Q   When you discovered a fraud had been committed had you any doubt by whom it was committed?

A   None whatever.

Q   By who was it committed?

A   I have no doubt it was by Rowland Stephenson.

At midday David Remington began to check the securities in the strong room. The situation was bad enough, but now he found some of the envelopes of their customers that should have contained valuable exchequer bills, government stock and foreign bonds were empty. He then found where Rowland Stephenson and James Lloyd kept the envelopes containing the exchequer bills belonging to the London Life Association (also known as the London Life Assurance Company) which was a special client of Rowland Stephenson. To his relief David Remington could feel that these were not empty but when he came to open them, all he found was blank paper.

This was it. The bank might have withstood the loss of £58,000 and even the fraud in the account of the Bank of England but the missing securities were far more than the bank could withstand. The bank was ruined and they must stop trading immediately. The time was half past one and the shutters came down for the last time on the banking house of Remington, Stephenson, Remington, Toulmin & Co. that had been trading for over a hundred years.

No further payments should have been made after this time but there was one exception. David Remington explained that a customer called Mr. Jamie

Butler, an Oporto merchant, had withdrawn his deposit of £1,000 during the pressure on the bank the previous week but had been given *'every guarantee'* by the partners and so had reinvested the money back into the bank. Mr. Butler arrived at the bank at 2 o'clock. He 'manifested such a dreadful degree of painful feeling' that he was ushered into a private room where, 'we remonstrated very strongly against payment and indeed positively refused on account and of the impropriety of so doing, but were induced to do so in consequence of the very painful situation of his feelings, and which worked upon us also at the same time.'

He was very lucky. As Cobbett's Weekly reported 'the street was so much crowded at half-past two o'clock, that the city authorities were obliged to send down officers to disperse the multitude'.[54]

William Remington, as senior partner, had the task of immediately informing the Committee of London Bankers that the bank had been forced to cease trading. The Committee acted immediately and dispatched their solicitor, Mr. Thomas Gates, from their office nearby at 56 Lombard Street. He was very experienced in the world of banking and this was not the first time a bank had gone under and needed his help. When he arrived at 4 o'clock the partners showed him Rowland's cheque for £58,000 and the empty exchequer bill envelopes. The collapse of the bank he would deal with in the usual way but it was the missing exchequer bills that really worried him; they were negotiable and as stolen property could be sold through the City of London financial markets and thereby cause chaos. The exchequer bills were named and numbered. The name of the bearer might be changed but the number could not and Mr. Gates was keen to find out which clients had lost exchequer bills and more importantly the numbers. Those exchequer bills held by the bank in the normal way were easily identifiable through the ledgers, but the problems came with the large number of exchequer bills belonging to the London Life Association. These had been held separately by Rowland Stephenson and James Lloyd and the only record was in a ledger found after breaking into Lloyd's locked desk. The contents of this ledger would be examined closely by the Commission for Bankruptcy at a later date.

The bank was formally declared bankrupt and the Commissioners began the task of not only investigating the cause of the collapse but also establishing the claims of the very many creditors who came from far and wide.

CHAPTER EIGHT

THIS IS NOT A RIGHT THING

U P TO THE BEGINNING of 1828 there was no shortage of clients for the banking house of Messrs. Remington, Stephenson, Remington, Toulmin & Co. They had a good reputation with the solid father and son, William and David Remington, the hard working Joseph Toulmin and the colourful Rowland Stephenson, M.P. There was also the fact that the bank was offering the attractive 5% interest while most were offering only 4%.

There is no evidence that the other partners in the bank acted in any way like Rowland Stephenson. They had however been naïve and complacent and there had been an incident in April 1826 when they turned a blind eye to his casual use of bank funds. Remington's needed to be seen to be solvent and all the partners had an interest in keeping their partner, Rowland Stephenson, afloat.

An anecdote published at the time describes the attitude that some bankers had towards their banking houses,

> 'Talking of bankers' said a friend of ours the other day, 'I'll tell you a curious fact relating to that craft—When old T-----, the banker, felt his health fast declining, he called for his son and said, 'William, I have sent for you to talk to you very seriously. By my will you will find out I have divided what I have equally among you, but I am not worth a shilling. Our bank is rotten and has been rotten for years'.
>
> 'Good God' said William 'I always thought you very rich. Have you not a large sum, Sir, in the iron box?'
>
> 'Ah, William' said the old man, 'that box was to fool the clerks. The iron box, William, is empty, and has been for years. Continue however, my dear boy, to attend to banking, some lucky turn may happen; the bank is all I can leave you; make the most of it; keep the secret and the secret will keep you for years. Don't sell a single carriage or put down a single horse; a banker is thought nobody unless he lives like a Prince.'

William did as his father bid him, made half a million, enjoyed a good reputation but crashed at last and paid three shilling and six pence in the pound.'[55]

Rowland was undoubtedly a very affable and congenial man with many
friends and admirers. He was generous and loyal but there is also no doubt that
his banking practices could be described at one end as relaxed and openhanded
and at the other as sharp and felonious.

The English Chronicle, following the flight of Rowland Stephenson, began
printing verses for the amusement of their readers. This excruciating doggerel
was based on nursery rhymes and entitled *Mother Goose Tales* and the first
appeared on 6 January 1829,

> I sing a song of sixpence a balance all awry –
> My 'friend and benefactor' a piping of his eye;
> When his mouth was opened, the clerk began to sing
> 'Is not this a pretty dish? Suppose we both take wing!'
> 'The folks are in the counting-house counting out the money,
> 'Five bankers in the parlour are looking rather funny!'
> 'The clerk then in the carpet-bag was packing up his clothes,
> 'Send out and call a jarvey, ere somebody turn nose!'

> *(Jarvey = driver of a hackney coach; turn nose =to inform)*

At half past one on 27 December 1828 the bank had ceased trading and
William Remington had informed the Committee of London Bankers that the
bank had failed and Rowland Stephenson had absconded. The first concern of
the Committee was to find the absconding banker and they certainly acted
without delay. Word of the failure of the bank had certainly reached Dover
High Street by the Monday morning when Christopher Good tried unsuccessfully to cash the two cheques at Fector's Bank.

The banking house known as Remington's dated back to at least the beginning
of the eighteenth century and was originally known as Knight and Jackson. By
1729 the bank was doing 'considerable business'.[56] In 1763 the firm became
Knight, Batson and Co and was now situated at 69 Lombard Street. In 1794
the bank was trading under the name of Stephenson, Batson, Remington and
Smith and by 1815 was Remington, Stephenson, Remington and Toulmin,
having five partners, William Remington, Joseph Petty Toulmin, Rowland
Stephenson, David Remington and Henry Stephenson.

Henry Stephenson had been taken on as a gentleman clerk in 1816. At Christmas 1825 Rowland Stephenson had taken his young cousin to meet the drawing clerk at the Bank of England. He was introduced as a new partner so that in future he could draw cheques and endorse bills on the Bank of England. To celebrate his entry as a new partner David Remington gave him a pipe of wine, (a cask containing two hogsheads, equal to 105 gallons). Henry was paid £80 a year up to Christmas 1825 and this was increased to £300 a year when he became a partner. The senior partner, Mr. William Remington, however, for some reason, never accepted Henry as a partner. A brass printing plate was made so that cheques could be stamped out, headed with the names of all the partners including Henry, but William Remington forbade its use and the plate was put away and lost.

Joseph Petty Toulmin was also one of the partners but never gave evidence to the Commissioners, having been taken ill with a stroke shortly after the collapse of the bank. He was 64 when the bank collapsed and had been a partner since the end of the eighteenth century. He was widely respected, keeping regular hours at the bank and a low profile. He was known to arrive punctually at 9 o'clock and leave at a quarter past four, six days a week. He lived comfortably in a house on Clapham Common with his wife and four children and employed five servants.

Joseph Toulmin probably had little to add to the investigation and nothing to fear from the Commission. He did, however, have to make a personal appearance at the Court on 16 March 1829 so that he could be declared officially bankrupt and was made to surrender his gold watch and £21.

William Remington was the senior partner. He told the Commissioners that he had been a partner since Christmas 1792 when he joined the firm whose partners at that time were then Edward Buckley Batson, Rowland Stephenson (the Elder), John Stephenson (the father of Rowland, the younger), Edward Stephenson (Mary Eliza's father) and John Smith. William Remington had a wide selection of clients and was a well-respected figure in the City.

His son, David Remington, lived at 76 Old Bond Street and had been taken on as a partner in 1815. He described his work at the bank to the Commissioners as 'to superintend generally'.

Rowland Macdonald Stephenson, aged twenty, gave evidence on Monday 5 January 1829. He was Rowland Stephenson's eldest son and had been taken on as a gentleman clerk at the bank in 1827 after he left Harrow School. He appears to have known very little about his father's work practices but was questioned at length concerning the events of Boxing Day and whether he had any idea of his father's present whereabouts.

Rowland Stephenson was not there to give evidence and nor was James Harman Lloyd, Rowland's enigmatic clerk. Lloyd was 28 years old in 1828. Little is known about him except that he was the son of James and Susanna Lloyd of Tewkesbury, Gloucestershire where he was christened on October 19th 1800. Lloyd seems to have worked, and lived, at the bank for at least ten years and was on very good terms with Rowland, especially after the death of Mary Eliza. They certainly socialised together, often being seen at the various eating houses in the City and he was a frequent visitor at Marshalls. Not everyone approved of the familiarity. 'We understand that James Lloyd was a constant guest at his master's table, and was frequently remarked for his obtrusive manners by the gentlemen who have met him there'.[57]

The questioning of the witnesses by the Commissioners concentrated on four main topics.

Firstly the Commissioners wanted to know what had happened on the Friday and Saturday when the bank failed. They were also anxious to find out where Rowland Stephenson had gone.

Secondly the Commissioners wanted to know how Rowland Stephenson had been able to abstract so much money from the bank for so long without being detected or prevented. They were particularly interested in how the books appeared to be balanced at the end of the day. It was Henry Stephenson, Rowland's young cousin, who had to answer for this and most uncomfortable it was for him.

Thirdly, they wanted to know what were the daily working practices of the bank, particularly as regards the dealing in loan notes and Exchequer Bills. The clerks, Thomas Digby and Edward Hall, as well as the partners, especially David Remington and Henry Stephenson, were summoned to describe this. Clients of the bank, William Greenwood and Philip Cox, described their personal dealings with the bank and their banker, Rowland Stephenson.

Lastly, the Commissioners wished to unravel the dealings of the bank with the London Life Assurance Company. From this company they interviewed Henry Brooke, Richard Heathfield, Benjamin Scott and Joseph Rainbow and stockbrokers William Hankey, Joseph Knibbs, Henry Thornton and Ellis Reeve. From Saint Bartholomew's Hospital in whose name some of the abstracted exchequer bills were found to be, they interviewed the Almoners, Thomas Helps and Thomas Hodgkinson, William Wilby, a clerk, and John Wood, the hospital solicitor.

Some witnesses were open and gave a clear account of what happened while others were less so. The examination of John Tate gives an example of what the Commissioners were sometimes up against. He was a clerk at the banking house but also a partner at the stockbrokers, Messrs. Williams & Co. and was interviewed six times from February 1929 to March 1831. He had dealings with the clients in the country but knew exactly how the bank dealt with exchequer bills. Rowland's use of exchequer bills, especially those he bought on behalf of his client, London Life Assurance, was central to the collapse of the bank.

On his second appearance before the Commissioners on 28 February 1829 it had already been clearly established that the partners regularly ordered the purchase of exchequer bills and government bonds.

Q   Were those orders given verbally or in writing?
A   That I do not know.
Q   Did you ever see any in writing?
A   Never.
Q   So they were given verbally?
A   Indeed they were.

Whether the Commissioners rolled their eyes in frustration is not recorded.

In all the interviews there was no mention or description of the private life of Rowland Stephenson, nor was there any speculation as to why he appeared to have removed so much money.

There was no evidence that Rowland Stephenson had acted rashly or dishonestly in his banking career until 1826. Indeed the account of his life referred to earlier in 'Fifty Years of Biographical Reminiscences' by Lord William Pitt Lennox paints a picture of the most hardworking and proficient banker, successfully mixing his flourishing professional life with a happy home and hectic social life. Lennox had finished his description of Rowland Stephenson thus, 'That Rowland Stephenson carried on under the cloak of religion, respectability and morality the most nefarious transactions and made away with monies entrusted to his care cannot be denied. A more plausible or agreeable acquaintance I never had'.[58]

Rowland Stephenson's wife, Mary Eliza, had died in 1821 and it may have been the loss of her steadying influence that propelled him into extravagance. He became an avid, almost compulsive, collector of objets d'art and property and his conduct at the elections that he contested was always described in the newspapers as 'lavish'.[59]

Henry Stephenson was interviewed at length on five occasions starting on 3 January 1829. He described his job at the bank; he lived above the offices with his wife and each morning unlocked the front door of the banking house. He then checked over the business of the day before. He attended the counter during the day and at closing time it was his responsibility to '*check the copy*' which entailed counting the cash and cheques of the day so that all the books balanced. There were various books and ledgers used but his main responsibility was to check the copybook and this book was to be a focus of attention by the Commissioners, as were the actions of Henry Stephenson when the books did not balance.

On 8 February 1831, as the Commission for Bankruptcy ground on, Henry Stephenson was summoned yet again to give evidence, this time to tell the whole truth concerning the first time Rowland Stephenson appeared to have abstracted money from the bank.

In April 1826 while checking the copy in the morning, Henry had discovered that there was £1,000 missing and that Rowland Stephenson must have removed the money the night before. Not knowing what to do he had a meeting with William Remington, his son David, and Joseph Toulmin in the counting house of the bank, where he hoped for privacy and not to be disturbed.

When told that £1,000 was missing and that it seemed Rowland was responsible for taking it, David Remington declared, 'This is not a right thing', and instructed Henry to speak to Rowland Stephenson about it. Henry replied that he had no influence over Rowland and begged the other partners to confront him with his misdemeanor. William Remington then turned the blame onto Henry Stephenson for allowing the abstraction to happen and severely reprimanded him. At this point a member of staff entered the counting house and disturbed the meeting, which broke up without a conclusion. Henry was left with the impression that William Remington would speak to Rowland Stephenson about his abstraction but he never did.

David Remington was also interviewed on the same subject in 1831. He remembered the matter differently:

Q   You said that in April 1826 the abstraction of £1000 was discovered. Did that appear in the copybook?

A   I cannot say how it could appear in the copybook, the copy appeared to have the £1000 in it.

Q   In fact there was no such £1000 note in the assets?

A   There was not.

Q   When the abstraction of the note was discovered by the firm, did you mention it to Henry Stephenson?

A   I believe it was my father who mentioned it to him.

Q   Was it mentioned to Henry Stephenson in your presence?

A   I do not recollect.

Q   Is there not a private counting house at the bank?

A   Yes.

Q   Speaking as to the time when the abstraction of the £1000 note was discovered, do you not recollect yourself, Mr. Toulmin and Mr. William Remington having talked with Henry Stephenson about the note in that private counting house?

A   As far as my memory serves me my father reprimanded Mr. Henry Stephenson for his conduct.

Q   In the private counting house do you mean?

A   Yes, to the best of my recollection.

Q   You were of course present then?

A   I do not recollect the circumstances.

Q   How do you recollect what you father said if you did not hear it?

A   My father told me he did so reprimand him.

Q   Will you swear that you were not present?

A   No, I cannot recollect the fact.

Q   Did you ever speak to Mr. Henry Stephenson yourself about it?

A   I do not remember.

Q   Did you speak to Rowland Stephenson about it?

A   No, I do not recollect speaking to him about it

Q   Did your father ever speak to Rowland Stephenson about it to your knowledge?

A   Not that I remember.

Q   Did your father ever tell you he had mentioned it to Rowland Stephenson?

A   No, I do not think he did.

Q   Did Mr. Toulmin mention it to Rowland Stephenson?

A   I do not recollect.

Q   I presume that your father and Mr. Toulmin often talked about the abstraction of this £1000?

A   I do not remember any conversation.

The astonished commissioner continued,

Q   Is it usual for one partner of a banking firm to abstract £1000 in this way?

A   No, very unusual.

Very unusual indeed but perhaps more unusual for someone to have such poor recall of the event when his trusted partner removes from the bank a sum of money that is today equivalent to well in excess of £50,000.

If William Remington had reserved his reprimand for Rowland Stephenson rather than Henry the affair might not have progressed. As it was Rowland felt he could continue to prop up his own financial affairs with money abstracted from the bank and pay it back when he could while Henry had realised he could not rely on the support of the other partners.

David Remington on another occasion testified that it was not Henry Stephenson who noticed the abstraction but himself when he examined the copybook on James Harman Lloyd's desk. Whether this is true or not is difficult to say but he never examined the Copybook again and if he had he might have had quite a shock.

For the next two and a half years Henry Stephenson was left to check the copy, night and morning, unsupervised. This certainly surprised the Commissioners and they pressed David Remington on this subject a number of times,

Q   Speaking of April 1826, did Mr. Henry Stephenson at that time always assist in making up the copy?

A   Yes he did.

Q   Was it not his business at that time to lock up the assets of the firm on each day?

A   Yes.

Q   That was, I presume, after he had checked the copy?

A   Yes

Q   Then was not Henry Stephenson the person in whom your firm confided for the accuracy of the copy and the safety of the firm's assets?

A   Yes

Q   Did any member of the firm ever attend and check the copy themselves?

A   Never, but in the absence of Henry Stephenson.

Q   You said £1000 note was entered in the copy in April 1826 where there was no £1000 note to justify the entry.

A   Yes I did.

Q   Was not that false entry Henry Stephenson's doing?

A   I do not recollect the entry now to speak to that fact.

Q   Must not Henry Stephenson have checked it?

A   Yes

Q   Then he must have known therefore it was a false entry.

A   Yes.

Q   Who checked the copy and locked up the assets after the abstraction of the £1000 was discovered?

A   Henry Stephenson.

Q   Did the firm trust him after the abstraction was discovered, the same as before?

A   Yes they did. I understood from my father that after he had reprimanded Henry Stephenson for what he had done in consideration of Rowland Stephenson's situation in the house he consented to overlook what had passed

* * *

Q   Had you objected to Henry Stephenson being continued in the situation?

A   I did not object to it.

Q   Did Mr. Toulmin ever object to it to your knowledge?

A   I do not recollect his making any objection.

Q   What time did the partners in general leave the banking house?

A   My father and myself left at 4 o'clock.

Q   What time did Mr. Toulmin usually leave?

A   About quarter past four.

Q   Was this the practice of the partners in April 1826?

A   Yes.

Q   Did they continue to do so after the abstraction of the note was discovered?

A   Yes, to the best of my recollection.

Q   Did you, or your partners, after the abstraction of £1000 note was discovered take any precaution to see that the copy was faithfully checked by Henry Stephenson?

A   Having come to the resolution of continuing him in the confidence we did not take any precautions.

* * *

Q   After the abstraction of the £1000 had been discovered did you or your partners ever in any way leave Rowland Stephenson at liberty to act as he has done?

A   By a misplaced confidence Rowland Stephenson found means to act as he has done.

Henry Stephenson at first testified that Rowland began to abstract again in the autumn of 1828 but as more evidence was given to the contrary he changed his story until the whole truth came out when he testified in 1831,

Q   You have mentioned in your former examinations that Rowland
    Stephenson frequently abstracted money. Did he continue to do it
    immediately after April 1826?
A   It was not immediately after. I felt the latter end of May or the
    beginning of June, it might have been the beginning of May 1826.
Q   Did he continue to make further abstractions after that time?
A   I do not think the copy was ever straight after that time, except
    when I was out of town as far as I can remember?

So there it was. Rowland Stephenson, stretched by his professional and personal
spending, his uncontrollable collecting, and his costly commitments, was continuing to unofficially borrow money from the bank almost immediately after the
events of April 1826. His young cousin, Henry, who was very much under his influence, knew that he was removing money one day and then replacing it the next.
For the subsequent two and a half years the money ebbed and flowed into the copybook, sometimes the book balanced and Rowland had paid all the borrowed money
back, but other times the short fall was in excess of £20,000. Rowland was using
the bank's money as a private fund to dip in and out of as and when he needed to.

When Henry was asked how Rowland informed him how short the copy
would be, he answered,

A   Sometimes Rowland put a cheque in the copybook and other
    times Rowland just told me how much the copy would be short.

This arrangement continued until the autumn of 1828. The copy was rarely
correct except for the time when Henry Stephenson was on holiday. He had
three weeks annual leave when he and his wife would go the family home at
Farley Hill. Rowland was careful to behave while Henry was away so that the
clerk standing in for Henry would be able to balance the copy and suspect
nothing of previous borrowings. Sometimes however it was a close run thing
and in May 1828 Henry was going away and the books were not balancing.

Q   Look at those signatures marked A on May 28th 1828 and state in
    whose writing it is.
A   I believe it to be mine.
Q   Attend to the contents of that page and explain what it means.
A   That if I went away someone else must check the copy, which
    I presume, must have been short. The ledger is marked in the
    following words –' if you stay away tomorrow you will miss both.'
    The whole of that page except the date is in Rowland Stephenson's
    handwriting.

Q   Do you know what is meant by 'you will miss both'?

A   That the copy would be short and of course he would be found out.

Q   You knew of course it was your duty not to connive at this.

A   I did

Q   Was any other person except Rowland Stephenson and yourself privy to the transactions?

A   Yes Mr. James Lloyd.

Q   Look at the writing on the back of the cheque for £58,000 and state whose writing it is.

A   It is Mr. Lloyd's.

As previously stated Rowland's financial needs were increasing in 1828 and he required more and more money to pay off creditors. He just about managed to balance the books for Henry's holiday in September 1828 but then things began to escalate as Henry described,

A   I went into the country in September and returned on October 11th and it was about the middle or latter end of October the extractions began again. To the first taking might be £20,000, £25,000, £30,000. He afterwards repaid some and took more, so that it ultimately came to this sum of £58,000.

Q   As it was your duty to check the copy why did you not between the first taking in October and the month of December mention the subject to any one of the Mr. Remington's or to Mr. Toulmin?

A   I constantly spoke to Rowland about it and told him I would give over checking the copy and then he told me he would replace all the money.

Q   But as these abstractions, which began in October, and continued until December had increased to £58,000 and upwards and as cheques were sometimes initiated and sometimes not, why did you not mention the subject to one of the Mr. Remingtons or Mr. Toulmin?

A   Because I know Rowland would not wish me to do it.

Henry's role in the abstractions was closely scrutinized. Was he a willing accomplice, reaping the rewards of a capital felony or a duped junior partner under the influence of his older cousin? With the memory of Henry Fauntleroy hanging in front of 100,000 people in his mind Henry faced an uncomfortable interrogation,

Q   Did you at any time receive any of the money, which was so taken?

A   No I did not, that I swear positively.

Q   Have you any account containing entries of the sums you received from Rowland?

A   No I do not think I have.

Q   Are you sure that there is not any paper in existence containing entries of any sums you received from Rowland?

A   I have made entries on memorandum slips of paper of sums, which I have received from Rowland for interest and I may have done so of other sums I have received from him.

Q   State for what purpose he paid you money.

A   It was sometimes to pay for things for him and at other times for things for myself.

Q   What is the amount do you believe you received from Rowland?

A   Between two and three thousand pounds.

Q   Do you swear that you have not received £5,000?

A   I have been in the habit of receiving money from him ever since I have been in Lombard-street when I was about 17 years old, but I do not think I have received from him £5,000 from the time I went to Lombard-street to the present time.

It had finally dawned on the Commission, once they had wrung the truth out of David Remington and Henry Stephenson, that there was no sudden removal of £58,000; Rowland had not stuffed his pockets with bank notes on Christmas Eve. This was an accumulated abstraction of £58,000 and Rowland had left a cheque for Henry in the usual way to let him know how short the copy would be. Up to the last Rowland hoped he could put the money back, however temporarily, to balance the books again.

A   On the evening of Monday the 22nd of December I checked the copy and found that there were £58,000 notes short but in lieu of them Mr. Rowland Stephenson's cheque was placed there with other notes in the book. When the book was given to me to check I spoke to Mr. Rowland Stephenson. I asked him if that cheque was to be passed, he told me that the next day he expected the money to cover it, hoping to receive £20,000 from Mr. Thomas Welch and £30,000 from Mr. Thomas Hornor. He told me likewise that he had £15,000 upon his own account. The next evening I spoke to him again he told me then he was expecting every hour to receive the two above sums and likewise again on the Christmas Eve that he had been disappointed but expected to receive it without doubt the following morning.

But money came there none.

CHAPTER NINE

THE LOAN NOTES

R OWLAND'S CLIENTS, FRIENDS AND business associates were summoned to the Commission for Bankruptcy one after another to describe their dealings with him. There emerged a picture of Rowland acquiring loan notes in the form of promissory notes, bills of exchange and accommodation notes which he then used, with other assets, to borrow money.

William Greenwood gave evidence on 17 January 1829. He had been a client of the bank for many years, as had his father before him. In 1822, attracted by the 5% interest, he deposited £27,000 at the bank through Rowland Stephenson who was the only partner he dealt with. Mr. Greenwood received his interest promptly until 1827 although he did admit that he found the accounting of the bank rather casual and unreliable; entries in his paper book were incomplete and the records of some transactions were on scraps of paper signed by Rowland Stephenson. In July 1827 he had to make two or three applications to the bank to receive his interest and even then he was not paid in cash but was surprised to receive a promissory note that had been signed by a Mr. Robert Wright. In the summer of 1828 rumours were circulating about the solvency of the bank and he decided to withdraw all his money but received instead another promissory note of Mr. Wright to the value of £23,400, as well as the offer of the deeds of one of Rowland's houses in Romford. William Greenwood was not at all happy with this arrangement and declined, insisting he be paid in cash. He was still pressing for payment when the bank stopped trading on 27 December and he became one of its many creditors.

Philip Zachariah Cox of Harwood gave evidence on 15 June 1829 and confirmed Rowland's cavalier attitude towards his clients' money and poor record keeping. Mr. Cox had been a client of the bank for many years and, like Mr. Greenwood, dealt only with one partner, Rowland Stephenson. There had been a run on the banks of London in 1825 and to support the bank he had given power of Attorney to bond the banking house for £5,000 at 3%. The bank survived the crisis but in December 1828 this power of attorney was reused by Rowland Stephenson to sell the stock to the separate benefit of himself and not the bank. This was carried out without the knowledge or permission of Mr. Cox. Since there was no record in the bank's stock book the unfortunate Philip Zachariah Cox later found himself trying to claw his money back from the personal estate of Rowland Stephenson and not the estate of the banking house.

A flavour of Rowland's style of banking was fully described in this extract from the English Chronicle of January 10th 1829. Mr. Samuel James Arnold had been the manager of the Drury Lane Theatre where Rowland was an devoted member of the audience and had a permanent box.

> Mr. Arnold, of the English Opera-house, has sustained a considerable loss by the failure of Remington and Co. Mr. Rowland Stephenson, as a lover of the drama, made the acquaintance of almost all the leading professors. His patronage extended to managers, authors, and actors. Mr. Arnold became one of his friends. Such was the banker's kindness for theatricals, that he invited performers, whose circumstances were not very affluent, to take all their spare cash to him; however small the sum, he was willing to receive it, and to employ it to the best advantage for their profit.[60]

In November 1828 Rowland noted that there was a handsome balance of £2,600 in the account of Mr. Arnold. He wrote,

> Dear Arnold – as I perceive you have a heavy balance on our books, I have ventured, without your knowledge, to appropriate it for you in a way, which will prove advantageous.

This came as an unpleasant surprise to Mr. Arnold and caused him some alarm as he too had heard the rumours about the solvency of Remington's. He wrote back to say he was not happy about this and wished to withdraw all his deposit but Rowland replied that he had deposited the money where it was not easy to withdraw immediately. An even more alarmed Mr. Arnold wrote again insisting on withdrawing all his money from the bank. Rowland now wrote back to say that not only was the £2,600 available immediately but that he could lend him any further sum he should wish.

The newspaper continued,

Mr. Arnold was half inclined to blame himself for the steps he had previously adopted. He contrasted his own misgivings with the generous confidence of the banker, and was ashamed of the suspicions, which he had, as he now concluded, too readily indulged. His previous mistrust was completely set at rest, and, fearing that it would be unpleasantly remembered by Mr. Stephenson, he did not like to draw out the whole of his cash. To show that he had still confidence in the house and in his friend, he determined only to reclaim £2,000.

The £600 he had so politely left behind was lost when the bank collapsed.

The newspaper concluded, 'The conduct of Mr. Stephenson in this business was singularly artful'.

Rowland may have been 'singularly artful' but he also may have genuinely felt he could still give his friend a generous return on his deposit even if he had to juggle a few assets to do it.

One can view Rowland Stephenson as being in the centre of a web of money dealing, a web that had on its periphery banks, stock brokers, Saint Bartholomew's Hospital, the London Life Association and many clients and friends like William Greenwood and Robert Wright. Exchequer bills, promissory notes, government and foreign stock were bought, sold or offered as security with the signature of endorsement frequently changed as it was passed from hand to hand. This was no place for the unwary and the amounts that circulated were by no means small. The most conservative estimate of Mr. Greenwood's loss of £27,000 is equivalent to £1,336,200 today's currency.[61] (National Archives Currency converter). It is not surprising that William Greenwood became rather anxious for the safety of his investment when he was offered dog eared promissory notes, signed by someone he had never heard of.

On the frantic afternoon of Boxing Day, 1828 Rowland Stephenson had tried to return all the promissory notes that belonged to Robert Wright and Thomas Hornor. Robert Wright, the builder, gave evidence to the Commission on four occasions in January 1829. Apart from his testimony about the events of Boxing Day, he also described his financial dealings with Rowland Stephenson and was asked about the promissory notes that had been passed to William Greenwood and others. At this point Wright's memory failed him until the examiner became more aggressive.

Q   Was there any transaction in the year 1827 respecting a promissory note for £24,000 or any such sum?

A   I have certainly placed implicit confidence in Mr. Stephenson and I have given him promissory notes without ever receiving consideration.

Q   Question repeated.

A   I certainly did it very imprudently and without taking any account. I really do not know any more but that Mr. Stephenson asked me to give him a note for the amount which I did, and never received any consideration.

Q   What date was the note?

A   I have not even got the date. I never received any such sum or any part of it.

Q   Have you any entry in any book or memorandum respecting this note for £24,000?

A   No.

Q   State when you gave Rowland Stephenson the note for £24,000.

A   Really I cannot, I did not take any account of it.

Q   Do you mean to say that you put your name to a note for such a large sum as £24,000 without having any entry respecting it or being able to speak to the time when it was done?

A   I really do. I had no improper intention whatever. Mr. Stephenson asked me to do as I did.

Q   Was this the largest security to which you ever put your name for him?

A   I believe it was.

Q   Have you often put your name to notes or bills for Mr. Stephenson?

A   Not lately, but I have several times.

This was where some of these promissory notes were coming from, supplied by Robert Wright to his friend to use as a security but without money changing hands or records kept. It was imprudent indeed and would eventually cost Robert Wright dear.

Another client of Rowland Stephenson was the trusting Adam Murray who inadvertently wandered into the murky world of notes, loans and bills and this would take him eventually to the Court of the King's Bench on October 22nd 1829 where he featured in the case of Murray v. Hodgson.

This was an action on a promissory note made by the defendant for £8,000, dated 23 November 1825, payable eight months after that date, to the order of Rowland Stephenson, and by him endorsed to the plaintiff, Adam Murray.

The defendant, Mr. Frederick Hodgson, 'was a gentleman of large fortune, and a member of Parliament. He, to his misfortune, had been on terms of great intimacy with Mr. Rowland Stephenson. They had been connected together for a long time, partly for purposes of business and partly for pleasure'.[62]

On 23 November 1825 Frederick Hodgson gave Rowland Stephenson a promissory note to the value of £8000 as a returnable down payment for the purchase of a property called Pitt's Place, near Epsom. The purchasing price remained open to negotiation and the difference was to be paid or repaid according to what the agreed price finally was.

The promissory note was made payable on 26 July 1826 and this was the date stipulated for the completion of the purchase of the property. Mr. Hodgson moved into the house and the note was taken as a security by Rowland Stephenson and was kept with the other similar notes in a tin box in the strong room under the care of Mr. Digby at the bank.

Mr. Baker who was the solicitor acting for Frederick Hodgson, was not satisfied with the title deeds of the estate and the conveyancer, Mr. Venner, examined the title deeds of the estate and described them as 'defective', finding 'innumerable objections'. It is not stated what these objections were but Rowland may have offered these deeds as security for some other loan and Mr. Venner and Mr. Baker were worldly wise enough to have nothing to do with the property or indeed Rowland Stephenson. Consequently the sale of the Pitts Place fell through and by July 1826 Frederick Hodgson had moved out and the day of payment of the promissory note, July 26th 1826, had come and gone without renewal, thus invalidating it. Mr. Hodgson thought that was the end of it, but it was not.

At the bank on the morning of 26 July 1826 Mr. Digby checked the notes held by the bank to find those that had come up for payment. When called to give evidence to the commission he stated that he had found this promissory note amongst others that had come due on that date. He asked Rowland Stephenson if it should be presented to Mr. Frederick Hodgson for payment.

Rowland replied, 'No! Mark it 'received'.

The ledger was duly entered but in the handwriting of James Harman Lloyd: 'Eight £1000 bank notes received from F. Hodgson' Where had the eight £1,000 notes come from?

As it happened, earlier that week, Adam Murray, attracted by the 5% interest, had come to see Rowland Stephenson with a view to investing £8,000. Adam Murray was 'a surveyor, who had conducted himself with great reputation and integrity, and by his industry had realised a competency for himself and his family', but, 'Mr. Murray was not a man accustomed to business except the business of his own profession. He had had nothing to do with accommodation bills and promissory notes, and was unacquainted with transactions such as those with which Mr. R. Stephenson had unfortunately been too much engaged.'[63]

Into the web he walked. He handed over his eight crisp £1,000 notes to Rowland Stephenson who gave him in return the promissory note of Frederick Hodgson. Into the accounts of Remington & Co. went the £8,000 to prop up the abstractions for another day.

Had poor Mr. Murray known more about promissory notes and the sharper practices of the City he might have noticed that the date on the note had been changed and the signature of Rowland Stephenson was superimposed onto a signature rubbed out.

Eighteen months later during the fateful week of Christmas 1828, Adam Murray had heard that all was not well and hurried to the bank on the Saturday morning to withdraw his money. David Remington later testified that when Adam Murray presented the promissory note he had to point out to him that this was not a promissory note of the bank but of Mr. Frederick Hodgson personally to Rowland Stephenson and advised Murray to take the note to Hodgson which he immediately did. Mr. Hodgson was surprised and sympathetic but he pointed out that the note was 'outdated and nothing more than waste paper'.[64] Poor Adam Murray lost no time returning to Remington's only to find the shutters down and the bank failed.

Adam Murray was advised by his lawyers to bring a claim against Frederick Hodgson as his only hope of recovering his lost money. The judge pointed out to the court that the legal question was simply 'Who between them was to bear the loss of this £8,000?' The case lasted all day with legal argument exchanged by the lawyers; the Attorney General, assisted by Mr. L. Gurney and Mr. C. Manning represented Adam Murray while Mr. Hodgson was represented by Mr. J. Brougham, assisted by Mr. F. Pollock and Mr. L. Chitty, an array of the legal profession as eminent as it was expensive.

At the end of the arguments the jury took three minutes to find for the defendant.

Adam Murray was ruined, all for the difference between four and five per cent.

CHAPTER TEN

EXCHEQUER BILLS

O F THE MANY HOURS the Commissioners spent questioning witnesses, most time was spent on the subject of the exchequer bills held at the bank, and the dealings of Rowland Stephenson with the London Life Association. They had established that the bank collapsed not only because of a prolonged abstraction of funds by Rowland Stephenson amounting to £58,000, but also by the removal from the house of large quantities of exchequer bills. Regular customers of the bank had lost exchequer bills but the London Life Association had lost all their bills except those, amounting to £11,000, that were found in an envelope in James Lloyd's desk. The Commissioners had established that the exchequer bills were being either sold on to other clients or exchanged for money that Rowland was replacing in the bank so as to lessen the deficit caused by the abstractions. This was successful enough until December 1828 when the deficit had become so high it was no longer possible to hide it.

The bank held many exchequer bills for its clients and the purchasing of the exchequer bills for the regular clients was the responsibility of David Remington.

Q   Do you know anything respecting the mode of purchasing exchequer bills for your customers?

A   Our customers used to give directions to me to make purchases of exchequer bills which we used to comply with by giving over to our broker to purchase them verbally. When they were purchased the broker's clerk, or the broker himself, used to bring them and deliver them to the cashier at the counter and he would place them in a drawer called the Discount Drawer. The exceptions were those purchased for our bankers in the country and then he used to place them on Mr. Tate's desk, and those purchased for the London Life Association, which he gave direct to Mr. Rowland Stephenson.

Q   After the bills were taken out of the discount drawer, what became of them?

A   Many of our friends in the country had them sent down to them, sometimes by being cut in half and sent at two distinct times by the post, or sent to them by the first convenient opportunity when a parcel was going down to them.

Q   Do you know anything with respect to the exchequer bills belonging to the London Life Association?

A   I do not know anything respecting the exchequer bills belonging to the London Life Association further than that Mr. Rowland Stephenson had them delivered to him personally by the broker or the broker's clerk and I considered that he so received them as a trustee for the London Life Association.

Q   Do you know where he placed them?

A   I do not.

Q   Were they placed with the general exchequer bills of the house?

A   They were not.

The London Life Association was uniquely placed to be relieved of its exchequer bills. The Association was established as a mutual life assurance company in 1806 and had its office at 48, St Paul's Churchyard. Political uncertainty and the Napoleonic Wars were persuading the middle classes to think about their financial security and the Association offered a very attractive insurance scheme that balanced the cost of premiums with the possible benefits. The Association steadily grew until 1811 when it moved to 35, Canon Street, a short walk to their bank, Remington's. In 1822 Rowland Stephenson took over the banking responsibilities of the London Life Association and he also became a trustee of the Association, acquiring one of the keys to one of the two locks that would open the tin box that contained their securities.

Richard Heathfield was the Secretary of London Life Association from June 1821 until 11 July 1827. He testified on 6 May 1829 that on 5 July 1828 the Association ordered the purchase of £20,000 exchequer bills and then £10,000 more on 14 July 1828. This was performed in the normal manner through their banker, Rowland Stephenson. The bills were paid for by money belonging to London Life Association, which was held at the bank in the tin box. This box, he confirmed, had two locks and each lock, two keys. The keys to the first lock were held by Mr Davies of the London Life and Rowland Stephenson and the keys to the second lock by a Mr. Harrison and Sir Claudius Stephen Hunter. Apart from cash the strong box contained many City Bonds and foreign stock belonging to the London Life and Rowland had to remove these occasionally to receive the interest at the city hall. The tin box, marked LLA, did not contain their exchequer bills because Rowland kept them elsewhere in the bank.

Mr. Heathfield was adamant that the London Life Association rarely dealt with exchequer bills and there was only three occasions that he knew of when they were bought, the two occasions in July 1828 when £30,000 were purchased and once before in 1823 when £5,000 of bills were acquired.

His testimony was confirmed by his successor as Secretary to the Association, Henry James Brooke. He was not just a lawyer working in commerce but had also been accepted as a member of the Royal Society in 1819 in recognition of his work on crystallography. His most important innovation was the use of spherical trigonometry into the calculation of the crystal interfacial angles. He may have found the complexities of a crystal to be a light relief compared to the convolutions of the Associations financial dealings with its banker.

The Commissioners interviewed Mr. Ellis Reeve on 5 March 1829. He was a stockbroker in Roper's Head Alley and acted as broker for Remington's.

Q   During the six years since Mr. Stephenson became a trustee of the London Life Association did you ever purchase exchequer bills for the London life Association?

A   Yes a great many times in the name of the London Life Association and as far as I can recollect I received the instructions from Mr. Rowland Stephenson.

This confused the Commissioners. The secretary of the London Life, Mr. Heathfield, had stated clearly that they had bought exchequer bills only three times but Ellis Reeve said he bought on behalf of the London Life Association, exchequer bills 'a great many times'.

The discrepancy explained how the London Life lost so much money through the removal of exchequer bills that they did not know they owned.

When Mr. Gates and the City of London Committee of Bankers began tracing the exchequer bills that had belonged to the London Life they were able to ascertain some of the bill numbers. From this they traced missing exchequer bills that had been sold to Saint Bartholomew's Hospital. The Commissioners therefore interviewed some of Rowland's colleagues at the hospital. Thomas

Helps and Thomas Hodgkinson were almoners of the hospital and confirmed that the hospital had bought exchequer bills which were bought through their trusted Treasurer, Rowland Stephenson, and were kept at the bank in a tin box that required keys to open three locks.

William Wilby was interviewed on 2 July 1830. He was the Receiver of rents at St Bartholomew's Hospital. He gave a very cagey account of the record keeping at the hospital and the dealings with the bank but did give this interesting insight:

A   On the 24th December, the day before Christmas Day 1828, Mr. Stephenson said to me 'The hospital has a large balance in my hands' and I said 'A handsome balance?' and he then opened his desk and showed to me an envelope, which he said, contained exchequer bills belonging to the hospital.

Q   Where was Mr. Stephenson at this time?

A   At the banking house at the place where he usually sat.

Q   Did you communicate to anyone connected to the hospital the fact of those exchequer bills having been produced to you?

A   I did think it was to Mr. Helps and Mr. Hodgkinson.

Q   When did you make that communication?

A   On that day.

Q   What induced you to make that communication on that day?

A   Because I was pleased to find that the exchequer bills belonging to the hospital were so safe.

Q   Had you any reason before that time to doubt the safety of the exchequer bills?

A   There had been rumours about the house.

Q   Did that rumour induce you to go to Mr. Stephenson to make the enquiry?

A   No, I went to Mr. Stephenson to get him to sign some cheques for money due that day.

The Commissioners had now confirmed that the management of exchequer bills was highly suspect and went on to interview the partners and staff at the banking house, concentrating on how exchequer bills were handled at the bank.

Thomas Digby kept the cashbook at Remington's and confirmed that exchequer bills were bought on the instructions of Rowland Stephenson from Mr Ellis Reeves, the stockbroker, in the name of the London Life Association. He said that when the bills were brought to the bank Rowland Stephenson or his clerk, James Lloyd, always took personal charge of them. He also said it was customary for exchequer bills belonging to all other clients to be entered into the cash book and the bills placed in the 'discount drawer'.

Mr. Thomas Gates, solicitor to the Committee of London bankers, who arrived at the bank on the Saturday afternoon, testified to the Commission on 1 April 1829. He was shown the evidence from James Lloyd's desk and was asked about the ledger that he had been shown marked LLA that had been found in Lloyd's desk,

Q Have you in your possession a book, which at and after the time when Stephenson absconded was in the house of Remington & Co?

A I have.

Q How did you obtain possession of it?

A Having been employed by the Committee of London bankers and the house of Remington & Co. being a subscriber to the fund, and believing that committee as having also gone into the banking house at the request of the senior Mr. Remington, and when there, at the request of himself and the two other partners, who were in attendance, had been directed to do what was necessary for the apprehension of Mr. Rowland Stephenson, who it was supposed had absconded, and taking the course that suggested itself to me, the book was found in one of the desks of the banking house, which desk I have since been told was the one used by Lloyd. This happened on Saturday the day on which the house stopped.

Q Does the book contain any entry respecting exchequer bills?

A It contains entries the nature of which I am ignorant, there is no entry of any article which is defined as an exchequer bill, but I have been informed the code refers to them.

Q Do you mean that the details of exchequer bills are not entered in the book?

A I do.

Q Are the words the London life Association in the book?

A No.

Q Are there any words to that effect in the book?

A I believe there are not words in the book to that effect.

Q Is there anything in it besides?

A Letters.

Q Do you mean alphabetic letters or letters of correspondence?

A I mean alphabetic letters. There was a code employed.

Q Were any, and what, persons present when the book was found?

A   Yes. The whole establishment of the banking house was present except Stephenson.

Q   Was it locked up?

A   I think the desk was forced open in my presence and I received the book from the hands of a clerk whose name I do not recollect.

Q   Where is the book?

A   It is now in my pocket.

Apart from the book an envelope was also found in James Lloyd's desk that contained eleven exchequer bills, each worth £1,000 and marked 'London Life Association'.

Witness after witness who were employees at the bank testified that the exchequer bills of the regular clients went into the discount drawer and those of the London Life Association always went to Rowland Stephenson. Since he was a trustee of the Association this was not thought to be unusual.

The Commissioners had now established how Rowland was acquiring exchequer bills for London Life and that they were kept separately from other exchequer bills in Lloyd's desk with the ledger written in a code that no one else understood. These exchequer bills were not disposed of through the usual channel of the stockbroker, Ellis Reeve, but through various other brokers, particularly a stockbroker named John Knibbs and the stockbrokers, Williams and Co.

John Knibbs had borrowed money from Rowland Stephenson as well as giving loans on exchequer bills. He gave evidence on 8 January 1829,

Q   What are you?

A   I am a stockbroker.

Q   Have you had pecuniary transaction with Rowland Stephenson for any and what period of time?

A   Yes, from the year 1825 and at intervals until the present time. In December I borrowed £5000 on £5000 exchequer bills from that date until the 21st January at 5% interest. After that I borrowed £10,000 on £10,000 exchequer bills of which £10,000 was paid back. I also purchased by his order £5,000 exchequer bills

The Commissioners then painstakingly examined each transaction,

Q   Had those £5,000 exchequer bills ever to your knowledge been in the possession of Stephenson before?

A   I do not know for a certainty they have. I cannot say for certain they have not.

Q   Did you pay £5,000 to Stephenson?

A   No. I paid it to Lloyd who brought me the bills, that is I gave him my cheque for it on Lubbock and Co. And the cheque passed through the house of Remington's.

Q   Of whom did you borrow the money?

A   I borrowed the £5,000 off Mr. Norris of No 8 Old Ascot Street.

Each transaction was the same. James Lloyd brought the exchequer bills to the house of Mr. Knibbs and was paid for them. To confirm the methods used, the Commissioners went through the same process for the dealings in November when again there was much selling of exchequer bills. The interview with John Knibbs continued,

Q   Have you since Stephenson absconded seen or registered any of the exchequer bills?

A   On the 30th December, the money lender, Mr. Norris who had the option of calling for the £5000 he had lent me on the £5000 exchequer bills, gave me notice that he should bank his money on the following day, the house of Remington having stopped payment. Knowing I could not get the £5,000 from them, I went on the market on my own responsibility and made a contract to sell these bills on the 31st December. Before the sale could be completed the numbers of my exchequer bills were posted up in the stock exchange and it seemed that all these bills really belonged to the London Life Association, consequently the sale fell through.

The dealings with Williams & Co. were also important as there had been the sale of £30,000 of exchequer bills on the Monday before Christmas and this money had not found its way into the accounts of the bank and had caused the discrepancies at the Bank of England on the following Saturday morning.

On the Sunday 21 December Rowland was desperate to shore up his critical finances. Through his friend, Edward Down, the broker, and William Thornton, partner at Williams & Co, he arranged to obtain a loan on £30,000 of exchequer bills. Edward Down takes up the story.

Q   Did you on Monday 22nd December receive from Rowland Stephenson any exchequer bills?

A   I did

Q   State what you received, and under what circumstances and for what purpose.

A   I received them for the purpose of getting a loan upon them. It was £30,000 exchequer bills. I took them to Messrs. Williams & Co house and when Mr. Thornton had counted them over he handed me £30,000 bank notes, which I took over to Mr. Rowland Stephenson and I handed them to him himself before all his clerks.

Q   When you took the exchequer bills to Messrs. William & Co did you not represent them as coming from Messrs Remington &Co?

A   I brought them from the banking house of Remington & Co. I received them from one of the partners, certainly I said that I had brought them from Remington & Co. and I asked for the loan of £30,000 as a loan to Remington &Co and Mr. Stephenson came over afterwards and confirmed it. The arrangement for the loan had been previously made on Sunday between Mr. Thornton myself and Rowland Stephenson

Q   Explain what you mean by arrangement having been previously made on the Sunday.

A   Rowland Stephenson applied to me and asked if I could do anything for them in the way of procuring him money. I told him that I would apply to Mr. Thornton, who is my banker, as the only channel. I saw Mr. Thornton and I told him that the house of Remington & Co. wished for a loan of £30,000 upon £30,000 exchequer bills. He said with that security there could be no objection and requested me to call on him on Monday morning about 9 o'clock, which I did.

Q   Which of the partners of Remington house did you communication on the subject?

A   With Mr. Rowland Stephenson.

Q   Did you mention the subject to any of the other partners or Remington & Co.?

A   No.

Q   When you handed the £30,000 bank notes to Mr. Rowland Stephenson in the banking house, were any of the other partners present in the banking house?

A   I am not certain that any of the partners were present. My impression was that Mr. David Remington was there, but he says he was not, this was at a quarter past nine and he says he did not come till past 10, so he could not have been there.

Mr. Thornton confirmed this story and more light was shed on the transaction by David Remington when interviewed on 11 March 1829

Q   Look at the list now produced marked with the letter F, does the same contain a true and correct list of the numbers, dates and amounts of exchequer bills so deposited with Messrs. Williams & Co. upon which £30,000 were advanced as above mentioned

A   It does contain a true and correct list of the same.

This confirmed that the exchequer bills sold to Williams & Co. on that Monday morning were in fact the exchequer bills that had been bought by the London Life in July 1828.

David Remington was asked to explain further.

Q   You have stated in your communication at this place on the 5th March instant that you had heard that bills to the amount of £30,000 had been placed in the hands of Williams, the brokers, by Rowland Stephenson, to receive in exchange bank notes to that amount, do you mean by bills, exchequer bills?

A   Yes I do.

Q   On what day were those exchequer bills so deposited at Williams the brokers?

A   I have reason to believe it was on Monday 22nd December.

Q   Did not Rowland Stephenson after he had obtained £30,000 pay it with your banking house on the partnership account?

A   £30,000 so brought to our house is made received in our cashbook by the cashbook keeper as received of the bank on Monday, the 22nd December 1828.

Q   Was the money in point of fact received?

A   No it was not.

Q   Then why was it entered in your cashbook as received by the bank when it was not so?

A   I can give no positive answer to that question not being myself concerned in such entry but I have no doubt that Mr. Rowland Stephenson gave direction to the cash book keeper to make the entry in the way described.

When they added up all the exchequer bills that were absent from their envelopes they calculated that the London Life Association had lost £39,000. Their regular customers too had lost exchequer bills and the grand total of abstracted exchequer bills was £79,000.

The Morning Herald added up what they thought Rowland Stephenson had abstracted:[65]

Cheque left at the bank covering abstraction	£58,000
Exchequer Bills	£79,000
Bank of England	£40,000
Assorted clients	£83,000
Total	£260,000

Two hundred and sixty thousand pounds is conservatively estimated to be equivalent today to thirteen million pounds.[66]

The conclusion of the Commission of Bankruptcy, after they had heard all the evidence, was that Rowland Stephenson had abstracted funds in various forms from the bank without the permission or knowledge of the partners. Fortunately for Henry the conclusion of the Commission was that he was the duped junior partner, particularly since he could show evidence that Rowland had absconded owing him and his sister, Mary Frances, £14,700.

He had been a party to the abstraction of the £58,000 but they decided that he had not made any material gain and had always believed his cousin would repay the money, which indeed he frequently did, only to abstract even more.

Henry Stephenson was never prosecuted.

Not all the victims of the collapse of Remington's felt their only recourse was through the Commission of Bankruptcy. The acquaintance of Rowland Stephenson who had 10 years earlier enquired why he wished to be an M.P. was Joseph Wilfred Parkins. He was now in America and was none too pleased when he heard that he had lost £16,000 worth of exchequer bills and swore to track Rowland Stephenson down himself. Parkins was well known and the Times reported his full loss, 'Poor ex-Sheriff Parkins! He whom we have known acting in so many concerns, is here passive, or suffering, having exchequer bills to the amount of £16,000 in the house. But if R. Stephenson be fled to America, and meet with this customer of his banking house there, we should think he would have no easy time of it'.[67]

CHAPTER ELEVEN

JOSEPH WILFRED PARKINS: THE EX-SHERIFF OF LONDON

WHEN JOSEPH PARKINS LIGHT-HEARTEDLY commented on the unsuitability of Rowland Stephenson to stand for Parliament little did they know how their lives would become inexorably entwined.

They had probably first met on 7 June 1820 at the anniversary dinner of the Cumberland Benevolent Institute at the Crown and Anchor Tavern on the Strand. Rowland Stephenson had just become a steward and Joseph Parkins was an ardent supporter. Rowland Stephenson and Joseph Parkins would never have become friends; Rowland was an urbane music loving banker while Parkins was a rough tough street fighting exhibitionist.

Christopher Parkins, a whitesmith (a worker in tin and pewter) married Ann Barnfather at St. Cuthbert's Church Carlisle on 1 May 1769. Their first child, Joseph Wilfred, was born in early 1770 and was baptised at St Cuthbert's Church on 25 March 1770. Christopher had been married previously and Joseph later claimed he had many brothers and sisters. Christopher's life came to a violent end, either in a dual or more likely by his own hand, in 1785 and his departure precipitated his large family into poverty.

Little is known of Joseph Parkins' childhood but the year after his father's death, Joseph at the age of sixteen joined the East India Company and left England to make his fortune and, like Edward Stephenson seventy years earlier, make a fortune he undoubtedly did.

He arrived in India around 1787 and for the next 30 years worked for the Company. The only reference to these years in India is found in some letters of the American, John Higginson Cabot, who was trading in and around Calcutta in 1808. He represented the family firm, Merle, Cabot & Co. who were merchants

based on the island of Mauritius. On 5 February 1808 Parkins and Cabot agreed
to jointly invest in a business venture. The contract stated that they would take
the American brig, Creole, from Isle of France on Mauritius to Calcutta via
Madras, with a cargo in which Cabot and Parkins had each invested $20,000.
Unfortunately when they arrived in Madras, trade relations between England
and America were very poor and Cabot was unceremoniously arrested by the
British and taken as a prisoner to a 'damp unwholesome cell'[68] at Poonamallie
where he would stay from 12 May to 28 September 1808. He complained bitterly
of the behaviour of his associate, Joseph Parkins, whom he accused of not doing
enough to have him released and of being privy to his arrest. Parkins pleaded his
innocence and melted away, taking the ship and its valuable cargo with him to
Calcutta.

When Parkins returned to England, sometime around 1815, he described
himself as a retired East India merchant and let it be known that he was living
on his fortune, estimated to be in excess of £300,000.

He first came to public notice in June 1818 when he stood for Parliament in
his hometown of Carlisle. He stood as a Whig against two other candidates, J.C.
Curwen and Sir James Graham. His election address, apart from describing
his leaving Carlisle as a common sailor thirty years previously, emphasised 'his
perfect independence of all parties, his advocacy of Parliamentary reform and
his disinterested wish to serve his country'.[69]

The election took place on 19 June and by 3 o'clock Parkins knew he was hopelessly outvoted, not helped by 'considerable complaints about his parsimony, carrying his notion of purity of election to such an extreme that it was impossible for his cause to proceed'.[70]

After the declaration of the result a rumour spread rapidly in the town that there had been some collusion between the two main candidates, Mr. Curwen and Sir James and that they had agreed to poll the same number of votes. When they won the election and were chaired by their supporters there was a riot. Sir James' chair was torn to pieces by the mob and the windows of The Bush public house, 'smashed, and as Sir James, in his carriage, galloped off to Edmond Castle, the mob streamed across the fields to intercept him at Botcherby, and immense piles of stones were gathered up for his benefit; but Sir James managed to escape'.[71] Uncharacteristically Parkins took no part in the disturbance.

He also contested Arundel around this time and but was beaten by T. R. Kemp who was a minister for a 'dissenting congregation' in Brighton. Parkins wisely decided to abandon parliamentary politics and instead to stand for election in the more ceremonial role of Sheriff of London, a position for which he was even less well suited.

There were then, and still are, two sheriffs of the City of London, elected annually by the liverymen, at a ceremony called the Midsummer Common Hall, held in the Guildhall. A liveryman is a full member of a livery company of which there were over 70 in 1819. The livery companies varied from the Worshipful Companies of Mercers, of Grocers and of Drapers to the Worshipful Companies of Playing Card Makers, of Horners and of Spectacle Makers. The sheriffs did have ceremonial duties at that time but they also had important judicial responsibilities, not least attending the Old Bailey where prominent seats were reserved for them on the bench so as to attend the judges and there was the more sombre task of attending executions at Newgate.

The Midsummer Common Hall of 1819 was held on 6 June and Joseph Wilfred Parkins was nominated for sheriff, describing his occupation as a haberdasher. The Lord Mayor entered to heckling from the audience; he was not at all popular due to some tax changes which had adversely affected the livelihoods of the liverymen. He immediately retired, as was custom, to allow the election of sheriff to take place. Standing for election were Alderman Waithman and Alderman Rothwell, and Messrs Buckle, Thompson, Martin, and Kaye. A Mr. Peacock then handed in a note to the Recorder who was the most senior Old Bailey judge, nominating Joseph Parkins, seconded by Henry Bradshaw Fearon. Mr. Peacock gave a speech recommending his nominee, declaring that he was now in Carlisle with the benevolent intention of applying part of his great wealth to relieve the suffering of 'our distressed manufacturers in this fine old city'.[72] Cheers from the audience greeted this.

After more speeches and much hissing, William Thompson Esq., citizen and ironmonger, and Joseph Wilfred Parkins Esq., citizen and haberdasher, were duly elected.

Thus started a memorable year for the Corporation of the City of London.

The swearing-in of the sheriffs took place on 28 September 1819 at the Common Hall. The event was again overseen by the Recorder. The ironmonger, William Thompson, had withdrawn and had been replaced by Alderman Rothwell whom Parkins had defeated at the elections in June. The Lord Mayor had already ruled that Alderman Rothwell was to be the senior sheriff, because he had the priority of being an alderman, and Parkins was to serve as junior sheriff. Not unexpectedly, Parkins was none too pleased about this and wrote a long letter, published in the Times of Saturday, 25 September 1819, giving, in great detail, the reasons for his objection to this arrangement.

The Lord Mayor arrived at half past one in full ceremonial attire but again to a welcome of 'loud hooting and hisses and with every expression of dislike and displeasure from the crowd of liverymen. His Lordship was literally assailed by cries of 'Fire, Fire! Murder, Murder' and several more coarse expressions were used by some of the crowd'.[73]

At 2 o'clock Alderman Rothwell, also fully attired, appeared in his carriage at the door of the hall, preceded by his supporters and a band playing 'God save the King'. Five minutes later Joseph Parkins arrived alone on horseback.

The ceremony began when the Lord Mayor 'ascended the hustings a little after two o'clock and was greeted by more shouts of, Fire, fire!'

Order was restored and the Crier proclaimed Richard Rothwell and Joseph Parkins as having been chosen as sheriffs for the ensuing year and called them forward for the purpose of being sworn in. Alderman Rothwell was the first to present himself to be sworn as senior sheriff but at this point Parkins pushed Alderman Rothwell out of the way and announced, 'I was the first chosen therefore I should be the senior sheriff'.

The mayor declared 'By the law of the land and by municipal law, Mr. Alderman Rothwell has a right of precedence and is to be sworn in first'.

Parkins protested against such a principle, and presented a sheaf of papers to the Lord Mayor, which he said was his protest against such proceedings.

'Swear in Alderman Rothwell', said the Recorder.

Parkins was not going to have this and again appealed to the Lord Mayor, demanding that he should have precedence over the Alderman.

'I am not competent to form any opinion or judgment upon the matter. The question must be referred to another tribunal', said the Lord Mayor.

'My Lord, I have a duty to perform to the Liverymen of London, and I demand that my protest may be received.' replied Parkins.

'I cannot receive it'.

Parkins immediately banged his papers on the desk in front of the Lord Mayor. He made five separate points as to why he should take preference over Alderman Rothwell but his basic claim was that he had won the election in June and Rothwell had not.

Satisfied at having made his protest, the swearing-in could take place with Alderman Rothwell being sworn in first and taking the senior sheriff's chain of office. The audience of liverymen had not been impressed by Parkins' behaviour and did not applaud his taking the oath as they had enthusiastically for the senior sheriff.

The court then turned to what should have been the simple task of electing the under-sheriffs. Alderman Rothwell presented Frederick Turner of Bloomsbury Square, Attorney-at-law, as a fit and proper person to serve the office of under-sheriff. As Mr. Turner came forward to be sworn in, Parkins announced loudly,

'I object to the nomination of Frederick Turner, and I present as a fit and proper person to fill the office, Mr. William Jackson, Gentleman, of Mary-street, Fitzroy-square'.

'I object to Mr. Jackson' retorted Alderman Rothwell.

Parkins replied, 'I object to Mr. Turner for many reasons. It is impossible that I can consent to his nomination'.

The Lord Mayor, becoming impatient by this time, took advice from the Recorder who said that Mr. Jackson appeared not to have any profession or business and 'that circumstance invalidated his claim in a very essential degree'.

Parkins replied, 'He is written down as a Gentleman. That is quite sufficient designation.'

After more argument the Lord Mayor suggested the two protagonists retire to discuss their differences.

The two sheriffs then left the chamber only to return almost immediately with Alderman Rothwell announcing 'My Lord Mayor, my colleague and I have been out a very short time. I have however ascertained that he and I can never agree in the appointment of the under-sheriff.'

The crowd had by this time grown weary of the argument and was becoming restive. The Lord Mayor wisely decided to postpone swearing in the under-sheriff to another occasion and the meeting rapidly broke up.

A trial of strength now began between the pugnacious Parkins on one side and the Lord Mayor, Alderman Rothwell and most of the Corporation of London on the other.

The next morning which was Michaelmas, Sheriff Parkins arrived early at the Old Bailey and took the senior sheriff's chair with his unofficial under-sheriff, Mr. Jackson, beside him. The rightful senior sheriff now arrived and squeezed himself between them, leaving the junior sheriff and deputy's seats empty. And there the three sat on each other's knees, squashed together, throughout the morning proceedings.

Being Michaelmas Day, the election of the Lord Mayor by the liverymen of London traditionally took place in the afternoon at the Common Hall. By 2 o'clock there were 10,000 liverymen present in and around the Guildhall. They came to use the proceedings to voice an angry protest against the Peterloo massacre that had occurred in Manchester six weeks previously. 18 people, including 2 women, had been killed and over 400 injured when a peaceful meeting had been violently broken up by the drunken and ill trained Manchester and Salford Yeomanry who could not be controlled even by the 15th Regiment of Hussars, summoned to restore order.

The Common Crier called for silence for the mayoral election but was shouted down by calls of 'No Election, Questions of grievance first'. As the Crier persisted, there were louder calls of 'No! No! Manchester, Manchester'.[74]

A liveryman named Thompson ascended the platform and informed the meeting that he had a series of resolutions to submit. The Common Sergeant remonstrated to no avail; Mr. Thompson declared he would hold firm until midnight and to emphasise his point took out of his pocket a white night cap and put it on his head.

Sheriff Parkins, who was presiding over the meeting with Sheriff Rothwell, was sympathetic to the argument of the Liverymen having had a first hand account of the outrage in the Saint Peter's Field, Manchester from one of his brothers, Robert Parkins, in a letter dated the day of the massacre.

79 Walter Street, Manchester
August 16th

I take up my pen to relate to you one of the most daring, cruel outrages that ever was committed on a defenseless people. I was within ten yards of the hustings, when the, Cavalry surrounded the stage on which Mr. Hunt, Mr. Johnson, Mr. Knight, and many other gentlemen, whom I personally knew, were standing, with several ladies. At this time the main body of the

Cavalry made a charge on the people who were assembled, and cut down all before them; and if I had had a pistol, I would have leveled that villain C----y, but I had nothing but a small walking-stick in my hand, with which I parried off several blows that were aimed at me, and thank God I received no material injury. I never saw a man behave with more fortitude than Mr. Hunt did on that most trying occasion.

After reading the Riot Act, and ordering the people to disperse, the military came on without any notice whatever. If you will do a praise-worthy action, come down and back Mr. Hunt, and your name will then be handed down to posterity with the blessing of thousands of your suffering countrymen.

Your brother, Robert.[75]

Parkins now spoke up and assured the company that they might depend upon his exertions in support of their rights and liberties and that there could be no election until the resolutions had been heard. The Common Sergeant was determined not to allow the protest to proceed but the defiant Sheriff Parkins invited Mr. Thompson to speak which eventually he was able to do. He announced eight resolutions of which the most important were that the will of the people must be heard, the Common Hall of Liverymen should express its 'abhorrence of the late sanguinary proceedings at Manchester, and that reading of the riot act at a peaceful meeting was a violation of the law under which the authorities had hypocritically pretended to have acted.[76]

At a quarter past four Mr. Thompson declared, 'Now I believe we have had enough of it' and the election of the mayor proceeded undisturbed. Alderman Bridges was at last elected Lord Mayor but the events preceding his election humiliated him and he held Sheriff Parkins personally responsible. He therefore began proceedings at the Court of Aldermen to have Parkins relieved of his position.

To this end on 15 October he began an action against Sheriff Parkins.

The Lord Mayor, considering it to be a part of his office to notice any infraction of the ancient and accustomed usages of this city, derogatory of the State and dignity thereof, feels it incumbent upon him to report to this Court the conduct of Joseph Wilfred Parkins, Esq., one of the sheriffs of this city, and the circumstances attendant thereon, on the 28th, 29th, and 30th of September 1819'.[77]

In a long speech the Lord Mayor outlined all the shortcomings in his junior sheriff, such as arriving at the Inauguration of sheriffs on horseback, arguing who was to be senior sheriff and, worst of all, inciting a riot at the Lord Mayor's election. Parkins rebutted this in an equally lengthy and rambling speech, declaring, 'his aversion to and contempt of unnecessary parade'.[78] The case was adjourned.

On 28 October Parkins again usurped the senior sheriff's chair at the Old Bailey but Sheriff Rothwell retook his seat while Parkins was busy ushering in the senior judge, Mr. Baron Wood. This left the second judge, Mr. Justice Park, to enter the chamber unattended. The following day Judge Park complained bitterly of being treated in this manner, 'all because of an argument between the sheriffs'.[79] This affront to the judiciary was taken very seriously and was dealt with at the Common Council on November 4th. Sheriff Parkins was accused of, 'having offered an insult to one of His Majesty's judges, calculated to lessen that respect and reverence which should be paid to one of the judges of the land, to attend upon whom in that instance was the duty of the sheriff'.[80] Mr. Justice Park was unimpressed by the explanation that Parkins had put forward in a letter which mainly reiterated his grievances. The court decided to appoint an inquiry into the matter which later concluded Sheriff Parkins should be severely reprimanded for his insulting behaviour.

Joseph Parkins was incapable of keeping his name out of the newspapers. Some people admired him but most derided his antics. He was however a force to be reckoned with not least because of his readily resorting to litigation in court or to fist fighting in the street.

In January 1820 seats had been introduced into Hyde Park near Stanhope Gate, where ladies could sit and watch the perambulations,

> the Persian ambassador being a favourite to be seen, as was Sheriff Parkins, a fool of most excellent quality, who astonishes the peaceful setting of the park with his warlike appointments. Aloft in an awful state, he drives about the Park in a two-storied curricle, armed at all points and looking as if he were going on a journey where he expected to meet a highwayman at every step, a most terrifying spectacle. But when the sheriff appears on horseback, he goes to quite the other extreme and calmly and peacefully ambles his nag, dressed in nankeen tights, black silk hose and dancing pumps.[81]

As if this was not enough to draw attention to himself, Parkins was well known for having his phaeton drawn by two quaggas which were a variety of zebra. The quagga, which became extinct about 1870, was 'a strong, somewhat heavily built animal, slow of pace but with a soft and sensitive mouth, and not as feral as a zebra'.[82]

Parkins continued to cause annoyance to the establishment by his attitude and unpredictable behaviour. On Tuesday 11 January 1820 at the London Sessions in the Old Bailey the court was occupied in swearing in constables at which it was the duty of the sheriffs to summon the grand jury and to attend the court's ministerial officers. The Recorder noted that there was only one sheriff present, Sheriff Rothwell.[83]

'Where is Mr. Sheriff Parkins? Why is he not in attendance?'

'He is in the Guildhall, Sir' replied an officer.

The Lord Mayor ordered the City Marshall, Mr. Wotner, to fetch Sheriff Parkins immediately. The officer soon returned to say that Sheriff Parkins could not come as he was busy at the hall keeper's office.

'Tell the sheriff that the Court orders his attendance'

The reply came back, 'Mr. Sheriff Parkins desires me to say to the Lord Mayor that if his attendance is required an official written notice should be sent to him to that effect'.

'Go to Mr. Parkins again and let him know that it is not the Lord Mayor but the Court that requires his attendance, and that if he refuses, it is at his VERY GREAT PERIL' This was the Recorder speaking, one of the most important judges in the land.

At last there were shouts of 'Make way for the Sheriff'.

A smiling Sheriff Parkins entered and walked up to the Lord Mayor and said 'Did you want to speak to me, my Lord'

'No, Sir'

'You are ordered by the court to attend' said the Recorder in his very authoritative voice.

Leaning over the Lord Mayor, Parkins began to say to the Recorder 'Sir, I wish ... '

'I shall hear no altercation' spluttered the near apoplectic Recorder.

Sheriff Parkins remained on his feet glowering at the Court when Alderman Hunter, also presiding, said 'You have been ordered by the court to attend here and you had better say nothing'

'Well I am here'

'Well, then, sit down and hold your tongue.'

Parkins wisely sat down and said nothing.

He was already no favourite of the judges. It was rumoured that shortly after he was elected sheriff, he had ordered the distribution of free soup to the poor at lunchtime while supplying just bread and water for the judges' refreshment. This may have been an exaggeration of an argument between Parkins and the

Grand Jurors at the Old Bailey regarding their wine allowance and 'dinner money', which Parkins had cut and given the money to charity. This was the subject of yet another of his long and rambling letters to the newspapers.

Joseph Parkins was now beginning his long enthusiastic association with litigation in various forms. A libelous pamphlet in Dublin cost him a thousand pounds in damages and on 5 Feb 1820 he found himself summoned to the Court of Requests to answer a debt of £1. 13s., the balance of a bill incurred at a public house. Parkins arrived so late at the court it was thought he was not going to defend such a paltry amount but at last a shout went up 'Make way for the sheriff' while two small boys stood at the entrance and whistled the tune of 'See the Conquering Hero Comes'. The plaintiff, the publican, testified that on 18 May 1818 Parkins, accompanied by Lord Cochrane and others, had celebrated his intention to stand for election in Carlisle at his Inn on Newgate Street. The publican said the company was very rowdy. 'the conversation was not under the most strict discipline, and there appeared a general inclination to drunkenness and pugilism.' Parkins had only paid £5 of a £6.13s bill so that £1. 13s was outstanding. Parkins defended himself in his usual manner accusing the landlord of lying and supplying too much 'Negus' (a drink invented by Colonel Francis Negus in 1717, made of port and hot water with spices and sugar, much enjoyed by Jane Eyre on her arrival at Thornfield Hall) The landlord pointed out that more negus had been ordered by Parkins and 'your friends drank everything I sent up except the glasses, and I believe your friends would have eaten them too if they had not smashed them'. The court found for the plaintiff and Parkins grudgingly paid. As he left the court he turned to the publican and snarled, 'I'll make an example of you.'

The Lord Mayor continued to try to dismiss Parkins but as much as Parkins was incorrigible he was also tenacious. On 28 April 1820 at the Court of Common Council, a motion was considered to deprive Sheriff Parkins of money that the sheriff was due from fines and amercements. His deputy sheriff pointed out that at the start of his tenure Parkins had declared he would 'not put into his pocket one shilling derived from the fines and amercements usually paid to sheriffs'.[84] The Lord Mayor railed against Parkins, describing the letter of defense he had provided as 'containing not a single sentence which was not full of sophistry and impertinence; it was obviously written to show how much he gloried in insulting every person in authority in this City'. It was then pointed out to the court that it might find itself into a difficult situation if they adopted the motion. If Parkins was not paid the fines, he might not then pay his expected share towards the cost of entertainments on Lord Mayor's Day. A motion to leave the decision to another day was rapidly passed.

With his notorious year as sheriff drawing to a close, Parkins did not wish to be out of the public eye and on 11 September 1820 he entered the Hounslow races. He rode a horse named Alfred and wore white French trousers, a black tarpaulin jacket and, instead of a cap, a red spotted handkerchief. Alfred was unplaced.

At last on 20 October the Lord Mayor having searched for precedents in this situation made a decision on Parkins. The Court of Common Council did have the power to remove the sheriff, and the committee considered the charges against Parkins fully proved; it was therefore decided that since his year was nearly over, all dues usually paid to sheriffs would be withheld, and that Parkins should be required to perform his residual duties as sheriff in the normal manner without payment. On the same day the newly elected sheriffs for the coming year were presented at the Court of Exchequer. The Lord Mayor gave a laudatory speech on the conduct of Sheriff Rothwell and then pointedly sat down. Sheriff Parkins was heard to say in a loud voice that it was indeed a compliment to be omitted in the congratulatory speech of such a scoundrel. The meeting then rounded off the tenure of Joseph Parkins with a blistering attack on his behaviour which 'has been such in many respects to excite the just displeasure of this Court and the greatest regret at his appointment; that the dignity of the office has, in his hands, been forgotten, and the Livery of London been exposed to animadversion, by his inconsistent and unbecoming behaviour'.[85]

There must have been a sigh of relief echoing through the halls of civic government as the carriage of Sheriff Parkins was drawn away from the Guildhall for the last time by his two quaggas. So ended the eventful year of Sheriff Joseph Parkins, forever to be known now as ex-Sheriff Parkins.

He continued to appear in court at regular intervals for brawling and libel. Parkins had a weakness for lost causes and befriending the downtrodden but his support always ended with disillusionment. He became a fervent supporter of Queen Caroline, the Prince Regent's estranged wife, who had returned to England in 1820 on the death of King George III. She wished to be declared Queen of England and this caused a wave of popular support and unrest. Parkins chaired meetings to support her cause against the new King. She died three weeks after the coronation of George IV but by that time Parkins had moved on to fight other battles.

In 1820 Parkins received an intriguing invitation,

My dear Sheriff,

I feel that I am out stepping the usual bounds of female delicacy by thus opening my heart to a stranger for such I am to you; although your personal qualifications and superiority present your beloved image constantly to my enamoured senses. It is in vain, Sheriff, that I endeavour to surmount the affections I bear to you; thus I throw myself on your honour and feelings as a gentlemen and a man of honour, convinced that a heart like yours will always hold sacred the confidence of a lady. Sheriff! How shall I tell you that I find it impossible to live any longer without you? Virtue has hitherto been my chief observance, and I respect its precepts – but love constant as the return of day, triumphs over me. Sheriff ! Meet me on Saturday at the Grosvenor Gate, Park Lane. If you are inclined to profit by these sentiments no obstacles shall prevent our mutual happiness; but be delicate and spare me in the first and second interview. Be mine Sheriff and the world will no longer interest a thought. Be exactly at three o'clock in Park Lane and I will meet you. My parasol is blue with a white edge. That will direct your attention. Commit this to the flames the moment you receive and recollect, dear sheriff, my honour, my happiness, and all my hopes, are in your possession.

Olive

P.S. Ride tomorrow morning slowly around Bedford Square and I shall know that this letter has reached you safe, which will occasion no further trouble until we meet on Saturday.[86]

History does not reveal whether Joseph Parkins shared Olive's blue and white parasol that Saturday afternoon but they certainly did meet at some point and there were rumours of an affair, even an engagement. Like other friends of Parkins, he soon fell out with her and publicly vilified her.

Olive Serres (nee Wilmot) was born at Warwick on 3 April 1772. She was brought up by her uncle, James Wilmot, vicar of Barton under Heath near Stratford-upon-Avon. Olive received a good education but developed a reputation for 'high spirits'. She first came to public notice in 1789 when a burglary took place at the Rectory while the Reverent Wilmot was conveniently absent. Olive gave evidence that she had awoken to find five men in her bedroom. She managed to escape by jumping out of a window into the churchyard, dressed only in a counterpane. Her dramatic evidence at the trial of the robbers five months later sent two men to the gallows at Warwick Assizes but her reputation for high spirits gave rise to rumours as to her exact role in this episode.

Packed off to London to study art she married her drawing master, John-Thomas Serres in 1791. The marriage lasted for 13 years but her wandering eye and extravagant tastes finally pushed Mr. Serres too far and having been appointed Royal Marine Painter in Edinburgh, he left. Olive moved to Brighton where she met the Prince of Wales who temporarily fell for her charms and appointed her Royal Landscape Painter. This royal connection shaped the rest of her life.

In 1817 at the age of 45 she began her campaign to be recognized as a member of the Royal family; she was, she avowed, the illegitimate daughter of Henry Frederick, Duke of Cumberland, youngest brother of George III. Her claims became more extravagant with details changing regularly. She began to style herself the Princess of Cumberland as more and more mysterious documents surfaced to prove her claim. Her assertion was extravagant, as indeed she was, but she had had supporters before the gullible Parkins. To help Olive's precarious finances the Duke of Kent, another brother of King George III, had made her an annual allowance of £400, which lasted until his death in 1820. The ending of this allowance may have prompted Olive to write her alluring letter to Parkins after which she came under his protection. He read all the documents and became an ardent supporter. In November he invited her to the Guildhall and introduced her as the Princess of Cumberland, fuelling more rumours about these two characters whom many thought deserved one another.

She now hired a carriage, which she had decorated with the Royal coats of arms and dressed her servants in Royal livery. Sheriff Parkins was pushed aside as her advisor and his place taken by one Nugent Bell, a 29-year-old law student. She made it known that she preferred a more refined gentleman to help with her affairs than the coarse ex-Sheriff.

Once Joseph Parkins had been cast aside he began to set about denouncing Olive as an imposter. He wrote endless letters to the newspapers and to the King and to anyone else who might listen, accusing her of forgery and mendacity. Parkins took the trouble to visit the family home in Warwickshire where he met Thomas Wilmot, her brother, who said he would be only too delighted if his sister could prove she was related to someone else.

Her financial state declined rapidly and on 15 January 1822 she contested a debt from the Fleet Prison and was released. She now called herself merely 'Olive' and said she had no more than two pounds to her name and was entirely supported by her friends. On 13 March she again appeared in the insolvent debtor's court. At midday her case was called just as she arrived in a carriage attended by servants with crimson liveries. When her name was called she breezed into court wearing 'a dress of white satin, which was extremely large, and a bonnet which was also of white satin and was surmounted by a plume of feathers. An India shawl was thrown loosely over her shoulder. She appeared to be highly painted'.[87] As was usual with her appearances in court the proceedings were more about her royal claims and indisputable documents than her debts and the case was adjourned.

One of her supporters, Sir Gerard Noel, was induced to move in the House of Commons for an investigation into her royal claims. Sir Robert Peel set the matter straight, describing her as an imposter and the documents as 'obvious forgeries, which conveniently appear just as the signee dies'.[88] After this she had to remove the royal crest from her carriage and her footmen were forbidden from wearing royal livery, which at least saved her a little money.

By 1826 she was living above a stocking shop at the corner of Fleet market where she remained until her death on 21 November 1834. She was buried on 3 December in the churchyard of St James, Piccadilly and was entered in the register as 'Olive, Princess of Cumberland'. She died in absolute poverty and had been in and out of the King's Bench debtor's prison for most of the last ten year of her life. As with all conspiracy theories there is just a little thread of possible truth that runs through the tale of Olive Wilmot but one of her greatest mistakes was to spurn the attentions of the vengeful Joseph Parkins.

Despite minding a lot of other people's business Parkins was still finding time to make regular appearances in court. For a change from libels and assault, Joseph Parkins appeared at Marylebone Court on 3 August 1822 on a warrant of, 'with being the father of a male child, born of Hannah White'. Parkins appeared at the appointed hour and 'bustled into the courtroom'.[89]

Hannah White took the stand, cradling her infant that she said she had delivered on May 25th 1822 at Marylebone workhouse and the infant was now chargeable to the funds of the parish. 'Fresh coloured and remarkably good looking'[90] was how the Times described her.

'And who do you charge with to be the father of this child?'

'That gentleman', she replied, pointing at Parkins.

Her testimony continued that her name was Hannah White but during the pregnancy she had changed it to Mrs. Jarvis so as to obtain lodgings. She first met Joseph Parkins in Hyde Park on an evening in August 1821, at about 8 o'clock. Parkins was on horseback with a servant. She said she saw him on a couple of further evenings and while they were together in the bushes, the groom held his horse. She solemnly denied having intercourse with any other man during that time.

Parkins then took the oath and said he had never seen Hannah White until he had arrived in court that day but the two magistrates were unimpressed by the pleas of Parkins' counsel and made an order for the ex-sheriff to pay for the child. They asked the parish clerk what was the usual charge in such cases.

'From about one to four shillings a week'

'Then Mr. Parkins shall pay four shillings a week.'

Parkins spluttered that he would appeal.

The case moldered on for the next eighteen months with an unsuccessful appeal and reports in the newspapers of Parkins' failure to keep up the payments but his purse was not long troubled by Hannah White's child since he died in infancy. A curious, and probably apocryphal, epitaph features in a book entitled *Churchyard Gleanings*,

> Here lies the child of Hannah White,
> An eke of Sheriff Parkins,
> Begot one charming summer night
> When the ex was on his larkings.[91]

The ex-sheriff regularly got into fights, not all of which he won. On 1 July 1822 Horatio Horton was put on trial for assaulting Parkins in the previous May. Parkins said in evidence that he met the defendant in Bridge Street, Blackfriars and was struck him in the face with a stick. Parkins was then attacked by two dogs that bit his legs while Orton went on hitting him. Orton's defense in court was that he wished he had hit him harder and he was merely sentenced to two months in Giltspur Street prison.

There scarcely seemed a time that Parkins was not in court but he did make another unsuccessful attempt to represent the freemen of Carlisle in Parliament, 'and many are the burgesses in that ancient city who will remember his follies and whimsicalities on that occasion. The annals of electioneering, replete as they are with tomfooleries, could scarcely produce a parallel'.[92]

Poor Henry Fauntleroy had the added misfortune to have the ex-sheriff as a client and friend. When the friendship inevitably ended Parkins contributed to Fauntleroy's fall from grace,

'This spiteful enemy burst forth upon the stage of the sad tragedy of Fauntleroy like the comic villain of melodrama-too contemptible to hate, but with a humour too crapulous for whole-hearted laughter. Joseph Wilfred Parkins ....appears to have been one of the most blatant humbugs that ever belonged to the objectionable family of Bumble.'[93]

Joseph Parkins now invested his fortune in Remington & Co. and only dealt with the senior partner, William Remington whose even temper and long experience suited the temperamental adventurer.

Sometime around 1825 Parkins went to live in Paris where he deposited some of his fortune and bought property and in 1827, at the age of 57, Joseph Parkins left England for North America, content in the knowledge that his fortune was safe in the hands of his bank, Remington, Stephenson, Remington, Toulmin and Co.

Chapter Twelve

Alias Smith & Larkin

Now ride a cockhorse
Adown Charing-cross Road
In a dark-brown chariot and a grey horse!

Mother Goose Tales

T HOMAS WELCH RECOUNTED HIS role in the flight from London in his letter to the Courier newspaper on 9 January 1829. 'Rowland requested me' he wrote 'to accompany him a few miles that he might, when his mind was more collected, give me directions respecting his children. I consented and to Bristol was the road he determined to take'.[94]

The Stephenson carriage slipped out of Saint Bartholomew's Hospital through the Henry VIII gate for the last time at 4 A.M. on Saturday 27 December. There was no mistaking that it was the carriage of the treasurer since his crest was clearly visible on the doors and was drawn by his two striking grey mares. Inside the coach sat Rowland Stephenson, his clerk, James Lloyd and his friend, Thomas Welch. William Grave was driving the carriage and might have considered himself unlucky to be helping another employer try to escape the gallows. The departure did not, however, go unnoticed. Someone saw the carriage leave the hospital at this early hour and thought it suspicious enough to report the fact to one of the gentlemen who acted as financial security for the treasurer. He too was sufficiently alarmed to immediately send the hospital porter to wake Sir James Shaw, the president of the hospital,. He immediately came to the hospital where he was informed of the unusual events that had taken place. He was 'earnestly pressed'[95] to withdraw from Remington's a part of the balance held by the hospital, 'so as to lessen the danger of the situation in which they conceived themselves to be placed.' Although Sir James was very far from imagining that these suspicions were true he did agree to withdraw £5,000. A cheque was presented at the bank at 11.30 A.M. and paid in full, two hours before the bank stopped trading.

> There was an old woman got up at the turnpike
> To open the gate a mile out of town
> Where we were going to, she did not ask it –
> Into her hand I slipped a half-crown!
> 'Old woman, old woman, hip,' said I,
> 'Can't you contrive a bit of a lie
> 'Tell them we're off to the Isle of Skye!
> 'For they'll be after us, bye and bye',
>
> *Mother Goose Tales*

William Grave certainly knew his way along the Great West Road. He drove along Fleet Street, then the Strand and into Trafalgar Square, redeveloped and renamed in honour of the recent victory; Pall Mall, Piccadilly Circus to Hyde Park and into the countryside, beginning at Knightsbridge. If Rowland Stephenson was looking out of the window of his carriage it must have been a very sad journey, past the places he had loved so much. They travelled on through Hammersmith as far as Hounslow, 12 miles now from the treasurer's house. Thomas Welch continued, 'On my proposing to quit him at Hounslow, he ordered the coachman to proceed to Staines with the same horses and on the road requested of me, in the name of mutual and long friendship that had subsisted between us, to give him one and the last proof of it and accompany him until he was on board some vessel.'

The horses were changed at Staines and they passed through Reading where Rowland must have had nostalgic thoughts of happy times at Farley Hill; on they went to Hungerford, Calne, Bath until they reached Bristol at 5 o'clock that evening, having travelled 115 miles.

They arrived at the Gloucester Hotel, Hotwells Road and stopped for refreshment. They then continued west to the small town of Shirehampton where they found the Lamplighter's Hotel on the waterfront and arranged to stay the night. The small town of Shirehampton is on the eastern bank of the Avon and faces across the river to the town of Pill with a ferry connecting the two towns. Pill was famous for its pilots and pilot boats. The River Avon downstream from the port of Bristol is not an easy stretch of river to navigate and it was the Pill pilots who guided ships through the fast tides and mud flats out into the Bristol Channel. Pill pilots had a reputation for their independence and their stranglehold on the second largest port in England.

The Lamplighters Hotel was frequented by pilots from Pill since the hotel was the venue for the examination of Pill pilots in order to grant licenses. This was the perfect place for Rowland Stephenson and James Lloyd to find a pilot boat and a skipper willing to take two strangers out into the Bristol Channel.

> I had a little pilot boat no bigger than my thumb,
> There is a little place called Pill, and there I bid it come.

Mother Goose Tales

Thomas Welch, James Lloyd and Rowland Stephenson settled into the hotel. William Grave was ordered to return to London with the coach and arrived at Queen Square on Sunday evening. After his return, he was seen by Rowland Macdonald Stephenson who testified to the commissioners in his usual guarded manner on 5 January 1829; when asked about the whereabouts of the coachman he answered,

A   The coachman has returned, where he is now I do not know. I do not remember the day I last saw him, but it was some days ago.

Q   Did you see him when he returned?

A   Yes I did.

Q   Did he bring back the carriage with him, or did it go on with your father?

A   I think he brought it back.

Q   When and where did you first see the coachman after he returned?

A   In Queen Square, I know I did not see him on the 27th and I think not 2 or 3 days after.

Q   Who was present when you first saw him?

A   I think by myself.

Q   Did any of your family or domestics see him after he returned and before you saw him?

A   I think I first saw him, except for the servants at the hospital.

Q   What was the coachman's name?

A   William Grave.

Q   Has he quitted your service?

A   I do not know.

Q   Have you seen him since Saturday last?

A   No.

Q   Do you believe your father's horses were brought back?

A   Yes.

Q   Why?

A   I think the coachman told me.

Q   What do you believe has become of them?

A   I suppose he put them in the stable and I do not know whether they are there now.

Q   Was there any conversation between you and the coachman as to the place where he took your father?

A   No.

Q   Had you not interest enough in your father's welfare to enquire to what had become of him?

A   I did not ask him.

Q   Did you not hear him say anything as to the road or how far he went with your father?

A   No.

Q   Has anybody paid wages to the coachman since his return?

A   I do not know

Q.   Where can we find him?

A   I do not know.

William Grave had promptly disappeared and the newspapers noted the irony that he had previously been in the service of Joseph Hunton, and speculated that he was probably looking for employment that did not involve coach driving.[96]

Back at the Lamplighter's Hotel the three men set about finding a boat. To avoid the suspicion of the pilots Thomas Welch played the part of a physician accompanying his patient in a very delicate state of health. All other remedies had failed to help the poor man and as a last resort a bout of seasickness was prescribed to cure his severe abdominal pains.

The time spent at the Argyle Rooms had given Thomas Welch a taste for the theatrical and he used this to persuade patrons of the Lamplighter's how seriously ill his patient was.

> Rowland sat semi-collapsed in the public bar while his learned physician took his pulse, examined his tongue and enquired of the patient whether he still felt that excruciating pain in the region of the stomach. He then gave a grave and professional shake of his head and urged still stronger the vital need for his patient to take a short sea voyage.

Presently the skipper of the pilot boat Providence, a man named Peter Bull, agreed to take them into the Bristol channel for two guineas a day and the three men from London retired to bed, exhausted.

> Rowland and Jemmy were two pretty men,
> They lay in the bed till the clock struck ten,
> Up jumps Rowland, and looks at the boat –
> 'Come brother Jemmy, 'tis time we're afloat;'
> 'You go before with the bottle and bag,
> 'And I'll come after, and carry the swag.'
>
> *Mother Goose Tales*

At 7 o'clock on the following morning the poor infirm patient was helped onto the boat by his physician and by the young companion, James Lloyd, who was noted to be wearing green tinted spectacles. Thomas Welch settled Rowland in the small cabin of the pilot boat where he sat, wrapped in blankets and attended to by his shortsighted friend.

Thomas Welch, having fulfilled the promise to his benefactor and friend, returned to London by the mail coach and was in Regent Street by 7 on the Monday morning, well in time to organise the evening entertainment at the Argyle rooms.

Thomas Welch finished his letter to the Courier, 'I was totally ignorant when I accompanied Mr. Stephenson of the extent of his embarrassments in which he had involved others. I listened only to the dictates of gratitude, which impelled me to render all the service the only one I was ever able to render him, to the man who had been so long my friend and so often my benefactor.'

There was a man in London town
And he was wondrous wise
And he went with us in the chaise
And kept shut both his eyes;
And when he saw that all was safe
With all his might and main,
He got into another chaise
And so came home again.

Mother Goose Tales

Not everyone was impressed. A correspondent signing himself Crito lambasted Welch as an accessory after the fact in this 'melodrama' and 'should share the same punishment of hanging as Rowland Stephenson certainly will'.[97]

The Providence set sail from Pill into the Bristol Channel on the morning tide of Sunday 28 December and once the boat was under weigh Rowland Stephenson amazed the crew with an instant recovery although there was certainly a lot of sea sickness to be had as the sea was very rough. On the afternoon of the following day they put into the port of Bideford, which is situated about ninety miles west of Pill on the north coast of Devon, two miles up the Torridge estuary.

If Rowland Stephenson hoped to meet with a ship bound for America in the Bristol Channel, he had been disappointed but James Lloyd was pleased to reach dry land having been very seasick and had lost his spectacles overboard. Peter Bull, the skipper, was anxious to return to Pill and left the two fugitives on the quay. Rowland did not wish to stay any longer than he had to in Bideford since there was a Customs House overlooking the quay. The Collector for H.M. Customs, was a man named Thomas Grant whom Rowland was wise to avoid. Grant later showed himself to be sharper than many of his superiors.

Fortunately for Stephenson and Lloyd they soon found the skipper of a small fishing boat, the Ranger. John Lee was willing, despite the weather, to take the men to Clovelly where his brother, William lived. He informed Rowland that his brother had a pilot boat, the Sally, and he thought he would be willing to take them back out into the Bristol Channel when the weather improved. Skipper Lee brought the Ranger safely into the small harbour of Clovelly in the early hours of 30 December. Rowland Stephenson and James Lloyd, now calling themselves Mr. Smith and Mr. Larkin, took a room at the Kings Arms, a public house by the water's edge and from where they had a good view of the comings and goings in the channel and could see any unwelcome activity in the little harbour.

Clovelly suited them well, being a very secluded village. Situated 12 miles west of Bideford, it is set into a steep cleft in the hillside with a single street that runs through the centre of the village dropping down four hundred feet in quarter of a mile to the small harbour. The inhabitants of Clovelly had a reputation for independence even more fierce than the pilots of Pill.

The two men kept a low profile in their room at the King's Arms until the weather improved which it did on Wednesday afternoon. Just before midnight William Lee took them out into the Bristol Channel to try to find a suitable ship but the Sally was blown back to Clovelly on the following afternoon. With no choice but to wait, the mysterious two men returned to the Kings Arms and settled down to spend a further night in Clovelly, contemplating what the New Year had in store for them.

They continued to keep themselves in their room, and it was later reported in the newspapers, 'they kept the windows of their room constantly closed with a brace of pistols on the table. They are also said to have a large bag of sovereigns with them, which no doubt they exposed for the same purpose.'[98]

The dapper little banker had not lost his charm and was soon on good terms with the landlady and her daughter. The landlady did admit later that she thought it curious that two men calling themselves Mr. Smith and Mr. Larkin should arrive at such a late hour, particularly when their hats had the names Stephenson and Lloyd written on the inside band crudely rubbed out.

On the Thursday evening the pilots and fishermen of Clovelly dined at the Kings Arms. The inn was very crowded and the two gentlemen guests were asked to eat next door with the landlady's daughter. Rowland sent two guineas around to the Kings Arms for the pilots to drink his health, a gesture that won the hearts of the locals who swore to do all in their power for a gentleman who had proved himself, as one was heard to say, 'a real gemman'.[99]

The local paper in North Devon was, and still is, the North Devon Journal and has always been published on Thursdays. In 1829 it took a day to arrive at Clovelly and there was only one copy for the village. The journal of 1 January 1829 was delivered to the Kings Arms on Friday morning and Rowland snapped it up. He became increasingly unwilling to part with it despite the pleas of the principal inhabitants of Clovelly who were assembled at the inn and very keen to catch up with the latest news.

In the crowd was Lieutenant Jones of the His Majesty's water guard, based at the Clovelly station. The water guard were a division of HM Customs and Excise responsible for detecting smuggling and to take responsibility at ship-wrecks, to safeguard cargoes and vessels from looting. He already suspected that these two strangers were up to no good and probably trying to escape the country. He discussed his misgivings with his friends and asked them if he should arrest the pair on suspicion. They agreed but in the total absence of any authority they thought the risk was too great and Jones decided not to detain them on his suspicion alone but to bide his time and await developments.

The assembled villagers were still waiting to read their newspaper and they persuaded the landlady to send a maid to ask if the gentlemen could spare it. She found Rowland engrossed but what the maid did not see was that Rowland's attention was upon a paragraph prominently displayed on the second page with the headline:

FAILURE OF MESSRS. REMINGTON, STEPHENSON AND CO. AND DISAPPEARANCE OF ONE OF THE PARTNERS.

Soon after the commencement of business on Saturday morning. the money market was thrown into a state of dismay by a report that one of the partners in a banking house in Lombard-street had absconded, and carried off with him a very considerable sum of money. On further inquiry this fact was established past doubt; and it was followed at two o'clock this day by a suspension of payments by the house of which he is a partner – that of Messrs. Remington, Stephenson, and Co. the partner who has disappeared is Mr. ROWLAND STEPHENSON, who is Member of Parliament for Leominster, and treasurer of St. Bartholomew's Hospital. We think it right to give names thus explicitly, both for the information of the public, and to prevent the suspicion that might otherwise fall on other persons, if they are withheld.

Besides the sum taken off in money, which amounts of £58,000, it is said that a large amount in Exchequer-bills (more than £30,000) has been abstracted from the banking-house; but at present it is a matter of inference only that these have been removed by Mr. Stephenson, for whom search has been made in every direction, but up to this time without any success. The account in circulation is, that Mr. Stephenson, at a late meeting of the partners laid claim to the money as belonging to him by right individually, and that being the case, he resorted to this method for obtaining what he considered to be his due. The explanation given by the other partners to their customers was, that they possessed what they considered an adequate supply of money in the house, but that owing to the event which had occurred, they were so little while to understand their real situation, that they thought it more prudent to stop.[100]

Not only was this the first account he had heard of the disastrous conse-quences of his disappearance but he also knew that some of the villagers might make a connection and undoubtedly the article would confirm the suspicions of Lieutenant Jones.

Stephenson remained indefatigable in his reading of the newspaper. Inside out, upside down, on he read. Never before or since has the North Devon Journal been so carefully scrutinised. Rowland passed the paper to Lloyd and when the landlady sent the servant again to obtain the newspaper said, 'Don't you see that my friend is reading it now'?

The patience of the awaiting crowd became exhausted and they finally dispersed muttering 'plentiful Devonian oaths and abuse of the two unmannerly newsmongers.'[101]

By Friday evening the weather had improved enough for the Sally to put to sea again and William Lee came to the inn to say they could leave by 10 o'clock. Rowland paid the bill, leaving a large tip for all the servants and remarking that the cost of their stay was very moderate. The landlady was pleased to receive a further generous tip in return for him keeping the newspaper which he said 'contained news of a good friend'. That settled, Stephenson immediately put the newspaper in the fire holding it down with a poker until it was entirely consumed and saying to Lloyd, 'Now that can tell no tales.'

To add to the mystery, before leaving the Kings Arms, Rowland gave a sealed letter to the landlady, addressed to a Mr. Thomas, with instructions to present it to someone who would come to collect it. If no one came within five days, she was to destroy it.

Mr. Smith and Mr. Larkin then boarded the Sally and set off with fourteen days provisions. Poor Lieutenant Jones with all his suspicions had been outwitted and deprived of the arrest of the two famous fugitives.

At dawn the following day the weather unfortunately deteriorated again. Stephenson felt his luck had stretched as far as it ever would in Clovelly and the good Lieutenant would be more persistent this time. They therefore spent all Saturday at sea, sheltering in the lee of Lundy Island. By early Sunday morning the weather had improved enough to cross the Bristol Channel to the Welsh coast and the Sally anchored in Angle Bay, a small inlet just south of Milford Haven.

On the Sunday afternoon George Rixon, a pilot of Milford Haven, was guiding the Kingston, an American brig, captained by a man named Wood, as far as the quarantine station off Milford. When they reached the anchorage he ordered the ship to stay there overnight.

So on the Sunday night, 4 January 1829, the little pilot boat, Sally, and the large brig, Kingston, rode at anchor about a mile apart. The crew of the Kingston may well not have noticed the Sally but one of the men on the Sally had certainly noticed the Kingston and viewed her as his salvation.

On the Monday morning while the crew of the Kingston were having breakfast the Sally came out from Angle Bay and approached the Kingston. Skipper Lee rowed a dinghy over to the Kingston and enquired of Captain Wood if two gentlemen could have passage. Catching a boat in this manner was not that uncommon and the practice was known as shouldering. In Great Expectations by Charles Dickens. published 30 years later but set in the 1820's, Abel Magwich attempted to escape by using the same technique to board a cross channel steamer in the Thames estuary. Fortunately for Stephenson and Lloyd, there was no Custom's four-oared galley to bear down on them from under the riverbank that had wrecked the plans of the unfortunate reformed convict.

The captain of the Kingston readily agreed to let the two passengers come aboard and for the sum of 80 guineas he would take them to his destination, Savannah, Georgia. Captain Wood was keen to return to the Custom House at Milford to register his new passengers but was dissuaded from doing so by some means. Whether it was the pistols or the money that changed his mind has not been ascertained but the captain was happy enough to disembark the pilot and immediately get the Kingston under weigh, proceeding out to sea on a fine NE wind which kindly blew for the next four days, sending the ship well on its way into the Atlantic.

Back at Clovelly, on the morning of Rowland's departure in the Kingston, a mysterious man appeared at the King's Arms, looking for Rowland Stephenson. Unknown to the landlady this was not the Mr. Thomas to whom the letter was addressed but Captain William Walter Stephenson. He was aged 36 and another brother of Mary Eliza. He was a captain in the English army and resided with his family at Ocle Court, Herefordshire. On behalf of the Stephenson family at Farley Hill he had set off to find Rowland with the intention of making him see sense and return home.

The intrepid Captain Stephenson gave evidence on Thursday 8 January 1829:

Q   Did you, Captain Stephenson, leave London this last week in hope of meeting Rowland Stephenson?
A   I did.
Q   Where did you go in search of him?
A   I went down to Bristol and Pill.
Q   Did you learn anything of him?
A   Yes, having heard before that he had left Pill in a pilot boat I took a pilot boat myself and went after him. I embarked on Friday morning last [*January 2nd the day that Rowland eventually managed to get away from Clovelly*]. I was obliged to lay to off Berry Island in consequence of wind and tide being against me. We made way again

about two o'clock and beat about the channel all that day and all that night 'til midnight on the Saturday. About an hour before I put in at Ilfracombe we met a pilot boat and learned that persons I supposed to be Rowland Stephenson and Mr. Lloyd had put in somewhere on the coast. I did not learn where distinctly. I put in at Ilfracombe if possible to find him. I searched all the places where he might be found, Barnstaple, Bideford, Appledore and Clovelly. I learned at Clovelly that they had been there and stayed 2 or 3 days and were gone. It had been blowing hard. I heard they were gone to Tenby but the intelligence came from a person who wished to arrest them [*Probably Lieutenant Jones*], and I therefore could place no reliance on it. I then proceeded to Wells in the county of Somerset. Mr. Pulsford lives at Wells. I had known Pulsford before; he is an attorney. I directed Mr. Pulsford to obtain any information he could about Rowland Stephenson's whereabouts and to communicate it to me. I came to London shortly afterwards.

Q   Have you heard from Mr. Pulsford or any person directly or indirectly respecting Mr. Rowland Stephenson since you left Wells?

A   No.

Q   Has anybody to your knowledge or belief heard from Pulsford?

A   I know nothing more directly or indirectly than what appears by the public paper.

Q   What were the instructions, which you gave Mr. Pulsford as to his mode of directing or addressing any letter to you?

A   Under cover to Mr. Bacot, Lincoln Inn Fields and I gave that direction unknown to Mr. Bacot.

Q   Have you applied to Mr. Bacot since to know if he has received any letter for you?

A   Yes, he had received none.

Q   Can you give any further information of you knowledge or belief as to the place, which Rowland Stephenson has gone?

A   The last intelligence I had was that he had gone to Tenby, since that I have had none.

Q   As you have stated that although you did not rely upon the representation first made you that Rowland Stephenson was gone to Tenby, but that from further information you received you amended your opinion, what was such further information?

A   I found a letter at Clovelly from Rowland Stephenson. I believe I tore it to pieces immediately. The contents of the letter were that they had gone to Tenby and begging the person that got that letter to follow them. The letter was directed to Mr. Thomas. When I reached the public house at Clovelly the daughter and servant maid of the house appeared much distressed, but when they ascertained that I was desired not to apprehend but to befriend Rowland Stephenson they took me aside and showed me the letter directed to Mr. Thomas and asked me if I was Mr. Thomas. I said I was not but I would see to the letter, which I did. I had no speculation of receiving any letter when I sought Rowland Stephenson.

Q   When you learnt that they had gone to Tenby and desired you to follow, why did you not follow?

A   Because I was not in possession of the facts respecting the letter to Mr. Thomas until near twelve o'clock on Monday, but I heard on Saturday at Bideford that an attorney had sent off a warrant to apprehend him. This would of course have 17 hours start on me, as everybody at Clovelly knew they had gone to Tenby. I set out for Wells as a sort of forlorn hope, in the hope that some information might be obtained.

William Walter Stephenson was not far behind his brother-in-law and they were both aboard small boats off the North Devon coast on the Saturday but not quite close enough to meet. By the time he received the letter at Clovelly William Walter was shrewd enough to know that by then Rowland would be well on his way to America and an uncertain future.

> Little Bo-peep
> Is gone on the deep
> And can't fell where to find him,
> Let him alone,
> For he'll never come home,
> Nor leave any cash behind him.

* * *

> See saw, saw the waves,
> Saw the waves asunder,
> A great knave a top of the deck,
> And a little knave is under.

Mother Goose Tales

CHAPTER THIRTEEN

THE CHASE

M UCH TO EVERYONE'S SURPRISE Rowland Stephenson and James
Harman Lloyd were still at large on Friday January 2nd, 1829, a week
after they had fled London. This prompted Robert Peel, the Home Secretary,
to write to John Wilson Croker, the Secretary to the Admiralty, requesting
that 'the whole Navy of England'[102] should be made available in the hunt for the
fugitives. Rowland's abstractions had not only bankrupted the bank but also
brought the City of London into disrepute and paralysed trading. It was a case
described by one commentator as 'bold, unblushing, unmitigated turpitude'.[103]

The authorities were, however, confident that Stephenson and Lloyd could
not remain free for much longer. A middle-aged banker, accustomed to the
better things in life, and a shortsighted clerk could hardly evade the authorities
for much longer. Rowland Stephenson was not now the popular dapper little
banker but referred to in the newspapers as the 'fraudulent banker',[104] the
'fugitive banker',[105] the 'bankrupt banker',[106] or merely 'delinquent'.[107]

Saturday 27 December 1828, within hours of the bank closing its doors,
Thomas Gates, the representative of the Committee of London Bankers, had
reported the events to Robert Peel, the Home Secretary who immediately sent
word by express mail 'to all corners of England'[108] so that that they hoped by
Sunday night 'the hue and cry will be raised along the whole British coast of
Stephenson's flight'.[109] To accomplish this he ordered the Admiralty to send all
the available information about Rowland Stephenson by telegraph. The system
of optical telegraph communication was started in 1795 by Lord George
Murray on behalf of the British Admiralty. Each telegraph tower, situated
on an appropriate high point, had wooden boards with six large holes, which
could be opened and closed by shutters, different combinations representing
different symbols. From London there were telegraph systems to Sheerness

and Deal in Kent, to Great Yarmouth in Norfolk and to Portsmouth and then on to Plymouth. For a message to travel to the west of England it would start at the Admiralty and then travel initially to the Royal Hospital, Chelsea and then Putney Heath and then to seven more towers before arriving in Portsmouth and thirty more to Plymouth. Optical telegraphy was faster than a messenger on horseback but was dependent on good visibility and required many operators. Napoleonic France had pioneered the technique when an engineer called Claude Chappe and his brothers had constructed a network of five hundred and fifty-six telegraph stations covering nearly three thousand miles. In 1792 a message of thirty-six symbols could pass from Paris to Lille, a distance of one hundred and forty-three miles, in thirty-two minutes. By this means, as well as messengers and dispatches, information about Rowland Stephenson was disseminated across England.

For the next few weeks the newspapers were full of the alleged crimes and the possible whereabouts of Rowland Stephenson. Sightings were quoted every day; a 'very reliable witness'[110] had seen him on the road to Marshalls on Friday night, another was certain he was staying with a friend in the City of London. On 30 Tuesday December the English Chronicle reported that he had fled to Liverpool and planned to take passage on a ship of the Liverpool Line. 'Police Officers were dispatched and apprehended him, drinking tea, in the Waterloo Hotel'.[111] Whoever it was sipping tea at the Waterloo hotel, it certainly was not Rowland Stephenson.

On the evening of Sunday 28 December Robert Peel and Thomas Gates met with Sir Richard Birnie. Born in Banff in 1760, Richard Birnie rose from being a saddler to become Chief Bow Street magistrate. He had distinguished himself at the violent arrest of the Cato Street conspirators in February 1820 and a year later had undertaken the daunting task of reading the Riot Act to an angry crowd following the death of Queen Caroline.

Robert Peel and Sir Richard Birnie cooperated throughout this time, organising the hunt for Rowland Stephenson. Once James Harman Lloyd's desk had been forced open by the partners at the banking house there was sufficient proof to say that 'he was in the confidence of Mr. Stephenson, and had participated in his later proceedings'[112] and it had become clear that he had gone too. Peel and Birnie began the search on the Saturday evening by sending Bow Street officers to the main roads out of London to enquire of the two fugitives and to the Channel ports to ascertain if the fugitives had left the country already by sea. Dispatches were also sent to all the European courts requesting no protection should be afforded to the criminals.

At this time despite the 'hue and cry' to find and arrest Rowland

Stephenson, there were some legal difficulties to define exactly what crime he had committed. The Lord Mayor did however on Wednesday 31 December 1828 have sufficient evidence to issue a warrant for his arrest. This was based on irregularities in the sale of the £30,000 London Life Association exchequer bills to Williams & Co. on the Monday before Christmas. The newspapers printed this announcement:

FOUR HUNDRED POUNDS REWARD—

Whereas ROWLAND STEPHENSON, a partner in the banking house of Messrs. Remington, Stephenson and Co of Lombard Street Bankers and JAMES HARMAN LLOYD, late clerk in the said banking-house, severally stand charged with EMBEZLEMENT, & have ABSCONDED. Whoever will apprehend and lodge in safe custody both or either of the above names persons, shall receive the reward of three hundred pounds for the apprehension of Rowland Stephenson, and one hundred pounds for the apprehension of James Harman Lloyd on application to Mr. Gates 56 Lombard Street. The said Mr. Stephenson is about 50 years of age, 5 feet 7 inches high, has gray hair, light coloured eyes, square features, a light brownish complexion with some colour, small straggling whiskers, & his figure although not stout is square for his height. Usually wore a black coat and waistcoat, drab kerseymere breeches, and top boots. The said James Harman Lloyd is about 30 years of age, somewhat taller and stouter than the said Rowland Stephenson, usually wore spectacles, being short sighted; has light coloured hair, full round face, and eyes of rather a light hazel colour. The said Rowland Stephenson is supposed to have left his residence at St Bartholomew's Hospital the morning of Saturday the 27th instant, in a dark coloured chariot, drawn by two light coloured gray horses. Dec 31st 1828

The reward was immediately raised to £1,000 for Stephenson's capture and £300 for Lloyd's

On Thursday, 1 January 1829, while Stephenson and Lloyd were still concealed in Clovelly, Thomas Gates and Mr. William Cope, who was the principal Marshall of the City of London, had a private meeting with Sir Richard Birnie. They were keen to make sure that the warrant issued for the arrest of Rowland Stephenson was valid throughout the kingdom to avoid there being any difficulty in apprehending Stephenson in whatever county he might be found. Sir Richard told Thomas Gates that he might command the assistance of any of the principal officers of Bow Street in pursuit of the 'delinquent'[114] and particularly recommended officers Bishop, Ellis and Ledbetter, veterans of the violent events surrounding the capture of the Cato Street gang. Sir Richard had by this time good intelligence from Bristol that the fugitives had sailed from the town of Pill down the Bristol Channel and had taken shelter somewhere along the north coast of Somerset or Devon. He therefore dispatched Officers Ellis and Ledbetter there while Chief Officer Bishop went to Falmouth. The very best of the London police force were now enlisted in the search.

On that same day it was confidently stated in the London newspapers that Stephenson and Lloyd had left for America on the Cambrian, an American ship, sailing out of Portsmouth. The newspapers were certain that the ship had left Portsmouth six days earlier and had then cruised off the Needles until a small boat had come alongside and two men had climbed aboard. The ship had then immediately sailed westward with a favourable wind. To confirm the story it was said that it was well known that the captain of the Cambrian was a friend of Stephenson and had regularly dined with him in the City. To add to the rumour, the Morning Herald declared that 'a person, answering the description of Lloyd, the absconding clerk, called at the office of the agents of the London line of packet-ships on Boxing Day and enquired if it would be possible for a person, leaving London on Saturday, to be on time to get on board the Cambrian off the Isle of Wight'.[115]

Apart from daily vilifications of his banking methods and speculation as to how he had embezzled the money, the newspapers now turned to the topic of where the money had been spent. More 'reliable witnesses'[116] came forward to tell of Rowland's late nights at the gambling tables of London and his days at the races. He did not have one mistress but six that he kept in his various houses in London.

The Times of 3 January 1829 reported,

> As the extent of his frauds becomes more and more developed every day, the wonder naturally increases as to what way these immense sums have been disposed of. He has probably, in his retreat, secured something like a provision for himself but there is little doubt that the greatest part has been lost at the gaming tables. For of his private friends of whom there are many in the city, seem to be at all aware what his private habits of living were: but among the servants about his own immediate neighbourhood, it was notorious that he regularly kept the carriage out all night, that engagements in his service have been refused on that account. His attendance at business in the city was nevertheless tolerably regular, but those who had any to transact with him that his manner was careless and absent.

Rowland Stephenson may have had many faults but there is no evidence that he was ever promiscuous or a gambler. The stories, however, pleased an avid public.

There was still more speculation as to where he was. With, as yet, little evidence many speculated that he would try to flee across the Atlantic.

ROWLAND STEPHENSON – We are able to state, from authority upon which implicit reliance may be placed, that Stephenson, the swindler, has been for many months, if not years, contemplating an escape to America; and in anticipation of consummating by flight his system of plunder, has been so long remitting large consignments of bullion to the United States. Long before any suspicion of dishonesty attached to this man's character, an American Captain remarked upon the subject of Stephenson's large remittance, as proving the extensive dealing of the house. The remark was addressed to a British Naval Officer of rank, now in London, as long as six months ago. We throw out this intimation that it may be followed up by those who have in their hands the means to prosecuting the inquiry.[117]

Yet another 'reliable witness' wrote to the Times describing Rowland's previous trips to America where he was said to have hunted with the Native American Indians and had become accomplished with the bow and arrow; he could easily live off the land there for many years to come.[118] There is however no evidence that he had ever been to America previously. Like many men of his time Rowland was a good shot and as a young man posed for a portrait with his gun and his dogs but he was certainly no backwoodsman.

On Saturday 3 January as their prey waited for better weather in the lee of Lundy Island, Robert Peel and Thomas Gates met again to discuss their response to this sad affair. Peel reported that the Admiralty telegraph had been working for days to distribute the latest information about the fugitives as far as they could. During the previous week he said inquiries had been made by his officers 'at all turnpikes and at all other places at which notice might be taken of the movement of travelers'[119] but nothing had been reported. Robert Peel added that the ship, the Cambrian, had been overtaken and searched at sea but no sign of Stephenson found; the man seen climbing aboard by the Needles was most probably the pilot getting off the ship rather than Mr. Stephenson getting on.

But Sir Robert Peel was still confidant and declared, 'If he has not escaped by miraculous speed, he never can escape'.[120]

Thomas Gates informed Robert Peel that the Committee of Bankers considered expense as nothing in this matter and those who were acting under their directions had been told to go on with the pursuit under any circumstances

and least of all to allow pecuniary matters to interfere with their exertions.
On the same day the Times commented:

ROWLAND STEPHENSON; – nothing but ROWLAND STEPHENSON
talked of in the city! If the old adage could be verified of 'Talk of a certain
personage and he will appear,' it would not be long before this man were
apprehended. It appears singular to us, we confess, that a man whose habits
of frequenting plays, balls, and operas and appearing to have been so notorious, should have been trusted as a banker. What must his partners, above
all, have thought? If they had been resolutely honest men, they would have
exposed his malpractices, and broken up the firm long ago. However, we
recommend the reading of his life and actions in our city report to those who
are curious about delinquents in the eastern regions of London. The occur-
rence will do good in one respect – it will teach men to look to the conduct
and character of their bankers as trusty traders.[121]

By this time it was accepted that Rowland Stephenson was trying to escape by
sea and John Wilson Croker, the secretary to the Admiralty, was charged with
organising the sea hunt for him. On Sunday, 4 January 1829 he sent a memorandum to Lord Northesk who was the Commander in Chief at Plymouth on
his ship, Britannia, moored at Homoaze, the naval station on the Tamar where
it flows into Plymouth Sound. He had risen to post captain in 1782 and had
commanded the Britannia at the Battle of Trafalgar. He was given the duty
of coordinating the search for the fugitive, Rowland Stephenson, along the
western approaches of England,

Directions to Lord Northesk.

To send the Bramble and Nightingale or any other vessel he may have at
hand with the gentleman who will deliver this to him, to proceed to the
westward of the Lands End to examine vessels outward bound from the
Bristol channel with the view of intercepting Rowland Stephenson and
the persons who have accompanied him – and in the event of their being
identified the officers commanding the vessel are to take the said Rowland
Stephenson and his attendants into their ship and bring them to the nearest
port where they are to deliver them over to the civil power.
    The officers he sends on this duty are to continue upon so long as the
state of the winds and weather permit. I also send two gentlemen who
know Rowland Stephenson charged with identifying him at sea.

J.W.Croker'[122]

Also on that Sunday, Admiral Robert Stafford wrote to Croker from his headquarters aboard the more famous veteran of Trafalgar:

HMS Victory
Portsmouth Harbour
4th Jany. 1829

Sir

I have to acknowledge the receipt of your letter of yesterday with its enclosures respecting the detention of the vessel called Corinthian on board of which it is supposed that Mr. Rowland Stephenson is endeavouring to make his escape to America; and signifying the direction of the Lord's Commissioners of the Admiralty to me to take measures stopping the said vessel if she should make her appearance and to afford any assistance which may be in the power to the persons mentioned in the enclosure to Mr. Peel's letter on their application to me which direction shall be attended to.

I request you will acquaint their Lordships that I am informed that the Corinthian arrived in Spithead yesterday morning at nine o'clock when the sails etc for her were put aboard and she sailed to the westward four hours afterwards; in consequence of which I have dispatched the Anya tender to ascertain whether she has proceeded through the Needles and if not to detain and bring her back to Spithead.

I am Sir, Your most obedient humble servant

Robert Stafford, Admiral[123]

The following day Admiral Stafford was able to tell John Croker that the Anya had overtaken the Corinthian. The ship was boarded and searched but again the fugitives were not to be found.

The second week of the search started on Monday 5 January. The Commission of Bankruptcy had begun hearing evidence three days earlier. They certainly had a lot of work to do, unraveling the affairs of the bank but initially they turned their attention to those witnesses who might be able to assist in the quest to capture the absconding banker and his clerk. The Commissioners interviewed Rowland Macdonald on Monday, 5 January and began by asking if he knew where his father was going. From the start Rowland Macdonald was determined not to give too much away,

Q	Have you any knowledge, belief or suspicion from any cause whatever as to what road the coachman took your father?
A	I have a suspicion as to the road he took.
Q	Where do you suspect your father went?
A	I think I heard Liverpool mentioned in the room before he started.
Q	Upon your oath, do you think he went in that direction?
A	No.
Q	Why do you not think so?
A	I have heard something to the contrary.
Q	From whom did you hear it?
A	From Mr. Welch.
Q	What did you hear from Mr. Welch?
A	That Liverpool was not the direction.
Q	State the whole that Mr. Welch said to you.
A	That my father took a decidedly different course than Liverpool.
Q	What else did he say?
A	I think he said he went over to Bristol, but I am not certain, but I so think. I think Mr. Welch said he went in the direction of Pill. My conjecture was that it would be some seaport.
Q	Why did you so conjecture?
A	Because I supposed the packing up of the clothes and everything that he was going to leave the country.
Q	Did not Mr. Welch tell you where he went?
A	I think he said to Pill.
Q	Did Mr. Welch say anything as to the place where he left him?
A	I do not remember. Pill was the last place he mentioned, I suppose he left him there.
Q	Did you see Mr. Welch the day he returned?
A	I do not remember.
Q	Did he tell you your father was in England or out of England?
A	I think he said out of England.
Q	Have you any doubt about it?
A	Yes.
Q	Did he say how he had gone?
A	I do not remember.
Q	Will you swear that he did not tell you whether he had not gone by any and what ship?
Q	I think he said there was a vessel going to sail that day or the day after by which he expected to go.
Q	What was the name of the vessel?

A   I think it was the Ann & Harriet.

Q   To what place?

A   To America.

When Thomas Welch was interviewed on 6 January he described the moment he left Rowland on the pilot boat, Providence, at Pill,

A   ... he went down into the cabin. I shook hands with him and left him. His intention was to overtake, if possible, a vessel, which he said, had sailed the preceding morning for America. The name I do not know and if he did not succeed in overtaking that vessel to meet if possible the Mary (sic) and Harriet which sailed from Liverpool according to advertisements in the paper on the 27th or rather he judged that it would have sailed on the 27th I left him about 8 o'clock the instant the anchor was weighed.

Q   Do you believe it was his intention to go to America?

A   I cannot now form any opinion with what he intended to do. My opinion then was that his intention was to go to America, but up to that moment I still had hopes of bringing him back to town. He was so agitated and in such a state of mind there was no reliance to be placed on his intentions, except I was satisfied he would either destroy himself to avoid meeting his partners or endeavour to escape.

The authorities thought it unlikely that the fugitives had been able to board the Ann & Harriet but the evidence did suggest a degree of preparation by Rowland Stephenson. The newspapers were now getting impatient for news of his whereabouts and his predicted imminent arrest was proving not so imminent. The Times, ever hopeful, declared that he was confidently expected to be arrested within hours at a solicitor's house near Regent Street, but then he might be residing in the Harrow Road.[124]

The newspaper also happily announced that 'the extent of debt incurred by Stephenson is indeed enormous'.[125] The tradesmen of Romford were all owed money and because of his 5% interest, many had been tempted to invest heavily in the bank. There was now a rumour that Rowland Stephenson, shortly before he absconded, had been seen carrying an iron bar into the bank with the intention of breaking open the strong room. Since Rowland and all the partners had keys to the strong room it was very unlikely he would resort to using an iron bar to rob his own bank.

Not everybody agreed that Rowland was the rogue that the newspapers were describing him to be. The Times of 5 January pointed out that 'there are persons to be met with who were intimately acquainted with the fugitive banker, credulous enough to believe that he is still able to explain favourably all that has occurred and that he will surrender himself under the bankruptcy along with the other partners. This will be treated by everyone, and justly, as a great absurdity'.[126]

With Stephenson and Lloyd still at liberty it was now time for the newspapers to apportion some blame for this 'disgraceful state of affairs'.[127]

The Lord Mayor came in for particular criticism for not having issued a writ until 31 December despite the fact that his chief clerk, Mr. Francis Hobler, had strongly advised against a warrant until a sound legal case could be made. Thomas Gates confirmed the defectiveness of the evidence on which to grant a warrant and the lack of material witnesses. The only case against Stephenson, which clearly showed illegal intent, involved the sale of exchequer bills, lodged for safe keeping at the banking house of Remington & Co. It was alleged that Rowland Stephenson had fraudulently sold these exchequer bills to the value of £30,000 through the broker, Mr. Down, to the brokers, Williams & Co. on Monday 22 December 1828. Unfortunately the only witness, Mr. Down, was out of London and did not reach town until Wednesday, 31 December 1828 when the warrant could be issued. The only other obvious crime at that stage was the theft of the exchequer bills of Joseph Parkins but his absence from the country also caused legal difficulties. The timing of the warrant however was unimportant since Mr. Gates had initiated the search as soon as he knew of the disappearance of Rowland Stephenson.

Sir Robert Peel had been informed that the Act under which Rowland Stephenson would be tried when apprehended, was the 7th and 8th of George IV. C.29 sec.49, which deemed it illegal for a person to appropriate securities, entrusted to them for safety. The punishment for this, if found guilty, was not the death penalty but transportation for 14 years. This would not have disappointed Robert Peel since he was keen to reduce the number of executions and he also knew that the crime and the punishment were not as important as the loss of faith in the City of London and it was imperative to bring Rowland Stephenson to justice as soon as possible to maintain trust in the system.

On Monday night Lord Northesk wrote to John Croker,

Britannia, in Hamoaze
10 PM, 5th January 1829

Sir,

With reference to your letter of the 4th Instant which has just been delivered to me by the gentleman charged with identifying Mr. Stephenson, and the persons who have accompanied him; I request you will be pleased to inform the Lords Commissioners of the Admiralty that I have directed the commanding officers of the Meteor steam vessel and Nightingale schooner (the only vessels at my disposal) to receive each one of these gentlemen and put to sea without a moment's loss of time for the purpose of carrying into execution the orders contained in the letter above referred to.

Later; The gentlemen have embarked, and the vessels will proceed as soon as circumstances will permit.

I am Sir,

Northesk, Admiral[128]

Wednesday, 7 January brought news from Bristol. A letter was published in the London newspapers saying that Stephenson, the 'fraudulent banker' and his clerk, Lloyd, had been seen on Saturday 27th December going on board a ship called the Minerva, 'a fine, sharp, American built vessel'[129] whose skipper was Captain Wallace. It was reported that HMS Nimrod with 20 guns under Captain Radford and HMS Ranger of 28 guns under Captain Walpole had sailed in pursuit, one to try to overtake the Minerva and the other to go straight to New York to inform the authorities there of Stephenson's flight.

Later editions of the papers that day described an 'intelligent man' who was at Clovelly on Monday 29 December and had seen Stephenson and Lloyd come into the harbour in a Pill pilot boat late at night. He described their stay in Clovelly including the attempt to leave on the Wednesday night and concluded that they had left on Friday. He also reported seeing the Sally return on Monday morning but William Lee, the skipper, had declined to say what he had done with his passengers. The intelligent man concluded it most likely that they had fallen in with a ship heading out into the Atlantic and they were now well on their way to America, as indeed they were.[130]

To be fair to the Bow Street officers, who were part of a very small force, they were not far behind the fugitives. Bishop, the chief officer at Bow Street, had been sent to Falmouth the previous Friday but had been redirected to Clovelly. He arrived there on Wednesday, 7 January and was joined by Officers Ledbetter and Ellis.

The three policemen interviewed the boatman, William Lee. He told them of his trip to Milford Haven and how Rowland Stephenson and James Lloyd had successfully boarded a ship going to Savannah and that the ship was called the Kingston. They interviewed the hapless Lieutenant Jones, still fuming that he had let such a fine catch slip through his fingers and lost his chance to obtain the reward, but he had little to add. The landlady of the Kings Arms described the appearance of her two guests whose names, she said, were Mr. Smith and Mr. Larkin but she informed the officers how she had noticed other names on the lining of their hats that had been partially erased. They were quiet and respectable men, she said, and, like William Lee, she had no reason to suspect they were fleeing from the law. She did not mention their arrival in the middle of the night nor the pistols they kept close at hand. The landlady did admit to the officers that Rowland Stephenson had left a letter addressed to a Mr. Thomas that she was to destroy if no one collected it within five days.

'Where is it then? Have you destroyed it?'

'A nice gentleman from London came and collected it'

This revelation certainly surprised the officers since they had thought they were the first on the scene and how could someone from London have found out that the fugitives had been hiding in Clovelly?[131]

With no regrets the three officers took their leave of Clovelly where the inhabitants seemed to welcome criminals and where their only concern was that Mr. Smith had taken their weekly newspaper. The police officers decided to proceed to Milford Haven to confirm the story of the boatman but they knew that if the fugitives had boarded the Kingston two days earlier they were now long gone. On the afternoon of Thursday 8 January 1829, having scaled the steep hill out of the village, they climbed into a post chaise and bumped along the Hobby Drive to the coastal road. They turned left and crossed the Torridge Bridge at Bideford and followed the river downstream to Instow then followed the River Taw upstream crossing it at the bridge in Barnstaple and then on to Ilfracombe where they were surprised to find Mr. William Cope, the City Marshall, had already arrived.[132]

A letter from Captain Symons of His Majesty's Steam Vessel Meteor to Lord Northesk explains how Mr. Cope had arrived at Ilfracombe before the officers. He had been one of the two gentlemen put aboard the ships at Hamoaze by Lord Northesk on the night of January 5th in order to identify Rowland Stephenson if apprehended at sea.

H.M.S. Vessel Meteor
Hamoaze
9. Jany. 1829

My Lord,

From the information we obtained of Mr. Rowland Stephenson at Lundy Island, Mr. Cope the City Marshall, not foreseeing the least probability of intercepting him, requested to be landed at Ilfracombe to endeavour to find out the master of the vessel that took Mr. Stephenson from Clovelly, and that he should not return to Plymouth by the Meteor. Immediately on landing him I proceeded towards the Lands End and yesterday landed at St. Ives to enquire of the collector of HM Customs if he had any information of the vessel that took on board Mr. Stephenson and while I was with him he received a letter from the collector of Bideford stating that Mr. Stephenson embarked in the Sally of Clovelly on Friday last and that on Monday the Sally returned again without him and it is supposed he embarked in some vessel between Friday and Monday morning and with the stormy north easterly winds was soon out of the Channel, or the Sally might have landed him on some other part of the coast; this, Mr. Cope will endeavour to find out as soon as he gets hold of the Master, having learnt the return of the Sally there appeared no other way I could be of service and therefore make the best of my way to Plymouth.

I remain your Lordships most obedient servant

W. H. Symons Lieutenant and Commander [133]

The Meteor had called at Lundy and Mr. Cope received information there. A sharp eyed inhabitant of Lundy must have seen the Sally sheltering in the lee of the island on the Saturday night before it crossed to Milford Haven. William Cope had correctly deduced that the fugitives had got away.

Officer Ellis returned to London to inform Sir Richard Birnie of the situation, while Mr. Cope and Officers Bishop and Ledbetter immediately took a boat from Ilfracombe across the channel to Tenby and from there they travelled by post chaise to Milford Haven where they finally arrived on Saturday 10 January.

In the mean time on 8 January the collector of HM Customs in Bideford, Thomas Grant, wrote to Lord Northesk with a suggestion,

Custom House Bideford
8.1.1829

My Lord,

In consequence of a letter I have this day received from Mr. Gates, the solicitor to the Bankers Committee in London informing me that three of H. M. Cruisers under your Lordship's orders are cruising off the Lands End with the view to prevent the escape of Messrs Stevenson (sic) and Lloyd, I take the liberty of addressing your Lordship in consequence of my being the only person at present, except the Bow Street Officers, who attended at my house last evening, that was ever acquainted with the circumstances of their departure.

It is unnecessary for me to trespass on your Lordship's time by describing all the circumstances respecting the Sally's trip and narrow escapes owing to bad weather, it will be sufficient to inform your Lordship that Messrs. Stevenson and Lloyd were put on board the Kingston bound to Savannah at Milford from the skiff, Sally, of this Port and the Kingston was under sail about 10.00 a.m. on Monday.

Another clerk from the same Bank left this town on Sunday last, hoping to join them at Tenby. The Bow Street Officers left here last evening about 7 p.m. for Ilfracombe and thence across the Channel to Milford and Tenby. I hope your Lordships will not think me too officious in suggesting a plan which I think might be of service – I have given of my whole time and thoughts to this affair since it first came to my knowledge that they were in this neighbourhood, and with all due deference to your Lordship's superior judgement, permit me to submit for your Lordship's consideration whether in the event of a fast sailing vessel being made ready for such a voyage that she might not reach Savannah before a merchant vessel with a full cargo that started from Milford on Monday last.

The Western Coast is lined with your cruisers and the well known excellence of our Bow Street Officers with other arrangements made respecting the arrival and sailing of all vessels from this coast, I think the parties cannot escape – I have acquainted Mr. Gates that I have taken the liberty of writing to your Lordship to this affect because much time would be lost in submitting such a proposition to my superior, Mr. Pell.

The Kingston appears to be a Brig about 230 tons with a figurehead and KINGSTON presented on her bow – this is the only description at present recorded of her.

I have the Honour to be with great respect
Your Lordship's
Ever Obedient Humble Servant

Thomas Grant, Collector H. M. Customs[134]

The man whom he describes as leaving Bideford on the Sunday before was not 'another clerk of the same bank' but Captain William Walter Stephenson, endeavouring to find his brother-in-law.

Lord Northesk did take some notice of the letter and wrote to Croker at the Admiralty,

Britannia in Hamoaze
10th January 1829

Sir

I transmit herewith for the information of the Lords Commissioners of the
Admiralty, a letter which I received this morning from the Collector of
Customs at Bideford, stating that a Messrs. Stephenson and Lloyd were put
on board the Kingston bound to Savannah, at Milford and that the vessel
was under sail about 10.00 a.m. on Monday last, the 5th Instant.

Deeming it likely that the Kingston will make the Island of Corvo, one
of the Azores, for the purpose of taking a fresh departure, and judging that
under all circumstance it is possible a Man of War by carrying a press of sail,
might arrive out there before a deep laden Merchant Vessel, I have, with
reference to the orders contained in your letter of the 4th instant directed the
Royalist Tender to put to sea, and proceed with all possible expedition to the
island above named in the hope of her intercepting the Kingston.

I herewith enclose for their Lordships further information a copy of the
order I have given to Lieutenant Robilliard, Commanding the said Tender
for his guidance on this service.

I am sir, Your Most obedient humble servant

Northesk, Admiral

P.S. 5 a.m. As it is now calm I have directed Lieutenant Robilliard, to wait
the arrival of the post this evening.[135]

The orders to Lieutenant Robilliard, Commanding H.M. Brig Royalist,
Tender to the Britannia were as follows,

By the right Honourable William Earl of Northesk G.C.B.
Admiral of the White Bear
Admiral of Great Britain and Commander in Chief of His Majesty's ships and
Vessels employed and to be employed at Plymouth

Warrants being issued for the apprehension of Mr. Rowland Stephenson of
the firm of Remington and Company Bankers, London, and of Mr. James
Harman Lloyd, Clerk to the said Bankers, who have absconded with property
to a considerable amount, and having received intelligence that the aforesaid
persons were put on board the Kingston bound to Savannah at Milford from

the Sally of Bideford and that the Kingston sailed at about 10 a.m. on the 5th instant for America.

You are hereby required and directed to put to sea in the Royalist under your command, and proceed with the greatest expedition direct to Corvo, one of the western islands, in the vicinity of which you will cruise with the view of endeavouring to intercept the Kingston, should she make that island on her voyage to America.

After arriving off the island of Corvo for three days and not falling in with, or gaining any intelligence of the Kingston, you will then proceed to the southernward and westward of those islands on your route back, and then to the westward and longitude 36 and to Southward and 36 north latitude, in the hope of falling in with that vessel, should she take a more southern course.

In the event of your meeting with westerly winds on your passage to Corvo, and not being able to make that island expeditiously, you will proceed at once to the southward, and cruise for a week within the limits above defined.

Should you succeed in intercepting the Kingston, you will take Messrs Stephenson and Lloyd into the Royalist and return with all possible expedition to England, making for the nearest Port, where they are to be delivered over to the Civil Power.

You will avail yourself of every opportunity to report your proceedings, always sending your dispatches under cover to the Secretary of the Admiralty, and on your return to this Port, you will furnish me with a copy of the ship's log, and full detail of your whole proceedings in the execution of this service.

The Kingston appears to be a brig about 230 tons, with a figure head and Kingston painted on her bow.

Having directed a chronometer to be supplied to the Royalist, it is my direction that you observe the greatest care in moving it from the Depot here, to the tender returning the same to the agents immediately on your arrival back in England.

Given on board the Britannia
In Hamoaze
10.1.1829136

Had Lord Northesk followed the advice of the humble custom collector at Bideford, the precious chronometer would not have been necessary for the simple journey direct to Savannah. The lumbering Kingston took nearly eight weeks to reach its destination, a journey that most ships managed in less than six weeks. The Kingston did not sail anywhere near the Azores.

Meanwhile Mr. Cope and the two police officers arrived at Milford Haven and interviewed the pilot for the Kingston, Mr. George Rixon, who described the two passengers as a man in his fifties who took a great deal of snuff and a younger man who appeared very short sighted. They certainly fitted the description of Stephenson and Lloyd but were calling themselves Smith and Larkin. Mr. Rixon also reported that the ship was laden with salt and was a heavy sailor and any ships sent by the government would overtake her before she was half way to Savannah. He omitted to tell the police that the heavy user of snuff had tipped him ten shillings.

The officers then discussed with Mr. Samuel Starbuck what to do next. Starbuck was the agent for Lloyds at Milford Haven and was very keen to help. He suggested that the officers engage a revenue cutter that was then lying in the port. It would be much faster than the Kingston and even with six days head start could easily overtake her. With regret the officers did not feel they had the authority to commandeer a government ship and after some consideration they decided to split up, Bishop and Ledbetter would take a Pill pilot boat that happened to be in port, and sail to Falmouth while Mr. Cope would go back to London to discuss the state of affairs with Robert Peel.

From Milford Haven Officers Bishop and Ledbetter sailed to St Ives on the north coast of Cornwall where they intended to continue their journey by land to Falmouth thus avoiding the even rougher journey around Lands End. HMS Meteor had called at St. Ives a few days before so that everyone in the town knew the details of the flight of the absconding banker. As the police officers approached the small harbour the skipper realised his Pill pilot boat was too large to run up onto the beach so they anchored and hailed a small skiff to put them on the shore. The skiff at the time was being used to unload a brig but the crew immediately stopped what they were doing and rowed over to the pilot boat, only too willing to assist the two gentlemen to shore.

Two gentlemen, arriving in a Pill pilot boat, at ten in the evening, was proof enough to the crew of the skiff that this was the fugitive pair, Stephenson and Lloyd. The £1000 reward was all but theirs. They carefully and politely helped onto dry land the two men who perhaps, on hindsight, were rather more heavily built than they might have expected of two London bankers. They took particular care of the luggage and were rather disappointed that there was no strong box but this did not lessen their enthusiasm or their certainty that this was the absconding banker and his clerk.

Two of the crewmen now stayed with the gentlemen and their luggage at a local inn while the other two went off to find the Mayor and tell him that Stephenson and Lloyd were within their grasp. The Mayor declared this to be a momentous occasion for the town of St Ives and immediately called for the Solicitor of the Corporation who recommended that in addition to the civil powers they should procure reinforcements from the Coastal Blockade Service. Stephenson and Lloyd were known to be armed and dangerous, so all due care must be taken.

In no time the inn and all the roads leading to it were well guarded and sentinels posted in all directions. A large force headed by a 'respectable gentleman'[137] set off for the inn.

Unaware of the excitement their arrival had caused, Ledbetter and Bishop were sat at a table in a small room in the inn, enjoying brandy and water. They needed some peace and quiet to recover from their trip across the Bristol Channel. Their duties in London rarely took them near the sea, let alone on it in a small boat. As they tried to relax they did notice that there seemed to be some agitation around the inn and faces peering in through the window. After their experience with the Devonians in Clovelly they were ready for almost anything from the Cornish in St Ives.

> After a while there was a gentle knock on the door.
> 'Come in'
> An elderly gentleman with a grave and important face entered the room and said, 'I understand, Gentlemen, that you want a post chaise to Falmouth'
> 'We do' said Bishop 'and a precious long time they are without letting us know whether we can have it'
> 'I am afraid,' said the old gentleman 'that you cannot get a chaise – indeed we have no means of travelling here except by saddle horses'.[138]

Bishop was losing patience and informed the old man that they had valuable luggage and saddle horses were out of the question. At the mention of valuable luggage the old man's eyes travelled around the room. His eyes moved from the portmanteau back to the two gentlemen.

It was now beginning to dawn on George Bishop that there might be a misunderstanding here. There also appeared to be rather a lot of people in the corridor outside the room and there was now a crowd of people outside the windows craning their necks for a better view. Bishop gave Ledbetter a wink since they had both deduced what was happening and were now in no hurry to disappoint their hosts.

Officer Ledbetter then told the old gentleman how surprised he was that two men asking for a post chaise should attract so much attention.

As the room filled with people, eager to see the arrest, the old gentleman spoke with great solemnity,

> The fact is, Gentlemen, we have great pain in informing you from the very suspicious circumstances under which ye have landed here this evening, we have good reason that ye are Mr. Rowland Stephenson and Mr. James Lloyd. We have positive information that you embarked some days since in a Pill-boat and we are assured that ye arrived here this night in a boat belonging to Pill. Our duty is a very disagreeable one; but that it requires that we should conduct thee before the mayor.[139]

Just as violent hands were enthusiastically laid upon him, Bishop rose and said in a commanding voice,

> 'Make yourselves quite easy, Gentlemen. I think my friend and I are more likely to arrest Mr. Stephenson than you are and if you are really desirous that no delay should take place in the pursuit, pray use your influence to obtain us a chaise. We are Bow Street Officers.'
> 'The devil you are' exclaimed the old gentleman.[140]

The crowd soon realised there might have been an embarrassing mistake. The Mayor's son was the first to grasp that these two broad-shouldered men were more likely to be police officers than City bankers and ran off to the Mayor's parlour to inform his father of the ludicrous termination of his well arranged plan for the certain capture of Stephenson. He found his father in tremendous expectation of the arrival of the criminal. Food had been prepared and friends invited to witness this exciting occasion.

The disappointment was great but all took it in good heart except the boatmen who had already planned how to spend their share of the reward. The Mayor soon found a chaise and the two officers vanished into the night leaving the people of St. Ives to wonder quite what had happened that evening.

Mistaken identity would occur again as they made their way to Falmouth. Near Redruth they stopped for refreshment and this drew the attention of two local constables who decided to follow them. Bishop had had enough of this by then and drew out a pistol but far from being deterred one of the constables shouted,

'Its them, its them. Help us in the King's name. Help us in the King's name' and seizing Bishop by the collar said 'Ah! Stephenson, you thief, have we grabbed you?'

'Yes, you have grabbed me,' said Bishop in a very ungentlemanly fashion, 'but if you don't drop my toggery I'm cursed if I don't blow your brains out, In the name of the Law'[141]

The tone and manner were quite enough to make the local policeman think again and the constables acknowledged they were deceived by the resemblance and very willingly helped the Bow Street officers on their way.

Officers Bishop and Ledbetter eventually arrived at Falmouth and immediately ordered the Swallow, one of the fastest packets on the River Fal, to make ready to take them to America. Before they could set sail, however, they received a letter from Mr. Gates telling them to return to London. The search for the fugitives by the Bow Street officers was over.

A few days later Lord Northesk wrote to John Wilson Croker at the Admiralty:

Britannia in Hamoaze
17th January 1829

Sir,

I transmit herewith for the information of the Lords Commissioners of the Admiralty, the daily return of His Majesty's Ships and Vessels at this Port.

The Nightingale Schooner has returned from the Westward without having been able to obtain any intelligence respecting Messrs. Stephenson and Lloyd.

I am sir, your most obedient humble servant

Northesk, Admiral'[142]

When the Royalist returned to Plymouth with no sightings of the Kingston in the Azores it was finally accepted that the fugitives had got away. To bring Rowland Stephenson back to justice the British government was going to have to try different tactics.

CHAPTER FOURTEEN

LONDON AFTERMATH

Oh Wellington and Stephenson
Oh morn and evening papers,
Times, Herald, Courier, Globe and Sun,
When will ye cease our ears to stun
With these two heroes' capers.

* * *

Sir Richard Birnie doth decide
That Rowland must be mad
In private coach, with crest, to ride,
When chaises could be had

* * *

Oh Wellington and Stephenson
Ye ever boring pair
Wheree'er I sit, or, stand, or run
Ye haunt me everywhere.

The Times 10 January 1829
Extract from the Poetic Works
of Thomas Moore, collected by Himself.

B Y THE MIDDLE OF January 1829 despite all the efforts of the Committee of Bankers, the Home Secretary, the Bow Street officers and the Admiralty, it was conceded that Rowland Stephenson and his clerk, James Harman Lloyd, had slipped through the net. The last hope, H.M.Brig, Royalist, had returned from the Azores and reported no sightings. The authorities were now left to sort out the financial problems that the failure of the bank had caused.

On Wednesday, 31 December, the bank was formally declared bankrupt; the Commission for Bankruptcy was set up and the four Commissioners chosen and Mr. Montague appeared as counsel for the bank.

The City remained in shock for the first few days of January 1829, prompting the Times to note,'Business at the Stock exchange remains almost suspended and the funds consequently neither rise nor fall'.[143]

This was not surprising, particularly with relation to trade in exchequer bills when advertisements like this were appearing in the Times daily,

NOTICE is hereby given, that the following

EXCHEQUER BILLS, Numbers 8739, 8740, ... total value £10,000 were DEPOSITED with Messrs. Remington, Stephenson, and Co. by Messrs John Smith and William Harding and that **NO** order or other authority was AT ANY TIME given by them, or on their behalf, to the said Messrs. Remington, Stephenson, & Co., or either of them, to sell, pledge or otherwise dispose of the same; and all persons whomsoever are hereby **CAUTIONED** against taking the same.

JOHN SMITH, for Self and William Harding, 8, New-Inn, London.[144]

The first meeting with the creditors took place on Friday, 8 January, at the Guildhall, London. Each claim against the banking house had to be individually assessed.

The meeting was due to start at 2 o'clock but an hour before the room was already 'crowded to suffocation'.[145]

Mr. Roots who appeared as counsel for a Mr. Fructuoso started the proceedings with a claim for £60,000. He said that his client had lent Mr. Stephenson the money and had been given three holding Bonds for £20,000 each. Mr. Fructuoso had also not been paid for 250 pipes of wine. The crowd were unimpressed by this claim and the meeting rapidly became unruly but order was restored and the claim accepted. Mr. Roots then began another claim. In 1826 Mr. Fructuoso had instructed the firm to buy foreign securities to the value of £54,000 but had received nothing in return. It had since been discovered they were now vastly reduced in value. The crowd found this very amusing and the Times reports 'loud laughter'.[146] The two counsels argued whether past or present value should be paid and the decision of the Commission was that it should be the lesser amount ('more laughter').

Another 15 or so creditors were heard during the meeting, including a Mr. James Ramsbottom, a brewer from Windsor, for £515; our friend Ellis Reeve, stock broker, for £1469 and various other individuals and small companies. The debts accepted for that day added up to between £100,000 and £120,000. Many creditors bitterly complained that they had never sanctioned Rowland Stephenson to interfere with their money that was lodged for safe keeping only at the bank.

All the partners including Mr. Toulmin attended the meeting and they

> afforded every facility in checking the accounts of the different creditors. On the part of the Commissioners great anxiety appeared for them to do their duty towards the creditors but we cannot say the same for the solicitor or his clerks. As for these clerks, their conduct was abominable; a more proud, upstart, ignorant set of fellows never existed. If a question was asked of either of them, they would scarcely deign to give an answer; and if they did answer, it was in language so abrupt as not to be endured; and for our own part do not see why a paltry lawyer's clerk should assume the dignity of a chevalier.[147]

The exhausted Commissioners closed the meeting at 6 o'clock.

Almost immediately after the collapse of the bank, questions were being asked in the press as to why the five eminent bankers who had examined the bank were so sure of its solvency. It had not escaped the notice of the many creditors that the bankers had restored trust in the bank by investing £100,000 themselves the week before the collapse but had been repaid hours before the bank stopped trading.

The Times described the difficult situation that the five bankers were having to explain,

> ... that they could entertain no suspicion of so great a crime as the abstraction of the exchequer bills and could not therefore have put a question which implied a charge of a capital felony against the gentleman with whom they were in consultation. They say that no account could appear more plausible or bear more the semblance of truth than that which Rowland Stephenson gave of the affairs of the house. His manner was perfectly easy and unconstrained and in adverting to the run on the bank which occurred on the Saturday previous he said as proof that the house still possessed great resources, they nevertheless had been enabled on that day to make advances to a stockbroker to the amount of £30,000 on exchequer bills. The cheque of the broker, with the bills themselves, was at the same time submitted for the inspection of the

bankers. They had no suspicion, nor could they possibly have suspected that the whole transaction so described to them was FALSE, that the exchequer bills themselves were part of the deposit of one of his own customers and the cheque was to be deposited with another banker on the following day as the security for an advance of money to Stephenson himself.[148]

The bankers defended themselves by admitting that they had taken much on trust, particularly they had presumed the envelopes with the name and number of exchequer bills written clearly on the outside actually contained those exchequer bills on the inside; they did not examine the inside of the envelopes more closely because they considered it very unlikely that anything would be missing as it was a capital offence to remove exchequer bills from a banking house.

Elsewhere there were other consequences of Rowland's sudden departure. Mr. Thomas Hornor had been depending on Rowland's financial backing so that the Colosseum could be completed and opened to the public. With Rowland gone there was no hope of any more money from the bank and Hornor was desperate to open the Colosseum to the paying public. A group of his friends met on 3 January to view the panorama, which was now all but finished but the other attractions still required more work and investment. Hornor still maintained he needed a further £60,000 to complete the project but they decided to open as soon as they could so that money could be raised to finish the project. The Colosseum was duly opened for a private view on Saturday 10 January. The Panorama was much admired as was the building in general. The modern accoutrements drew comment,

> The central column contains a small circular chamber, which is to be made to ascend, by means of machinery, with an imperceptible motion to the first gallery. Having arrived thither, the doors open, and such of the visitors as are unable or unwilling to ascend the stairs, or who prefer this novel mode of being elevated, walk out into the gallery to look upon the picture.[149]

This 'novel mode of being elevated' was one of the first public lifts in use in Europe.

Work did continue but without the investment of Rowland Stephenson and many unpaid bills due to the collapse of the bank. the building was never quite able to live up to its expectations. The London Literary Gazette however did give lavish praise and 'hopes the financial problems brought on by the disappearance of Rowland Stephenson will not stop the completion of the project'.[150] At the end of January it was opened to the general public and instantly became, for a short time, London's most fashionable entertainment although some of this popularity was put down to its spicy association with the absconding banker. By the summer the Times was telling its readers that the Colosseum was enjoying the patronage of high society including royalty, the Duke of Wellington, 'and the admiration of the tout ensemble.'[151] Not all the 'tout ensemble' were impressed; it was also described as 'that monstrous edifice recently erected in London'.[152]

On Saturday 10 January 1829 it was reported that the Governors of Saint Bartholomew's Hospital who had prided themselves on the dexterity with which they had withdrawn most of their deposit from the bank just before it stopped trading were now facing a request from the Commissioners that the money should be restored 'for the benefit of the creditors the sum which under undue preference and advantage they have obtained'.[153] The argument was based on the premise that Rowland Stephenson, as Treasurer to the institution, may have informed the governors that the bank was in trouble. The hospital strenuously denied this accusation and no money was ever paid back.

While this was being decided Saint Bartholomew's featured twice in court cases that followed the disappearance of their treasurer. On 29 December 1828 a case of theft was recorded. Constable Groom brought a man named Anderson, dressed in livery, in front of Mr. Halls, the magistrate at Bow Street, after Anderson had tried to sell a fish slice at a pawnshop for ten shillings, a great deal less than it was worth. The prisoner said Rowland Stephenson had given the fish slice to him. The Times reported thus,

> The prisoner, who said that his name was Anderson, stated that the fish-slice was given to him by his master, Mr. Stephenson about 3 or 4 months ago, on the occasion of his purchasing a new one from his silversmith at Charring-cross.
>
> Groom, the constable, stated that, upon his searching the prisoner, he found in his greatcoat pocket a case of loaded pistols, which he now produced.
>
> Mr. Halls examined the pistols and found that they were primed and loaded. The magistrate then asked the prisoner where and how he had obtained them.
>
> The prisoner replied, that he found them in his master's dressing room at Saint Bartholomew's hospital, where they lay upon a chest of drawers, but he could not say how he came to put them in his pocket. He had no notion that they were loaded.

Mr. Halls — But how came you to take them away? They were not your property, you know. What business had you with them?

Prisoner — Why, I was this morning desired to go out of the house, which is in a great state of confusion. Everything is about to be sealed up; and so finding the pistols loose about, and being portable I suppose I put them in my pocket.

Mr. Halls — You did very wrong in so doing, and I certainly will not part with you without further inquiry. The account which you give of the fish slice is extremely improbable, and the manner in which you account for the pistols is equally suspicious. Your master not being forthcoming, I scarcely know how to act'.[154]

At the end of the day it seemed simplest to the magistrate to let him go, forfeiting the fish slice and the pistols.

The second case was that of William Fulker, a footman at Saint Bartholomew's and Thomas Boreham, Rowland Stephenson's groom, who were indicted for stealing wine and saddlery from the Treasurer's House.

Benjamin Phillips constable for St Sepulcher's, gave evidence that at seven o'clock on the morning of 5th January in Cow-cross Street he had seen Fulker carrying a horse collar and two horse rugs plus some cyder and nine bottles of wine that he said had been given to him by the groom of Mr. Rowland Stephenson to take to the house in Queen Square where the family were living. When the constable was cross-examined he was asked where Mr. Stephenson was.

Witness. — I wish I could. (Laughter) I do not know where he is but I should very much like to know. (Cheers)

When Fulker was asked the same question he replied, 'I think it would be like looking for a needle in a bottle of hay. (More laughter)'.[155]

The case was soon abandoned.

The second meeting with the creditors took place on Friday 16 January at the Basinghall Street Chambers at one o'clock and once again

long before one o'clock the doors were thoroughly besieged; and soon after they were opened it was most inconveniently crowded, anxious creditors and active agents unceremoniously climbing over tables and the outer partitions, and pressing in the passages and upon the tables in front of the Commissioners to a most oppressive excess....for a long time it was all noise and no business.[156]

The depositions, already written, had to be signed by the witnesses, before any further proof of debts could be heard. It was however impossible for those wishing to sign depositions to get to the table because there were so many people in the room. Commissioner Shepherd then asked one of the clerks of the court to shout out the names on the depositions that he had prepared to be signed.

'I have already done so repeatedly; some have answered me but they cannot get near me.'
'Then call again, man'
'Mr. Suggett! Mr. Suggett!'
A voice from the crowd shouted back 'I am over here but I cannot get to you'. He eventually fought his way to the front and in the chaos signed the document twice in the wrong place with handwriting he later could not recognise. Everyone was now yelling and Commissioner Shepherd tried to shout above the clamour 'Silence, Gentlemen! Pray silence! Order, Gentlemen! Pray order. If you go on thus, it will be impossible for us to proceed; for the sake of public time we must adjourn the Court'
Several voices replied, 'We are so pressed on, we cannot get to the table. We would gladly sign and get out of here. And why do we have no clear way out for us?'
Commissioner Shepherd agreed, saying to the clerk 'Keep calling out the names 'til someone answers and when one does we must get him to the table'
'Mathews! Mr. Mathews! Mathews' No Mr. Mathews (the performer we believe) answered and then it was noticed that he had already signed and gone home.[157]

The clerks now set about making a way for people to get to the desk and most of the depositions were signed. At last the commissioners began to hear the claims of potential creditors. The first claimant began with a long speech as to why he should be paid immediately but at that point a shout went up.

'Take care of your pockets.'
'Why?'
'Because there are pickpockets in the room'
'Gentlemen, take care of your pockets.'

As people in the room examined their pockets, Mr. Patch of Finsbury Square asked if he could sign his deposition for £1,295 but the clerk was determined that he should first sign the list of assignees. The assignees were to be appointed that day and would take over the eventual distribution of money to the creditors. Because the list required a certain number of signatures of credito0rs the clerk was keen to get as many signatures as possible to hasten the appointments.

'Sign this first. It is the choice of assignees'
'For assignees? But I have not seen the list'
'Oh, 'tis all right'
Mr. Patch looked at the list and declared:
'But there is one of them I do not know'
'Well, do you want to sign it or not? They are all respectable gentlemen; what objection can you have to them?'
'But I only want to sign for my debt'
'Oh! You can sign for that afterwards'
Eventually the hapless Patch signed both and escaped the chaos.
A voice now shouted that someone had stolen four shillings from his pocket and then another cried that he had lost twenty shillings.
'And I have lost my pocket-handkerchief'
'What! Robbery upon robbery! Well, this is a pretty place'
'Is Rowland Stephenson among us?'
'Shut the doors!'
'What's the use of that? We can't swear to sovereigns and shillings'
'Oh! Never mind a little more robbery; let the business proceed.'
Order was restored and business was about to proceed again when Mr. Montague, counsel for the bank, exclaimed 'Hallo! Where is my list? Somebody has run away with the list of the depositions already handed in'
More laughter and a cry of 'What! Still more robbery.'[158]

Poor William Greenwood now appeared. He had given evidence to the commissioners on 17 January telling them of his long association with the bank but his failure to be able to withdraw his deposit in 1828.

His attorney, Mr. Edgar, after silence had been obtained, said – 'I wait, for the second time, to submit questions on the part of Mr. Greenwood, of Hampshire. We have come from Hampshire twice, to prove a debt of £16,000.'
Mr. Montagu, counsel for Remington & Co., replied, 'The question

cannot be gone into now, in the midst of all this confusion.'

'The case will not take five minutes.'

Mr. Montagu replied, raising his voice, 'When you speak of minutes, do you mean Chancery minutes, which but too often mean hours? I am instructed to oppose your claim most strenuously; I have the particulars of it here, and I have my law books ready. I must examine parties and must take down the evidence in writing; therefore an hour, at least, instead of five minutes, would be occupied.'

'But the case is so simple.'

'I say, Sir, it is most complex; and I have my case and law books here, to show such to be fact.'

'If it will occupy time, why not engage that time now, and not bring us a third time from Hampshire? At the last meeting we were told to attend at this meeting, and now our case is to be again postponed.'

Sir. G. Hampson now interjected, 'the debt is a disputed one, and, except in cases of emergency, we refer disputed cases to the assignees'.

Mr. Montague replied it would neither be just to him nor to the estate, to allow this debt of £16,000 to pass without the strictest investigation, and to that he should subject it. More legal argument followed and it was eventually decided that a third journey to the court would be necessary for the unfortunate William Greenwood.

Commissioner Turner now announced that they must choose the list of assignees. The list had been given to other creditors apart from Mr. Patch and they had all signed it without question.

The list of assignees was as follows:

Sir. Wm. Cranford, of Old Broad street, merchant.
Wm. Salton, of 30, Great Winchester street, merchant.
Wm. Strachan, of 2, Copthall Chambers, merchant.
George Robertson, of Great Winchester Street, merchant.

Since no other names had been put forward and there were no objections to be heard above the hubbub the list of assignees was formally accepted.

At last there was a hush over the room as the commissioners began their conclusions as to how much was left in the estate for distribution to creditors.

Commissioner Turner now spoke

As the assignees have been chosen it may be satisfactory to all parties present if I gave the heads of general departments of the affairs of the estate. According to papers I hold in my hands, and which have been prepared with much labour, it appears that the assets are £344,000; that the debts are £425,000. But there must be added to this sum the amounts abstracted by Stephenson, and for which the house is answerable. Sums abstracted by Stephenson amount to at least £70,000; that makes the debts near £500,000.[159]

It was then calculated that there would be from twelve to fourteen shillings in the pound paid to creditors of the banking house.

Mr. Montague replied that he accepted these rough figures but that they were, of course, still subjected to outstanding obligations, for which Stephenson might have rendered the house liable.

A gentleman asked hopefully if the statements included Rowland Stephenson's private debts. Mr. Montague was quick to reply that they certainly did not.'The meeting occupied nearly three hours and remained confused to the end.'[160]

On Saturday 17 January the assignees met for the first time and decided 'on the propriety' of sending to New York John Wilson, a clerk at Remington & Co., 'to render such ASSISTANCE and INFORMATION TO our agent, Messrs Goodhue & Co. as might be necessary towards effecting the apprehension of Mr. Stephenson'.[161]

It was now accepted that despite the best efforts of the authorities the fugitives were on their way to America. Jonathan Goodhue of Messrs Goodhue & Co was a well known merchant in New York and had acted as agent for the London banks. Mr Wilson was furnished with letters of introduction and full details of the abstractions of Rowland Stephenson from the bank which he was to give to Mr. Jonathan Goodhue as soon as he arrived in New York. He left London immediately and took a coach to Dartmouth where he boarded the brig, Thames, bound for New York.

There was another crowded meeting of creditors on Friday 6 February 1829 where further debts were accepted, the highest being £1,000. The meeting was crowded but more orderly since the assignees had taken the precaution of having a Mansion House officer present to deter pickpockets. The partners in the bank, including Henry Stephenson were now formally declared bankrupt.

A week later another meeting took place at which the court was receiving private debts that Rowland Stephenson had incurred and was as crowded as ever. The Times pointed out that on this occasion there were several elegantly dressed ladies present.[162] Business began and soon descended into the usual chaos. As the press of the crowd became intolerable, Commissioner Turner suggested they moved to a larger court and finally gained some order. The first debt was to a baker for £66, followed by unpaid bills from tradesmen, in and around Romford. An elderly lady, Mrs. Delemere, from the country claimed £600 owed by Rowland Stephenson for an estate in Romford that she had sold to him and never been fully paid. Others followed, the largest being £6,700. Many of the debts were for bonds given by Stephenson in exchange for his many properties in Romford.

The commissioners now moved to the main hall of the courts for a proclamation of Outlawry:

> ROWLAND STEPHENSON, come forward and surrender yourself to the major part of the commissioners, in a commission of bankrupt, named and authorised and now in prosecution against William Remington, Rowland Stephenson, David Remington, and Joseph Petty Toulmin, the commissioners being now present in order to take the SURRENDER of you, Rowland Stephenson, one of the said bankrupts and your not appearing on this proclamation is FELONY according to the statute.[163]

The proclamation was repeated twice in the presence of the Commissioners who stood, heads uncovered. Rowland Stephenson did not appear and therefore a writ of Outlawry was declared. He now joined the ranks of those beyond the law that had gone before him, like Robin Hood, Rob Roy MacGregor and Dick Turpin. The meeting was adjourned.

On Friday 20 February there was another meeting and more debts presented for consideration, some against the bank and some against Rowland Stephenson. A debt for £2,000 was considered arising out of a transaction between a creditor and Rowland Stephenson. From this debt the question arose whether the liability was a private one or against the bank. The letters regarding the buying and selling of stock from the creditor were addressed to Rowland Stephenson personally, rather than to the bank, and the Commissioners decided that this was a private debt and stood against the estate of Rowland Stephenson. The importance of this was that it was expected that the bank would be able to pay at least half its debts while Rowland 's estate would probably pay next to nothing. The partners of the banking house were present but were not ready to be examined so the court renewed their protection. Mr. Joseph Toulmin did not attend since he was confined to his bed by a paralytic stroke.

Meetings of the creditors continued to occur sporadically throughout 1829. On 18 June it was announced at the meeting that the remaining partners would be able to pay their private creditors fully but that that Rowland Stephenson's creditors would receive little more that one shilling and sixpence in the pound.[164]

The last meeting on 12 December predicted ten shillings and four pence for creditors of the bank and perhaps two shillings for Rowland's creditors.

These predictions now prompted many of his creditors to try to switch their claims. Over the next two years there were a series of court cases where debts were argued as to whether they were debts of the banking house or of Rowland Stephenson, none less so than the claim of Henry Peto, the builder of the Colosseum who had died and the case continued by his executors. £28,000 was owed by Thomas Hornor and guaranteed by Rowland Stephenson. The judge eventually decided in favour of the Commissioners who had decided that the debt rested with Rowland Stephenson personally.

A claim by a Mr. Batson whose draught for £21,000 was scrawled on a scrap of paper and signed by Rowland Stephenson failed to impress the Commissioners. The claims of the London Life Association met the same fate since Rowland was a trustee and key holder and the majority of the liability would remain his. Thomas Digby who had kept the cashbook at the bank made one of the last claims on 6 December 1832. He claimed £3066 9s. 6d against the personal estate of Rowland Stephenson after lending him £5,500 in 1828 and receiving in return the deeds of a property which turned out to be worthless. He too was disappointed.

Although Rowland Stephenson was formally declared bankrupt at the creditor's meeting on 6 February 1829, steps had already been taken to sell his valuable assets. On 22 January 1829 posters appeared in and around London and as far away as Dover, declaring that Mr. Shuttlworth, the well-known auctioneer of the time, with auction rooms in the Poultry, would conduct sales at the various properties of Rowland Stephenson.

'Elegant and Valuable Household Furniture'[165] was to be sold at the Treasurer's House, St Bartholomew's Hospital, at Marshall's, Howe Hatch, and the house at Clarence Place, Dover. These would be followed by a grand sale at the auction rooms in the Poultry.

In total it took Mr. Shuttleworth a staggering 22 full days to sell all the effects of Rowland Stephenson. With his compulsion to collect, Rowland certainly did not need the services of six mistresses or an addiction to gambling to spend all his money.

The sale at the Treasurer's House at Saint Bartholomew's Hospital took five days. The contents of the stables were sold on Thursday, 29 January and then the household goods on 9 February and for the three days following. There was to be much interest in purchasing the coach that had taken Rowland Stephenson to Bristol, partly because of its infamous connections but also, the Times speculated, in case there should still be a gold sovereign or two stuffed behind the cushions.[166] It made one hundred and thirty-six guineas. A yellow barouch 83 guineas, a yellow curicle thirteen guineas and a buggy and chaise 10 and 20 guineas each. The two grey mares fetched £400 along with five other horses, 'some aged'.[167]

In the Treasurer's House there was much interest, particularly from the ladies wishing to see the rooms where the now notorious banker had lived and the escape plot had been hatched. The Morning Herald noted,

> the house is furnished in a very splendid manner; the walls of the dining and drawing room are covered with pictures. Many persons before the sale commenced, went to the windows to view the furniture. One of the domestic servants pointed out a portrait to the company, which he said was an excellent likeness of Mr. Rowland Stephenson.[168]

A large quantity of household furniture and fittings were sold, a Broadwood piano, violins and violas, as well as a gentleman's wood turning lathe. The contents of the well stocked cellar were sold and included ninety dozen very superior Claret, sixty dozen fine old Port, two and a half dozen Madeira, ten dozen Sherry, twenty dozen Constantia, Hock and Champagne, a butt of superior Sherry and a hogshead of tawny Port in the wood.

> The sale was well attended. Among the company were some gentlemen to whom Mr. Stephenson was personally known. There were several pickpockets there but we did not hear if they were very successful. They, however, committed one dishonest act accompanied with violence; one of the gang struck a gentleman over the mouth, another knocked off his hat, whilst another picked his pocket of a purse, but it contained we understand something less than a sovereign. The party of thieves, believed to be Jews, escaped.[169]

The sale at Marshall's began on Monday 2 February and took six days. On the estate, live and dead stock were sold including 'thirteen handsome Yorkshire cows, two Alderney cows, assorted calves, a Herefordshire bull, thirteen strong grey draught horses, two ponies, many sheep, pigs and twenty peacocks and peahens of beautiful plumage, numerous ricks of wheat, sixteen tons of mangel wurzels and thirteen tons of potatoes, ploughs, harrows and many rabbit hutches'.[170]

An embarrassing situation occurred towards the close of the sale of outdoor goods when two agents of the Parochial Parish of Romford appeared and demanded payment of, 'certain rates due upon the property which had not been paid by the late proprietor. The claim was enforced with much perseverance but the assignees resisted for some time. The parochial authorities at length said they were compelled to the disagreeable necessity of seizing some of the stock'.[171]

By that time however most of the stock had already been sold but the agents were very determinedly loading sold and unsold goods onto the back of a cart. This prompted one of the assignees to put his hand in his pocket and pay the overdue amount; the agents left satisfied.

Final sale of Rowland Stephenson's Marshall's property. Yesterday the fourth and last day's sale of the late banker's household property, billiard and bagatelle tables, firearms, wine, etc., was completed at Romford. The attendance of company throughout the week has been numerous and respectable and the lots, 481 in number have all produced good, and some very good prices, especially those articles more immediately used by Mr. Stephenson, for which there was always spirited competition, the ladies being the foremost in the bidding.[172]

By the end of the week everything had been sold. 'Marshalls now presents a dreary aspect, and this recently splendidly decorated estate has scarcely a vestige of its former brilliant appearance'.[173] It was hard to think the house had been ringing with the laughter of Rowland's children less than two months previously.

The sale at Howe Hatch, took place on Monday and Tuesday 23 and 24 February. The goods sold featured such items as a Baker's patent mangle, 150 iron hurdles and many carpets. The sale at Clarence Place, Dover was much the same, including 'many excellent goose feather beds'.[174]

The sale at Shuttleworth's auction rooms in the Poultry started on 9 March,

Sale of silver. The service of plate, which belonged to Rowland Stephenson, was sold on the 9th of March. It consisted of four thousand ounces of the most modern patterns, including candelabras, goblets, tea, dinner and dessert services etc., of the most expensive description. There were one hundred and thirty-two lots and produced upon an average of about 3s. per ounce'.[175]

All the books of the libraries at Marshalls and the Treasurer's House were sold as well as busts of Isaac Newton and Napoleon. The paintings were sold separately and included a Who's Who of painters of the eighteenth and nineteenth century,

Mr. Shuttleworth respectfully announces, that he will sell by auction, at his sale room, Chapel Place, Poultry, on Monday April 13 and following day at 11 by order of the assignees, the valuable and genuine collection of pictures of Mr. Rowland Stephenson removed for convenience of sale from his seat at Marshalls and the Treasurer's Residence Saint Bartholomew's Hospital. Amongst the interesting collection will be observed some rare and valuable specimens of the highest class in the English School, particularly a splendid Portrait of David Garrick by Sir Joshua Reynolds, and others by William Hogarth, Thomas Gainsborough, Philippe-Jacques de Loutherbourg, George Morland, Sir Thomas Lawrence, George Henry Harlow, William Westall, M W. Sharp, George Clint, Alexander Naysmith &c. In the Dutch, Flemish and French Schools some pleasing specimens by Gerard Dow, Adriaen van Ostarde, Cornelius Dusart, Adrian van der Cabel, Hans Rottenhammer, Jacob van Ruisdael, Pieter Verelst, Jacob Toorenvliet, Anne-Louise Girded, Jean Antoine Watteau, Antoine Compel &c.[176]

Despite the quality of the works of art, the prices paid were disappointing,

Rowland Stephenson's paintings have been sold by Messrs Shuttleworth and Co. at their rooms at the Poultry. Sales produced nearly one thousand guineas, although many of them sold miserably cheap, at even less that the value of the frames'.[177]

Once the sale of all of Rowland's removable possessions had been completed, Mr. Shuttleworth began the process of selling the properties, both freehold and leasehold. On 30 May the Times printed a notice of the forthcoming sale by auction of the house at Clarence Place, Dover, described as 'an elegant and spacious mansion with coach house and stable adjoining the pier and commanding a fine view of the sea, the castle and heights and the coast of France'.[178] On 23 June notice was given of the sale by auction of Marshalls and all the properties around Romford including Harold Wood Farm, the windmill at Romford and 'numerous lands, residences, inns, public houses, dwelling houses cottages, shops, tenements and the manor of Cockermouth, to go ahead on July 2nd 1829.'[179]

All his other properties met the same fate over the summer of 1829. The bank itself lost all its assets and notice was given for the sale of the banking house at 69 Lombard Street, describing it as 'consisting of a lofty spacious and well arranged banking house with private office, strong room, stone stair case and every necessary appurtenance for a banking or commercial establishment;

excellent dining room, drawing room, and numerous bed chambers on the upper stories: with kitchen and suitable domestic offices in the basement; to be sold by auction on July 22nd'.[180]

Claims and court cases continued for months afterwards but at last on 18 November 1834 the assignees of the bank of Remington & Co. announced that they would pay in final settlement 11s. 3d. in the pound to creditors, after proofs amounting to £497,500 had been accepted. The individual partners, except Rowland, were all able to pay their private debts in full. It was widely reported later in the nineteenth century that all the creditors of Rowland Stephenson were fully reimbursed but the records of the Court of Bankruptcy do not substantiate this. The truth is that the assignees could only pay three shillings and sixpence in the pound to Rowland's unfortunate creditors.

CHAPTER FIFTEEN

SAVANNAH

R OWLAND STEPHENSON AND JAMES Harman Lloyd had climbed aboard the Kingston off Milford Haven on the morning of Monday, 5 January 1829. Laden with salt the Kingston heaved and groaned across the Atlantic. The slow journey gave Rowland plenty of time to reflect on his actions before and after Christmas 1828. There is no doubt he regretted his flight but had long since gone far beyond the point of no return. He had lost his home, his reputation, his family. He had lost everything but the clothes he wore and those stuffed into a carpet bag by his son on the fateful night. There was so much to weigh on his mind.

Progress of the Kingston was slow and by the time the ship arrived in Savannah events in London had moved on rapidly; the bank and bankers had been declared bankrupt and most of Rowland's possessions had already been sold. The Kingston took fifty-four days to reach Savannah. The Cambrian, which had been suspected of carrying the fugitives and searched in the English Channel, arrived in New York on 11 February, having taken only forty-two days and with it, brought the story of a dramatic failure of a bank in London.

Other ships crossing the Atlantic brought further news and rumours. The American government was informed that there were two fugitives on their way to the United State but was not told of their likely destination in time to intercept the Kingston. Later there was to be an opinion voiced in England that the United States could have done more to apprehend Rowland Stephenson before he ever landed in America and 'that the Republic meant to show that they cherished a spirit of national hostility towards England which was ready to break out'.[181] James Fennimore Cooper who was travelling in Europe at this time commented in a letter, 'I understood pretty distinctly that there were reports current in Europe that the Americans were so desirous of obtaining rich emigrants that they had rescued a criminal in order to reap the benefit of his gold'.[182]

The Times defended the authorities in America against the charge that they were indifferent to the flight of Stephenson. The newspaper contended that this was the reverse of the truth and, 'the American government had acted with great zeal and alacrity the moment they heard of the flight of Stephenson and Lloyd. Fast sailing ships were dispatched from ports along the Eastern seaboard to seek vessels coming from England. Warrants were granted for their apprehension and silver oars were furnished to board vessels at sea which might be disposed to pass without being liable to search'.[183] As the Mace in the Houses of Parliament is a ceremonial symbol of royal authority so the 'silver oar' is a symbol of maritime law. It became the badge of authority of the Admiralty Marshall and was brought into court on land when maritime disputes and crimes were heard. It was also carried as evidence of authority in the sombre procession to the low water mark, the demarcation of Admiralty authority, in order to carry out naval executions. In the context of these ships sent out from East coast of America it gave them the legal authority to stop and search all vessels. Somehow the lumbering Kingston slipped through; the luck of the dapper little banker still held.

The Times continued that, 'an agent was even sent to the Rocky Mountains in quest of him in case he was obliged to fly to the most desolate place of refuge'.

The journey from Milford Haven on the Kingston must have been very tedious for Rowland Stephenson and James Lloyd who continued to be known as Mr. R. Smith and Mr. J. Larkin. Not only was the journey very long but also every day added to Rowland Stephenson's anxiety as the possibility of a British naval vessel overtaking them increased. When the two runaways disembarked the Kingston onto the quayside at Savannah on Saturday, 28 February they could not have believed their luck. There was no reception party to meet them. They did not go far but found accommodation in a cheap coffee house near the port. They now had time to decide what to do next. At least they had arrived at a delightful city in which to make their plans.

Savannah was founded in 1733 by James Oglethorpe who travelled from England with one hundred and fourteen colonists in the 'Anne'. It is the oldest city in Georgia, the thirteenth and the last of England's American colonies. Situated on the Savannah River, it is sixteen miles from the Atlantic and remains an example of English eighteenth century town planning with wide open streets, shady public parks and tree lined squares. More Europeans settled in the city but no Catholics were allowed until 1748 due to a disagreement with Spain and the colony had the advantage of prohibiting lawyers until 1755.

The Savannah that Rowland Stephenson found in 1829 was thriving on trade in slavery, cotton and rice, the proceeds being used for many civic improvements. The city was cosmopolitan and bustling and the port area particularly busy where two foreign strangers could stay and remain undiscovered.

As Rowland Stephenson and James Lloyd thought about their next move their contemplations were galvanised on Tuesday, 3 March when the local newspaper, the Daily Georgian, printed the story of the failure of the London Bank.[184] This was followed the next day by a more detailed account that might have made Rowland's blood run cold. There was a full description of his flight to Clovelly, with some minor inaccuracies, but there were no inaccuracies describing the reward offered in London and his full description.[185] To add spice the newspaper speculated that if he was to be returned to England he would almost certainly be hanged but the most alarming information, however, was that another substantial reward was being offered. A bill dated 17 February 1829 was reproduced:

City Hotel, New York-

I, Joseph Wilfred Parkins, do offer **$1,500** to any person who arrests and delivers **Rowland Stephenson**, the defaulter, and $100 to the person who shall first inform me, through my solicitors Messrs Prime, Ward, King & Co. of this City. [186]

Two substantial rewards for his capture were bad enough but the fact that Joseph Parkins was sharing the same continent must have come as a very great disappointment. He knew Parkins only too well and he was certainly aware of his reputation.

Joseph Parkins had arrived in America aboard the Moro Castle on 6 July 1827, and had since been travelling. He had spent time in Canada and by the beginning of 1829 was living in New York and had now decided to return to England. His plans were to be changed radically by the news from England. On 5 January 1829 William Remington had written to Parkins, confirming 'the lamentable news'[187] that Rowland Stephenson had absconded and the bank had failed due to his abstraction of £218,000 of which £16,000 Exchequer bills belonged to Parkins. He added that there was a rumour that Rowland Stephenson was headed for America. Mr. Thompson, Parkins' agent in London, kept him up to date with frequent letters and advised him that Rowland was on the Kingston.

The ex-sheriff was not going to let Rowland Stephenson get away with this and when he was informed that the fugitive was coming to America, he had taken an immediate step to apprehend him by offering the reward.

Stephenson and Lloyd did not make a move immediately but waited from the Wednesday when the full story was first printed until the following Monday, 9 March. On that day they hired a horse and gig and in the afternoon they took the road out of Savannah, west towards Augusta, with the hope of going much further west where their identity might not be known. In Effingham County, sixteen miles from Savannah, James Lloyd was driving the gig. Being short-sighted, and having lost his green tinted spectacles in the Bristol Channel, Lloyd did not see a tree stump in the road and drove over it, upsetting the gig. Rowland Stephenson was 'considerably bruised and the gig broken'.[188] They picked themselves up and walked two miles to the nearest habitation which was a farmhouse, fortunately owned by the local doctor, Dr. Garbutt. The doctor took them in and dressed their wounds. Rowland was not well enough to travel so the doctor offered to let them stay until he was fit enough to continue the journey and the gig repaired.

By the next day Rowland felt a lot better and hoped to leave the following day. That night, about one o'clock, Rowland awoke to find a man thrusting a pistol into his chest, saying, 'You are the man, you are my prisoner'.[189] This was William Oates, deputy jailer of the city of Savannah. Three more heavily armed men, George Miller, William James and James C. Pierce joined him in the bedroom. They forced Rowland to dress and bundled him down the stairs and into a coach that was waiting at the front door. The coach was not very large and not in the best condition. Four hefty kidnappers, two prisoners and a coachman were too many, even with some of them hanging on to the roof so William Oates decided to leave James Lloyd behind, making it very clear that it was only Rowland Stephenson whom they wanted. Realising that James Lloyd was to be left behind, Rowland pressed twenty-two dollars into his hand, saying, 'This is all we have left'.[190]

They set off in the coach, which was still overloaded, two of the kidnappers perched on top with the coachman and the rest inside. The curtains were pulled and a pistol was pointed at Rowland Stephenson with the threat to blow his brains out if he made a sound. Rowland Stephenson described the journey later as being extremely uncomfortable particularly since the overloaded carriage broke down five times, even at one point losing a wheel. At daybreak they reached the northern outskirts of Savannah and drove along a track by the Savannah River to an old wharf made of floating logs. Here the carriage stopped and the kidnappers manhandled Stephenson over the logs and threw him into a small sailing boat. The kidnappers then parted company; Miller, James and Pierce returned to Savannah in the coach while deputy jailer Oates set sail downstream. The river winds its way south past various islands and then flows just east of the city of Savannah. Oates did not stop at the port but continued sailing downstream, south east, past more islands and on until the little boat reached the eastern tip of land called Tybee Island where he tied the boat up by the Tybee Lighthouse. A larger boat, named the Savannah, was moored nearby and its captain and crew were waiting for their arrival. The Savannah was a sleek pilot boat, renowned for being the fastest boat on the river and used for important, and sometimes illicit, commissions.

William Oates bundled Rowland Stephenson into the boat where he was tied up and locked in a small cabin. The captain of the Savannah was Wright White and he had with him Julius Proctor, the pilot, Finch, the boat hand and a cabin boy named Edward. With their captive hidden from view, they set sail into the open sea. Their destination was 850 miles away, New York.

Somehow James Lloyd returned to Savannah the same day and informed the authorities of the kidnap of Rowland Stephenson. A whaleboat was immediately dispatched in pursuit but it was no match for the fast Savannah and it returned to the city, empty handed, the following day.

His Majesty's consul in Georgia heard the story of the capture of Stephenson and wrote to the British Consulate General in Washington on 13 March 1829 informing him that, 'individuals supposed to be Rowland Stephenson and James Harman Lloyd have arrived in Savannah on February 28th but Rowland Stephenson had now been kidnapped, destination unknown'.[191] The Consular General sent a letter immediately to the Secretary for Foreign affairs in London, The Earl of Aberdeen, informing him of the events.

The question now arose, what was the British government going to do about it?

Chapter Sixteen

New York

Theourney from Milford Haven to Savannah had undoubtedly been uncomfortable and monotonous for Rowland Stephenson but it was nothing compared to the five and a half days he spent going from Savannah to New York, tied up and confined to a cabin in the bottom of the boat. It must have been a most wretched voyage as his captors would not allow him out of the cabin to walk on deck in case he was seen or he tried to escape. There was a lot of money at stake to get him safely to New York and his discomfort was the least of their worries.

Only weeks before he had been a man who had possessed so much and now he had nothing, absolutely nothing, wearing filthy clothes and lying in this stinking cabin. Even his carpetbag, containing what little he had brought from England, had been left behind at the farmhouse by the kidnappers.

The pilot boat Savannah left the Tybee Lighthouse on Wednesday, 11 March and made its way up the east coast towards New York where it arrived on the afternoon of the following Monday, 16 March.

Meanwhile, the emissary of the Committee of the City of London Bankers, Mr. John Wilson, who had left England on 17 January had arrived in New York on Saturday 14 March. He brought with him powers of attorney from the Court of Bankruptcy and full details of Rowland Stephenson's alleged abstractions which made dramatic reading. The New York newspapers were now full of Rowland Stephenson's misdeeds; they alleged he had stolen £58,000 cash, exchequer bills worth £68,000, Foreign stock worth £50,000 and much more, even the stories of his six mistresses and nights at the gambling tables were repeated. The New Yorkers may have enjoyed reading these revelations but there was one person residing in New York who certainly did not. Joseph Parkins was telling anyone who was prepared to listen that he had lost £15,000 exchequer bills as well as a great deal of deposited money. He was particularly angry that he had also lost 160,000 francs that he had very recently transferred to Remington's from the safe hands of his bank, Lafitte's, in Paris.

On the Monday afternoon the Savannah slipped into New York harbour and anchored off the Battery. Two men were seen disembarking into a small boat in which they rowed over to the quay, climbed the ladder and hurried off towards the downtown area of the city.

Jacob Hays gave an account of the afternoon's events. He was High Constable of New York from 1802 until 1848. Fifty years later the New York Times described him as, 'a singularly handsome, well dressed and brawny man who nowadays would be called Superintendant of Police, but then he was not only the city's Chief of Police but also a queller of riots, leader of the leatherheads and constables and a buttress against all ill doers that if anything went amiss, people would say 'Set old Hays at 'em'.[192]

According to Hays, on the Monday afternoon a legal gentleman by the name of Jeremiah Graham entered the New York court house. Mr. Hopson was the only magistrate available and Jeremiah Graham informed him that he represented two gentlemen who were waiting outside and wished for a private interview, 'as they had something of the greatest importance to communicate'.[193] Jeremiah Graham then departed and two gentlemen, smelling strongly of fish, entered the court house. They were, of course, Wright White and William Oates. In a very conspiratorial manner they told the magistrate that they had Rowland Stephenson under their 'care' and they wished for him to be arrested immediately and placed in prison. Mr Hopson was not the least impressed and told them that he could not possibly do such a thing without going through the formal process of the law. Benjamin Hays who was a deputy marshal and the son of Jacob Hays, was called from an adjoining office. Having heard the account of the two men he promised them that he would bring his father to the boat later to decide what was to be done.

The two men, disappointed by this response, left the police headquarters and instead of going back to the boat, they made their way to the house of James Buchanan, His Majesty's Consul in New York. Buchanan had previously been the Justice of the Peace for Ireland and had the reputation of being a gentleman of wide experience and well suited to the Consulate in New York where polite diplomacy would be necessary between the two nations who had had serious differences over the previous forty years. The affair of Rowland Stephenson was to test his diplomacy to the limit.

James Buchanan had published a pamphlet in August 1827 entitled 'The

Causes and Prevention of Crime in the United Kingdom'. He held strong views on 'modern' prisons that were being built in England and America where 'heavy expenditure is incurred for new goals and penitentiaries in which the positive comfort of the inmates is studiously and primarily regarded. This amply justifies an enquiry into the expediency of a system which divests imprisonment of much of its horror'.[194] He goes on to say, 'Prisons, instead of becoming a terror to all evil doers, prove sanctuaries for the idle and the profligate'. He looked upon the death penalty, not as a deterrent, but as an incitement to crime. He illustrated this point with his experience in a small town in Ireland. A felon was brought before him charged with burglary. He was found guilty and sentenced to death. The man appeared truly repentant on the scaffold and was duly hanged but when he was cut down he was not only alive but made a rapid recovery from the ordeal. Three years later the same felon was again charged with burglary and hanged, successfully, from the same gallows. Buchanan offered this as clear proof of the futility of the death penalty. His views on the easy life of over-indulged inmates in early nineteenth century prisons and the overwhelming desire of criminals to be hanged, some found open to argument.

His account of the unfolding events of the afternoon was thus, 'Two men came to my house when I was sitting down to an early dinner and told me they had in their custody Mr. Rowland Stephenson, and were desirous of handing him over to me to obtain the reward'.[195] They recounted to Buchanan how they had come to be in New York with Rowland Stephenson as their prisoner. They said that they considered the rewards, offered by Joseph Parkins and by the London Bankers, to be justification enough to imprison him. James Buchanan continued

> I immediately proceeded to the vessel which had been anchored in the bay and found the wretched man in a cold cabin, his arms and legs pinioned. Upon stating who I was and expressing my regret that my public duty enjoined upon me to interfere and expostulating with him that for the sake of his children he should brave his misfortunes by affording all the reparation in his power to those whose interests he had injured, the wretched man burst into tears and cried, 'Oh my children, my children! I cast myself on you – do as you please – I shall act as you point out – I surrender myself to you as Consul to His Majesty.[196]

Rowland must have thought that nothing the British government might do would be worse than the situation that he had been enduring since his kidnap, even since he had walked out of the bank ten long weeks earlier. At least he would see his children again and give his side of the story to a court of law.

At that point Jacob Hays arrived. He was experienced enough to know that this was a very tricky situation and decided that taking the cold, half starved Rowland Stephenson to the city jail was inappropriate. He suggested moving him to the house of Jonathan Goodhue who lived nearby. It was to his mercantile company, Goodhue & Co. that the assignees in London had dispatched John Wilson on 17 January and Goodhue had already received information, instructions and powers of Attorney from assignees of the Court of Bankruptcy in a parcel sent from London that had arrived on Wednesday 11 March. On receiving this package, Jonathan Goodhue had immediately dispatched an agent to Savannah to inform the authorities that there were grounds to arrest the fugitive. John Wilson, the clerk who had been dispatched from London had arrived in New York aboard the ship, Thames, on Saturday, 14 March. He too brought legal papers from London for Mr. Goodhue and was immediately sent back to sea on the Empress sailing to Savannah.

Jonathan Goodhue was therefore in possession of all the details of the alleged crimes of Rowland Stephenson as well as the power of attorney, which the authorities in London hoped would be acceptable to the New York judiciary.

After they arrived at the house of Jonathan Goodhue, Rowland Stephenson was allowed to wash, change into some clean clothes and given some refreshment.

James Buchanan continues

> I probed him closely as to the cheque drawn on the Bank of England, and the funds sworn to as taken from the Bank a few days previous to his absconding. He stated that the deficiency had existed for a long time, although not discovered before, and in a most solemn manner he declared that he had but a few sovereigns and was dependent upon Lloyd for buying him three shirts and some warm clothing since his arrival. Lloyd, he said, was so involved in his transactions he determined to accompany him; but they were no sooner on board than they found out their error but they could not then return.[197]

Poor Rowland, once he had boarded the Kingston and had time to think bitterly regretted his actions. He then had a long uncomfortable journey across the Atlantic to lament.

James Buchanan advised Rowland to return to England and under the circumstances he readily agreed. Jacob Hays decided the best option was for Rowland to spend the night at his house where the fugitive was unlikely to escape and would not be subjected to the ordeal of being locked up in a cell. At 9 o'clock the exhausted Rowland Stephenson went to bed in a small room at the top of the house of Mr. Hays on Lespinard Street in downtown Manhattan. The next day they would decide how to return Rowland Stephenson to London.

Events however did not go to plan. The arrival in New York of the now notorious Rowland Stephenson had not gone unnoticed and by that evening the city was buzzing with the news that he had been kidnapped in Savannah and brought to New York, 'trussed up like a chicken'.[198] To add to the excitement it was confidently declared that this was the work of the British, keen to remove Stephenson back to England and bypass any legal formalities in New York. The respectable citizens of New York were not under any circumstances going to allow this. He may have stolen a large amount of money, he may be a fugitive, but he was still entitled to the protection of the law, American law. Far from being a wild and lawless society where gun toting thugs could kidnap whom they wished, the feeling was that a great injustice had been done. Kidnapping foreign nationals in the middle of the night and bringing them against their will to New York was against the law and had to be shown to be against the law, particularly since the British were probably at the bottom of it. At 10 o'clock that night a lawyer by the name of Wyley, accompanied by a Mr. Allen, went to the police station to enquire as to the whereabouts of Rowland Stephenson. They were told that he was in custody elsewhere in the city on the grounds of a writ issued by a court in New York. The two men realised they had to move fast and went directly to the house of a magistrate. At midnight they obtained a writ of habeas corpus for Rowland Stephenson, commanding that he must be brought to the New York Recorder's Court at one o'clock the following day, Tuesday, 19 March.

The writ of habeas corpus is the principal safeguard of personal liberty and its use enables subjects to challenge unconstitutional imprisonment. If on application for the writ the court or judge is satisfied that the detention is prima facie unlawful the custodian is ordered to appear with the prisoner and justify it; if this fails release is ordered.

Mr. Wyley and Mr. Allen immediately went to the house of Jonathan Goodhue where they thought Rowland Stephenson was being held. Seeing a light in a window they repeatedly rapped on the door. Finally the sleepy merchant put his head out of an upstairs window and said Rowland Stephenson was not there. Undeterred, Mr. Wyley read out the decree of habeas corpus in a loud voice. By now there were lights in a number of windows in the street, unaccustomed to disturbance at this time of night, particularly at the house of the virtuous merchant. Wyley and Allen satisfied that James Goodhue had heard their decree did the same at the house of the British consul and then at the house of Mr. Hays. Content with their night's work they retired to bed with the expectation they were going to give the British government a bloody nose.

Whether Rowland Stephenson was woken by the voice of Mr. Wyley proclaiming the writ of habeas corpus outside the house is not known but Jacob Hays certainly did hear it and was probably pleased that the case was going to be heard in an open court of law and not settled behind closed doors by the British.

Soon after 10 o'clock the following morning the New York Recorder, the most senior judge in New York, was informed that the writ of habeas corpus had been served and the case was to be heard at one o'clock. The name Rowland Stephenson always seemed to attract crowds and by midday the Recorder's court was 'filled to suffocation by citizens and gentlemen of the legal profession'.[199]

In the short space of time since midnight Rowland Stephenson was now to be represented by no less than five lawyers, Mr. W. Wylie, Mr. M.C. Patterson, Mr. P.H. May, Mr. W.M. Price and Mr. A.S. Garr. Mr. Robert Emmet represented Jonathan Goodhue and Mr. Peter Jay represented James Buchanan and the British government. It was noted that there were also two other lawyers present, Mr. Ward and Mr. Hoyt, taking great interest in the proceedings.

The New York Enquirer described the scene;

> The City Hall was crowded out to the vestibule by an anxious assemblage of our citizens who exhibited signs of great indignation. Punctually at the hour appointed, Hays came in with Mr. Platt, one of the Sheriff's Deputies, who had Rowland Stephenson in custody on a civil process. Stephenson looked pale and dejected, but has the air of a gentleman, and every appearance of great mildness, and benevolence of character.[200]

After silence was called the writ of habeas corpus was handed to the Recorder who declared that the matter was simple as far as this court was concerned; there was absolutely no legal justification to hold Rowland Stephenson. The power of attorney from England was not valid and there was no truth in the rumour that a writ had been obtained in New York the day before. The Recorder pronounced Rowland Stephenson at liberty and he was free to leave the court.

Cheers rang around the room and the lawyers slapped each other on the back. A dazed Rowland could not believe his luck but before he too could celebrate his freedom the two mysterious lawyers, Mr. Ward and Mr. Hoyt, came to life. Mr. Hoyt stepped forward and announced in a loud and solemn voice,

'I have in my hand a capias ad respondendum against Rowland Stephenson at the suit of Joseph Wilfred Parkins'.[201]

The writ was handed to Mr. Sheriff Shaw and passed on to the Recorder who, having inspected it, said gravely 'I cannot discharge you from this.'

A capias ad respondendum is simply a writ commanding a sheriff or other proper officer to take the body of the defendant and to hold the same in custody, to answer the writ of the plaintiff. In this case, the writ was for the large debt owed to Joseph Parkins.

The New York Enquirer described the courtroom as being, 'extremely excited and Mr. Robert Emmet, the counsel for Jonathan Goodhue, now rose upon his chair and addressed the multitude with a view of allaying the excitement.' This did little to restore order.

Rowland Stephenson's team of lawyers now consulted with their client and Mr. Patterson, pointing at James Buchanan, the British consul, announced 'There is a dark feature in this transaction, the blame of which rests upon some gentlemen.' The New York Enquirer continued 'Mr. Jay, counsel for the British consul, suspecting this to be a reference to the British government, replied sharply and a sharp exchange of words ensued during which the Recorder several times interposed to allay the excitement. Mr. Patterson was cheered loudly by the assembled crowd.'[202]

James Buchanan was now given a chance to defend himself. He stated that upon his word as a gentleman, he had no connection with the removal of Stephenson. He had received a letter from two Marshals of Savannah, apprising him of the seizure of Stephenson and when he was told that Stephenson was aboard a vessel in the Bay had gone on board. He continued to say that he had accompanied Rowland Stephenson to the house of Mr. Goodhue, and saw him there last evening. He had advised him to go to Mr. Hays' house, as he would be kindly treated there. 'Rowland Stephenson was hospitably used at Mr. Goodhue's, and we drank wine together.' The Consul admitted that he had sent a letter and affidavit to the lawful authorities in Savannah to have Stephenson arrested but that he had given a pledge to save his life. 'I feel as much commiseration for his situation as any man could do'.[203]

Mr. Emmet now interposed on behalf of Mr. Goodhue, who stood beside him, and who also solemnly disclaimed any participation in the arrest of Stephenson or the means adopted for that purpose.

Mr. Wylie then stated, that he was authorized by Mr. Stephenson to declare, that he had been treated in a most ruffian-like manner when kidnapped. The New York Gazette continues with the dialogue in the courtroom:

Mr. Wylie— Mr. Stephenson says that he was arrested and dragged from his bed, in the night, by four men armed with pistols—

Mr. Stephenson—And swords also!

Mr. Wylie—Yes, by four men, armed with pistols and swords, and in this manner kidnapped and dragged on board a vessel—on board of which also he has been bound and treated with ruffian violence; a great shudder ran through the crowd.

The excitement was very great. There was but one feeling that an unlawful and violent trespass had been committed and this was expressed by all the citizens present. It was understood that Stephenson's Counsel would take proper measures to do justice to him and the violated laws of the country. Sheriff Shaw now took Mr. Stephenson by the arm, and he was led away to the Debtor's Prison, on the civil process of Joseph Parkins before mentioned.

Mr. May now rose to address the people, but the Recorder entreated silence; and the sheriff ordered the room cleared; the crowd, considering its density, retired with great good order'.[204]

At the end of the hearing Mr. Paterson applied to the court for a writ to apprehend the persons on board the pilot boat Savannah that remained at anchor in the bay. Officers of the New York Police Department were immediately dispatched to the boat but found there was no one aboard. They now laid in wait on the quayside to capture the crew but Wright White and his men were too smart for that and at 11 o'clock the police officers were very surprised to see the Savannah weigh anchor on the high tide and set sail. The harbour authorities hastily assembled a six man crew to row after it in a customs boat but they were no match for the sleek Savannah with a fresh north westerly breeze filling its sails.

It might be worth pointing out at this stage that there was no extradition law as such between America and England at this time. This was much discussed in the press on both sides of the Atlantic. The New York Herald addressed the subject on 18 March,

In 1819 a man named Washburn was brought before Chancellor Kent upon habeas corpus charged with being a receiver of stolen goods and a fugitive from Canada where the crime was committed. The Chancellor discharged him on the grounds that the evidence before the court was not sufficient to organise his arrest; but at the same time gave it as his opinion that 'it was the law of nations to deliver up offenders charged with felony and other high crimes and who have fled from the countries in which the crimes were committed.' This doctrine the chancellor maintained in an elaborate and able opinion which may be found in 4 Johnson's chancery reports'.[205]

The Times summerised the ambiguous situation, 'No man has a right to say "I force myself into your territory and you shall protect me", but at this time there is no treaty between United States and Great Britain which authorises an arrest for a crime committed in another country.'[206]

The New York afternoon newspapers of Thursday 19 March printed a statement that had been made by Rowland Stephenson to his counsel, Mr. Wylie, informing the people of New York of his ordeal,

On the 9th of this month, I left Savannah in a gig, accompanied by Lloyd, with an intention of going forty or fifty miles into the country. After riding about 16 miles, our carriage was unfortunately overturned, and being considerably hurt we had to remain at a Farm House until we should be able to pursue our journey. At this place we stopped two days and on Wednesday Morning last, at one o'clock, while I was lying in my bed, my room was entered by four men armed with cutlasses and pistols, who forced me into a carriage. After this vehicle had many times broken down, I found myself at Savannah; and notwithstanding all entreaties was hurried to the water's edge. In the course of this ride, the parties threatened me that if I made any noise they would shoot me; and even prohibited me from putting my head out of the carriage. At one time they requested me to get upon a horse and ride; but this was impossible. My strength had failed me.—I had become completely enervated,--and withal so tired, and fatigued, that I felt utterly incapable of a compliance. I accordingly resumed my seat in the carriage, & half asleep and half fainting, was put on board a small boat and thence transferred to the Pilot boat Savannah. The captain in this boat was named Wright White and acted to me as if he was compelled to sail to New York, at the instigation of a Mr. Oates, who stated himself to be the deputy gaoler of Savannah.—From this fact, on arriving at this port. I was taken into the custody of I know not who and conveyed I know not where.—It is true that at Mr. Goodhue's I was treated with considerable kindness and that I slept under the roof of the High Constable with a peace of mind that I had not experienced for many months previous. As regards the greater portion of my treatment, and the individual who acted in the case, I beg leave to decline stating; as I have no wish to implicate persons whose characters ought to stand fair in this community.[207]

He followed this up the same day with a letter:

To the Editors of the Journal of Commerce, New York.

Gentlemen—I have seen your paper this morning, containing some
remarks respecting my abduction from Savannah. Misused and maltreated
as I have been in England, both by individuals and the public press, I
earnestly request that the public will suspend their opinion in regard to the
failure of Remington, Stephenson, & Co. and my agency therein

In the meantime, I cannot sufficiently express my admiration of the
good feelings of this community, and of the unbought exertions of the
learned counsel, who volunteered on my behalf, and in support of the laws.

Your most obd't.,

Humble servant,

ROWLAND STEPHENSON.[208]

The New York Herald thought the moment right for some patriotic rhetoric:

Sufficient time has transpired to warrant us in saying that Rowland
Stephenson was violently and unlawfully seized without any form of law,
a few miles from Savannah, and conveyed to this port for the purpose of
sending him back to England. There is not a particle of doubt that a high
handed trespass has been committed and that the sovereignty of our laws has
been grossly violated by another country. In common with what we have no
doubt is the general feeling of the American public we are willing, nay, more
than willing, that Rowland Stephenson should suffer the penalties due to his
felonious acts; but let his person be secured by legal process not abduction,
and let justice be administered according to law. It is due to the American
character-it is due to justice-it is due to sovereignty of our laws and it is
demanded by that equality of rights upon which our government is founded
that this trespass on Rowland Stephenson, though a felon and a fugitive from
justice, should be promptly punished and the full force of our courts and
of public opinion put in requisition to expose and bring to light every man
from the British consul to the cabin boy of the Savannah who has participated in this nefarious outrage. Mortifying to the pride as this transaction is,
and cause of resentment as it is as connected with the Englishmen who have
dared to trample down our laws we are glad to record the steady enlightened
and just feeling which filled the breast of an American populace assembled

in and about the City hall to witness the delivery of Stephenson from the illegal bondage in which he was held, upon the highest authority of our land –the writ of habeas corpus. That feeling was all one way – a feeling not of sympathy for the unhappy and misguided Stephenson but of indignation that he had been unlawfully seized and surreptitiously brought hither. The British Consul, seeing around him a determination to protect Stephenson in his rights, and a strong abhorrence of the part he was supposed to have acted, wisely receded from the course he had resolved upon, and without debate yielded to the action of the writ of habeas corpus.[209]

Tuesday, 17 March saw Joseph Parkins enter the fray with a little mischief making. His letter was published in the New York Herald on 18 March,

IN THE MATTER OF JAMES BUCHANAN AND JONATHAN GOODHUE

State of New York
City and County of New York

Joseph Wilfred Parkins, at present of the city of New York, being duly sworn doth depose and say; that in the latter part of the month of February, or beginning of the present month of March, in a conversation which this deponent had with Mr. James Buchanan, the British Consul, the said James Buchanan informed this deponent that he had instructions from the British government and intended to take Rowland Stephenson & forcibly send him back to England. And further, that Jonathan Goodhue above named, last night informed deponent, that deponent could not see the said Rowland Stephenson; that the British Consul, James Buchanan, had taken him away from his house and intended to send the said Stephenson back to England; and that the said Buchanan had authority to do so and that he had a warrant for that purpose from one of the magistrates of this city. And the deponent further saith, that he verily believes it to be the intention of the said James Buchanan and Jonathan Goodhue forcibly to take and carry the said Rowland Stephenson out of the jurisdiction of the State of New York, contrary to law. And the deponent further saith, that he verily believes the said Rowland Stephenson hath been forcibly taken and detained, contrary to his will by the said James Buchanan and Jonathan Goodhue, and that in so doing an assault has been committed on the person of the said Rowland Stephenson.

J. W. PARKINS.
Sworn this 17th day of March 1829.[210]

Poor James Buchanan and Jonathan Goodhue found themselves trying to contest the truth with Joseph Parkins. If they did not know before what the ex-sheriff of the City of London was like to deal with, they soon would.

James Buchanan replied in an affidavit the following day,

> James Buchanan, his Britannic Majesty's Consul, maketh oath, that he has read an affidavit, purporting to have been made by J.W.Parkins in which it is stated that deponent informed the said Parkins he had instruction from his government, and intended to take Rowland Stephenson, and forcibly send him back to England, which statement this deponent declares to be false. And also, that as to the apprehending of Stephenson at Savannah, and bringing him on here, deponent was in nowise privy thereto, directly or indirectly, nor had deponent any intention of forcibly or otherwise removing him out of the jurisdiction of this state as stated by Parkins. Deponent further saith, that the letter that appeared in the public papers was drawn by deponent, at the express wish of Mr. Stephenson and was left with him for consideration, and that he would signed it, but as deponent saw no hope of preventing proceedings, he advised him not to do so. Signed March 19th 1829 sworn and subscribed this 19th day of March 1829 before me Zephaniah Platt.[211]

Jonathan Goodhue, priding himself on his good name, was also incensed. In the strongest denial that he or his company had anything to do with the kidnap, he released a statement that was reprinted in the New York Herald newspaper and was very critical of the other New York newspapers for jumping to conclusions regarding who was responsible for the kidnap.

> On the 10th of March 1829 this house of Goodhue and Co. received instructions by the packet from England. These instructions were from certain creditors of the house of Remington, Stephenson and Co and their solicitors to arrest Stephenson for debt if he was to be found in this country and there were enclosed powers of attorney for that purpose. Late on the evening of the 11th an agent was furnished with the necessary instructions and told to proceed by land to Savannah where it was believed Stephenson had landed. This agent left New York on the Union Line Express coach on the morning of the 12th of March, which was the very day that Stephenson was kidnapped and was already on his way to New York by boat.[212]

The newspaper pointed out that this fact alone was sufficient to exculpate Mr. Goodhue from all censure. Mr. Goodhue's statement added,

Late on March 14th the Thames arrived here on board of which was Mr. John Wilson, lately clerk at Remington's, who brought duplicates of the powers of attorney and documents before received. Early on the following morning Mr Wilson sailed for Savannah in the Empress being furnished with instructions to cooperate with the agent before mentioned. Due care was taken in making these instructions to state that Goodhue and Co. acting only as agents themselves wished their agent to take professional advice in any case of doubt. The moment this house knew of the arrival of Rowland Stephenson on Monday afternoon a messenger was sent in pursuit of Mr Parkins to inform him of it. Mr Parkins was not however at his lodgings. It was the result therefore altogether of accident that Mr. Parkins was not the first apprised of Stephenson's arrival in New York.[213]

Meanwhile in Savannah the arrest was announced of three of the kidnappers, George Miller, William James and James C. Pierce who had been identified by James Lloyd. Pierce was released but the other two were held in custody to face charges of abduction at the May sessions.

Rowland Stephenson remained incarcerated in the debtors prison while his lawyers worked on how to respond to the writ issued by Joseph Parkins. A further court appearance to challenge the writ was planned for the following Monday, 23 March.

During this time of waiting, Rowland Stephenson received an unexpected visitor to his cell. Joseph Parkins came to see him and 'a very affecting interview took place between them; the moment Stephenson recognised Joseph Parkins he exclaimed, "Hear my story – don't condemn me yet. I solemnly declare I am not the guilty man you suppose me"'.[214]

Parkins appeared to have had some sympathy for the man whom he was holding by his writ in prison but as often was the case with Joseph Parkins this feeling of sympathy did not last long.

The case of Parkins v Stephenson was heard at the Superior Court of New York before Chief Justice Jones and Mr. Justice Oakley on Monday 23 March. Mr. A. S. Garr, Mr. W.M. Price and Mr. Ogden represented the defendant, Rowland Stephenson and Messrs Ward and Hoyt again represented the plaintiff, Joseph Parkins.

Already that morning at a separate court of justice in New York, the powers of attorney sent to Goodhue and Co. were examined and found to be invalid in the American court of law and were dismissed. The representative of the London banks then made it known that they would not pursue the matter further, happy to leave Stephenson to the mercies of the ex-sheriff whom they doubtless knew by repute.

The proceedings before Justice Jones opened with an affidavit of Rowland Stephenson read out by Mr. Garr. This gave full details of the manner in which he had been brought from Savannah to New York. Mr. Garr continued by reading the notice that Joseph Parkins had published, offering a reward for the capture of the defendant.

Mr. Ward now answered by saying that the case rested on Rowland Stephenson having surrendered himself to Mr. James Buchanan and High Constable Jacob Hays in the presence of Mr. Jonathan Goodhue on the afternoon that he arrived in the Savannah. To prove this, Mr. Ward asked the court for time to obtain affidavits from these two gentlemen to show under what circumstances the defendant did surrender himself.

The affidavit of Joseph Parkins was now read out by Mr. Hoyt and was very short for a change. The firm of Remington, Stephenson and Co. of London was indebted to him for the sum equivalent of $76,000 and the defendant was a partner of that bank and instrumental in its failure.

Chief Justice Jones was unwilling to lengthen the procedures but asked if the affidavits from the three witnesses, Hays, Buchanan and Goodhue, could be procured by 2 o'clock. Mr. Ward thought he could but asked why there was such a hurry.

> Mr. Price – Then I presume it is no very great hardship to be abducted, and afterwards locked up in jail.

> Chief Justice Jones – If the defendant is entitled to relief, he ought to be discharged immediately. Besides, one of his leading counsels will leave the city this afternoon, and his valuable assistance will be lost. I shall require the affidavits by 2 o'clock.

> Mr. Ward –I will take all the chances, and get them if I can.[215]

At the appointed hour of 2 o'clock the lawyers assembled, and Mr. Ward stated that he had not been able to procure affidavits, as the gentlemen from whom he wished them had refused to testify on the subject.

There followed a prolonged exchange between the various interested parties; the judge was keen to see an early resolution, the counsel of the plaintiff was keen to see these witnesses dragged to the court and the counsel for the defendant keen to see him discharged,

> Chief Justice Jones —Are the gentlemen here? Do they decline making an affidavit?

Mr. Ward—I cannot get them to attend or make requisite affidavit. I should therefore request the aid of the Court to enforce their presence.

Ch. J. Jones – That cannot be. Parties must get their witnesses in a case like this as they can.

Mr. Ward – Will the Court have the kindness to look at the consequences of such a decision. The party will get out of prison, and the creditor to such an immense amount will lose the possibility of ever gaining a cent of it.

Ch. J. Jones – I cannot help it, unless you can show that we have the power to subpoena witnesses on a matter of this kind.

Mr. Ward – Does it not come within the great power of the Court?

Ch. J. Jones – We have not the power, sir. It might be a defect in judicial proceedings.

Mr. Ward – Then I shall ask the Court to let the case lie over until tomorrow.

Mr. Justice Oakley – Have you applied to these gentlemen personally?

Mr. Ward – I have; and used every exertion to procure their affidavits. Perhaps they might have been so occupied in business that they could not conveniently comply with my wishes.

Mr. Justice Oakley – Here is a large amount of money at stake, and there is something in Mr. Ward's assertion, that the gentlemen might have been so engaged in business that they could not devote the requisite time for drawing an affidavit.

Chief Justice Jones – I think the whole proceedings in this case so decidedly improper that it is with great reluctance I comply with the wishes of Mr. Justice Oakley, and adjourn the case until tomorrow.

Mr. Patterson – I hope no excuse of the kind will be taken tomorrow.

Mr. Justice Oakley – Certainly not. If other affidavits are not adduced he must be discharged.'

The Court was then adjourned until 12 o'clock the following day.

Joseph Parkins left the court on 23 March very dissatisfied. He always had scant regard for the legal profession but he considered this New York bunch a particularly lily-livered lot.[216] He much regretted not representing himself and he could have got the witnesses to testify, one way or another. He could see that Rowland Stephenson was going to slip from his grasp and he let it be known that he was not going to pay the reward to the kidnappers or anyone else. The English Chronicle remarked, 'Parkins, acting as expected, but now has got himself into hot water and the lawyer sharks of New York will give him an excellent dressing before they leave him. The Americans have begun to smoke this genius and he will soon become as fine a subject for quiz as ever he was in England, Ireland or France'.[217]

As had happened in England, the name Joseph Parkins was beginning to feature regularly in the New York press as a figure of fun as much as a combative litigant. During the trial an anecdote illustrating his curious behaviour was circulating New York. When Joseph Parkins first arrived in New York he went to the house of an Irish acquaintance and asked if he could stay the night.

'For a night, of course'

But night followed night and week followed week and still Parkins stayed. The Irishman's friends pulled his leg about the man who came and didn't leave.

'How is your friend, the sheriff?'

'A pleasant companion, the sheriff, is he?'

'When is the sheriff going to leave you?'

'Can't tell', replied the Irishman.

'Why don't you ask him, then?'

'The point is this. In Ireland we have a tradition of hospitality that does not allow me to ask that question until our guest has been with us for a year and a day; and then, Sir, we enquire if we are to have the pleasure of his company for a year longer.'

This was, indeed, what he did and Parkins took umbrage and stormed out of the house, saying all Irishmen were 'inhospitable pigs.'[218]

Parkins had been telling everyone how much he had lost and to be fair he had lost a lot of money. On 28 November 1828, almost exactly a month before the collapse of his bank, Joseph Parkins had written to William Remington from an address in Troy, New York. He grumbled that his agent in London, W.H.Thompson, has asked the bank for more money to pay out allowances giving pecuniary relief to individuals whom he seemed to support. Their needs had become 'greater and more urgent'.[219] Parkins expressed his displeasure to Mr. Remington for having given £50 to help. He continued by enquiring whether the bank had received safely $44,430 sent from Quebec, $4,300 from Calcutta and $33,111 from Messrs Lafitte and Co. in Paris. All this money was now lost until the assignees decided what pittance could be paid to the creditors of the bank.

The court reconvened at midday on Tuesday, 24 March for the final decision. The first announcement came from the counsel representing Joseph Parkins. They had not been able to obtain affidavits from Jacob Hays, Jonathan Goodhue or James Buchanan who all wished to distance themselves from the proceedings.

The Counsel for Mr. Stephenson based their application for his discharge upon the principle of law laid down by Lord Justice Holt, Lord Chief Justice of England and supported by many subsequent decisions, which they cited, 'that if a man is wrongfully brought into a jurisdiction and there lawfully arrested, yet ought he to be discharged; for no lawful thing founded on a wrongful act, can be supported'.[220]

The counsel for Joseph Parkins contended that his client, finding the defendant in the city, had a right to commence a suit against him, and cause him to be arrested and that was the basis of the argument.

Chief Justice Jones after consulting with his colleagues on the bench for a considerable time, gave his opinion and reproduced in full in the New York Herald,

> The summary was both able and eloquent. He said that the Court had looked over the authorities on the matter in question, since the adjournment, and that those cited and commented on by the counsel, had not affected their opinion .... 'And here was a case, of an individual, a foreigner, owing no allegiance to this country, who lands peaceably on our shores, and is forcibly brought from his legal castle to another state. How can this court entertain jurisdiction over him? There is no evidence that the plaintiff has been concerned in the forcible arrest, but though he be innocent, yet force has been applied and the victim has been brought here under it. Is it not plain that his presence and present confinement are the offspring of the forcible arrest?—
> ....he must be restored to the same security he originally possessed—he must be set free, and have liberty to return to the place from which he came, or at his option to have a domicile here, as secure as the castle of any citizen. If he remain here beyond a reasonable time allowed for his departure, he must submit in common with our citizens to the regular process of law. My opinion is that he must be discharged from all arrest and not be held even upon common bail'.

The rule made was that Stephenson should be discharged from the arrest
and he left the court accompanied by a friend.[221]

Three months after the events of Christmas, 1828, Rowland Stephenson
walked out of the court in New York a free man. The New York Herald
had pointed out, that he was not alone in the world and had left court in the
company of 'a friend'. That friend was a man named Captain John Myers.

CHAPTER SEVENTEEN

BRISTOL PA

R OWLAND STEPHENSON LEFT THE Superior Court in New York on
24 March 1829, well aware that although the British government and
the London bankers might have given up the chase Joseph Parkins was very
unlikely to leave him be. For the moment however Rowland was going to
savour freedom and fresh air and keep a low profile with his old friend, Captain
John Myers.

John Myers was born in Wales sometime around 1775. He was brought up
near the coast and at an early age went to sea on a local boat, trading between
England and Ireland. On 16 February, 1793, at the age of 18 while visiting his
parents he was impressed into His Majesty's Navy. At that time there were
45,000 men in the British navy, most recruited either as volunteers or through
a county quota system but some were coerced to join by impressment, which
had become common since the middle of the seventeenth century. Press gangs
were comprised of local thugs who were hired by the Regulating Officer to
search coastal towns and countryside for likely candidates suitable for life on a
ship of the line. They preferred young men with experience at sea but anyone
between eighteen and forty-five could be forced to join the navy. Young British
merchant sailors like John Myers, were particularly vulnerable to be snatched.
Although many deserted at the first opportunity, some, like Myers, remained
in the service. In 1817 John Myers published a book entitled,' The Life,
Voyages and Travels (Detailing his Adventures during Four Voyages around
the World) of Captain John Myers'.[222]
    The year after Myers joined the navy he was seriously injured in a skirmish
with the French and was treated for his wounds in Bristol. Three months later
he had recovered and sailed from Bristol to America on a ship called the Betsey.
For the next 12 years he sailed from continent to continent in the Betsey and

later in other ships of the British navy. He was taken prisoner twice by French privateers and in 1806 was involved in an incident worthy of Captain Jack Aubrey in the books by Patrick O'Brian. Myers at that time had left the navy and was a lieutenant on a privateer named the Tamar that was cruising near the coast of Madagascar. A privateer was simply a private warship allowed by its country of origin to attack enemy vessels during wartime and licensed to do so by official warrants called letters of marque. Possession of the letters of marque distinguished a privateer from a pirate. The privateers sought any enemy ships they could find with the intention of capturing rather than sinking them since, when the 'prize' was brought to a home port, the privateer would claim a substantial reward. The captured crews were generally well treated, even after a fiercely fought encounter, and were usually released unharmed. Since England was at war with France in 1806, Captain Wilson, in command of the Tamar, attacked and captured a small French ship called the Bon Fortune. Lieutenant Myers was ordered to take 14 men and sail this prize back to a friendly port. The following day Lieutenant Myers, having lost sight of the Tamar, was alarmed to see a much larger ship bearing down on their starboard beam. By its curious appearance, the ship was undoubtedly the much feared, Le Brave, a French privateer of 16 guns and a crew of 130. Resistance seemed hopeless and John Myers and his crew were resigned to be taken prisoner once again.

The wind, however, dropped and Le Brave's final approach was slow giving Myers time to form a plan. Le Brave had a reputation of taking many prize ships by coming alongside and overwhelming the enemy ship by force of numbers when almost the all the crew would board their prey and rapidly dispatch any resistance. Myers ordered his men to load the four guns on the starboard side and then threw the rest of their gunpowder overboard. At the same time he had a small rowing boat lowered and tied to the stern having filled it with firearms, primed and loaded. As Le Brave approached, the crew of Bon Fortune fired their small broadside, causing little damage to the sturdy Le Brave, which had picked up speed and was driving its bowsprit into the smaller ship's rigging. Leaving only four men on Le Brave and with shouts of 'Vive l'Empéreur!'[223] the French poured onto the deck of the Bon Fortune. Myers and his crew were not there to repel them since they had all slipped down into the cabin and climbed out of a port-hole into the waiting rowing boat. The two ships now drifted apart and Myers and his men quietly rowed their boat under the stern and over to the enemy ship which they boarded. They had no trouble dealing with the four men who had remained aboard Le Brave and this well armed ship was theirs. The little Bon Fortune was now in French hands but was defenseless. Myers hailed its new captain and said he was quite satisfied with the exchange and perhaps the captain would follow him to the nearest port that flew the Union Jack. To make his point he added that since the Bon Fortune had no cargo of value, he 'would as soon sink the ship as not.'[224] The French captain duly agreed and the two ships met up with the Tamar three days later. Disaster nearly struck when the Tamar, fearing an attack by the fearsome Le Brave delivered a broadside before Myers could signal the change of fortune.

All was well and John Myers remained in command of Le Brave for a few months before Le Brave was recaptured by the French frigate Tamise off Mauritius in the Indian Ocean. Le Brave still had some of the original French crew aboard who were very pleased to be back under French command. When they told the captain of the frigate the story of how Le Brave was captured, his amusement was so great that he gave a grand bal at Port Louis to honour his daring prisoner.

Released by the French, Myers continued his travels around the world. In 1807 he was on an American ship that traded between Barbados, Jamaica and America. He arrived on the East coast of America on 5 June 1807 where he was stranded on shore in Baltimore because of an embargo on American shipping. He spent the time exploring the east coast particularly the area around Philadelphia which he describes as 'the capital of Pennsylvania and the handsomest city of the United States'.[225] He was particularly taken by the area around the river Delaware as good for shipping and his 'most favourite place'.

By 1809 he was now on a ship traveling around Scandinavia and the ports of the Baltic and he then returned to America in February 1811. After another stay in Philadelphia he bought a house nearby in a town called Bristol but was then off on his travels again, eventually circumnavigating the world four times.

During his later travels Myers befriended Simon Bolivar. Simon Jose Antonio de la Santisima Trinidad Bolivar y Palacios (1783–1830) was a leader of several independence movements throughout South America and continues to be revered in many countries of that continent. John Myers' wide experience and frequent visits to London made him an obvious choice to become an agent and representative of Simon Bolivar Mining Company which had obtained a lease on 12 October 1824 to work the copper mines of Aroa in the Province of Venezuela, Columbia. The trustees of the company were Timothy A. Curtis, Esq. Governor of the Bank of England, Thomas Maude, Esq. Rowland Stephenson, Esq., Captain John Myers and Charles Stuart Cochrane, Esq. R.N. and the bankers for the company were Messes. Remington, Stephenson, & Co.

It was not the California gold rush but there was some money to be made and by the end of 1825, Cornish miners and other labourers, along with specialised machinery, had reached some of the most inaccessible parts of South and Central America. Hopes entertained by British shareholders of a rapid and generous return on their investment were dashed in 1826, as a number of the mining companies failed when capital was suddenly withdrawn. Another dent in the finances of Rowland Stephenson.

Rowland Stephenson and John Myers first became friends through the Bolivar mining company. He was probably the mysterious sea captain with whom Rowland had been seen dining in London in the six months prior to his departure and rumoured to be the captain of the Cumbria. What part, if any, John Myers took in the flight of Rowland Stephenson is not known but Myers certainly did cross the Atlantic frequently and would have willingly helped his friend. What is undeniable is that Rowland Stephenson, after his release from the debtors prison in 1829, was taken by John Myers to his house in Bristol, Pennsylvania.

Rowland had been running, hiding and in custody of one sort or another for just over twelve weeks, ever since the day he had walked out of the bank. He now had time to consider his future. The weight of what had happened to his charmed life must have been almost unbearable; he had lost everything and had not even had time to say goodbye to six of his seven of children. He was now notorious, the thief, the bankrupt, the absconder and worse. Scurrilous stories of his life were published on both sides of the Atlantic, with little regard to the truth or chance of redress. To make matters worse the American newspapers were now printing details of the sales of all his possessions by Shuttleworth's. He could read how his treasured collections were being picked over and sold under the hammer for a fraction of their worth. The worldly wise John Myers must have been a cheerful host and a supportive friend at this difficult time although Rowland probably did not wish to have to listen to too many sea-faring stories.

Rowland had various options to consider and one of them would have been to return to England. James Buchanan, representing the British government, had said his life would be spared but he still faced a lengthy prison term if found guilty and transportation for at least fourteen years was the most likely sentence. On the afternoon of his arrival in New York he appears to have readily agreed to return but now that he was stronger and under the protection of Myers he could look at alternatives. The British government had failed to extradite him to England and were unlikely to try again; the Commissioners of the Bankruptcy Court had made it known that they thought he would not come back to England, willingly or unwillingly, and had ceased all proceedings. There was, however, Joseph Parkins. He, in his usual pugnacious way, had let it be known he would pursue Rowland Stephenson until he 'received satisfaction'.[226] Rowland knew that Joseph Parkins was definitely not a man to give up the chase as was illustrated in his hounding of man called M'Vey in 1818.

On 17 February 1819 DANIEL M'VEY was indicted at the Old Bailey

> for burglariously breaking and entering the dwelling-house of Joseph Wilfred Parkins, about seven o'clock in the night of the 5th of February, 1818, at St. Marylebone, with intent to steal, and burglariously stealing therein, one diamond ring, value £150; one pearl breast-pin, value £6.; two bunches of pearls, value £116; one gold button set with pearls, value £2; one hunting-frock, value £2; one pair of breeches, value £1; five yards of plush, value £2 10 s.; 64 pieces of foreign gold coin, value £56 16 s., and £3 in monies.[227]

Joseph Wilfred Parkins was the first to testify in court and described the circumstances of his stolen property:

> I live in Riding House-lane, St. Marylebone. On the 5th of February, in the morning, I left my house for two or three days, and went into Hampshire on particular business. I left my house in the care of Edward Parry, who was my groom – there was no other servant left except the prisoner, whom I ordered to take a horse down to Egham that morning, for Sir Francis Burdett to attend the hunt, which was next day. He had been a helper in my service about a month. Before he took the horse, he was to take a bundle of papers to my agent in Threadneedle-street, to be sent to India – he was also to take my Macaw to Exeter Change, to be taken care of for me. After giving him these orders, I sent for Parry, and informed him that I expected a gentleman to call with a post-chaise for me, and to tell him he would find me in Somerset-street. Parry was to remain in the house till I returned. The prisoner did not sleep there as he lived at Pimlico – he was not an in-door servant.

Q   Did you give him permission to sleep in the house while you were
     away –
A   No; I did not expect he would be in town, as I sent him to Egham to
     wait for Sir Francis Burdett. I left the key of the house with Parry,
     as he was a regular in-door servant – I left town that morning. The
     prisoner came into my service on the 7th of January – he told me
     he was in great distress, and wanted clothes and every necessary.
     I never saw him with a watch.

Q. When you returned to town did you see him –

A. No. I left town on Thursday morning, returned late on Saturday night, and found he had entirely left me. He had given me no notice, nor had I in any way discharged him. In consequence of information which I received, I searched for valuable property which I had recently brought from abroad, and missed the property stated in the indictment, which was all safe in a bureau when I left town. The gold coin consisted of a quantity of Napoleons, Louis-d'ors, and fourteen large Portugal coins worth four hundred rials each, nine pagodas, and an antique gold coin.'

Joseph Parkins' taste for the long chase came to the fore. M'Vey had come from County Down and since the fugitive had last been seen boarding a ship at Liverpool bound for Dublin Parkins concluded correctly, that he was heading for his hometown. Parkins immediately wrote to Alexander Stewart who was the local magistrate in the area of Rostrever where the family of M'Vey lived. He had known Alexander Stewart from his East India Company days and Stewart was only too happy to help, particularly since Parkins was offering a reward. Stewart duly apprehended M'Vey and immediately summoned Parkins from England. M'Vey pleaded his innocence to the magistrate, blaming the other servant, Parry, for the robbery but when Parkins arrived he found his breeches, now very dirty, were among M'Vey's belongings. M'Vey was confined at Rostrever prison but unfortunately the constable who was in charge let him go, probably unimpressed by Parkins' manners and doubtful he would ever see the reward Parkins had offered. A furious Parkins in the presence of a large number of people 'used some unhandsome epithets towards Mr. Stewart'.[228]

Empty-handed, Parkins returned to England and he heard no more about his breeches until September 1818 when he learned that M'Vey was in Dumfries in Scotland. Parkins took an express coach to the city and pursued him from there across Scotland and back to County Down where he again caught up with him in Downpatrick. With the help of a soldier he arrested M'Vey whom he brought back to England. Parkins finally arrived back in London by coach, disembarking at the Peacock Inn, Islington where M'Vey attacked him with a poker, shouting that he would send him to hell before he was hanged. Parkins, well used to a fight, overcame M'Vey, handcuffed him and delivered him to Marlborough Street.

All Parkins' efforts might have been in vain as the events of the night of the burglary, when examined in court, were by no means clear. It seemed that M'Vey had persuaded Parry to take the horses to Egham for him. Parry had locked up the house and left but M'vey asked a neighbour to help him get back in through an upstairs window. Half an hour later a shot was heard coming from the house and M'Vey appeared at a window shouting *'Stop Thief'*. No one including the local watchman could remember seeing anyone run away. Parry had returned to the house later but was too drunk to recall anything.

The case might have gone M'Vey's way but a Peter Mungo Knight gave evidence,

> I am apprentice to Mr. Magene, of Prince's-row, Pimlico, opposite the Bag of Nails public-house. In February last the prisoner came to our shop – – it was in the evening. I do not remember what day of the week it was. He asked me if I bought old gold coin for my master and I said, sometimes and called my master. He produced a small Indian piece; my master said he did not know the value of it – he urged distress, and my master agreed to buy it. Next evening he brought several others, there were some Napoleons and pagodas – my master bought £9 or £10 worth. He received a silver watch, and I believe, a gilt chain and seal, and the rest in notes – I believe the watch was valued at 50 shillings. He produced a bunch of pearls, which he said he was going to give to his sister. He left no watch to be repaired, but bought one.

> Q   Did you inquire how he got the property?
> A   He said he was a soldier, and come from abroad – he was very shabbily dressed; it is very common for soldiers to bring these things.

Daniel M'vey was found guilty and sentenced to hang. Parkins made one last attempt to find his stolen property when he visited M'Vey in the condemned cell at Newgate. M'Vey remained adamant that he had sold the stolen goods to a man in Liverpool 'for a very inconsiderable sum'[229] and even swore this on the scaffold to the Reverent Deveraux.

Sometime after the execution Parkins was surprised by a visit from M'Vey's widow. She asked for his help and gave Parkins a letter that she had received from her husband written the day before his execution.

> Newgate Cell April 6th
>
> These words is from my hand – DANIEL M'VEY.
>
> My dear Wife, – These lines I refer to you respecting the property which I am suffering for now at this present times, and explanation of where you

will find the same property. You must go to Ireland, and stop at my sister's Catherine Vernon, within one mile of Glaskin-hill, seven miles from Newry, on the road to Bun Bridge. When you go there, send privately for my father, and you and him will go to the place where the property his (is), and you will find it about five regular paces or yards on the left hand as you enter the cave. The cave is about half a mile on the way to my father from my sister's: Harshay's – cave, there is one yard of separation between the pearls and 400 Napoleans. The pearls is five yards, and the Napoleans is four yards from the entrance, about four feet from the ground as you enter on the left hand side; there is 1,000 Lower dwars (Louis d'ors), 375 pagados; Swamacal (Sumatrical) pieces there is 666, and there is two rows of pearls, having 4,000 in each row, and the rose diamond ring, which you will find as I have mentioned. And I wish my father to share them between my wife, my sister, and himself, and I shall rest happy. Amen.

And when this you see, remember me, and God bless you all, Amen.

DANIEL M'VEY[230]

The letter was undoubtedly authentic and Mrs. M'Vey said she hoped Parkins would reward her, particularly since her relatives had also seen it and she was anxious that they might get to the hiding place first and not give her a share. Parkins immediately dispatched a copy of the letter to the local magistrate, Mr. Fevey, asking him to find and return his property. Ten days later he received a disappointing reply from Mr. Fevey saying

> that he had searched the cave that the holes were found as described but that the property had been removed from them. There were tracks on the floor, one of the stones of the side wall had been removed and a pair of pot hooks was found at the mouth of the cave, supposed to have been used for the purpose of carrying coals for the search. On enquiry he found that the father and the sister of M'Vey had sold their cottages and had removed to another part of the country. No part of the property has been recovered from that day to this'.[231]

If Parkins was prepared to go to such lengths to apprehend a man who had stolen a few foreign coins and his breeches he would go a lot further for a man whom he blamed for stealing so much of his money. For Rowland there seemed no alternative for the moment but to remain in Bristol, P.A., with John Myers.

Joseph Parkins, however, was seething in New York; not only had Stephenson got away without punishment he had also not repaid him a penny.

What made it all the more irksome was that it all might have been different had he not offered the reward.

On 10 and 11 April the Grand Jury in New York examined the circumstances of the abduction of Rowland Stephenson. Several witnesses including Jacob Hays, James Buchanan and Jonathan Goodhue were examined. A subpoena was issued on the first day for Rowland Stephenson to appear before them and testify about his abduction from Georgia but there was some question as to where he was living and the subpoena was never served. The conclusion of the court was that the kidnap was the work of opportunists keen to receive the $1,000 offered by Joseph Parkins. The British government, and James Buchanan in particular, were exonerated. The accusations of Joseph Parkins, sworn and printed on 17 March 1829, were held to be vexatious and without grounds. At the end of the proceedings a letter was read out from Governor Forsyth of Georgia in which he stated that the parties concerned in the abduction of Stephenson would be rigorously prosecuted, and if found guilty, appropriately punished. On 19 December 1829 the state legislature of Georgia, as a result of the abduction of Rowland Stephenson, passed a law: 'Any person who shall feloniously abduct or kidnap any white person from out of any local jurisdiction or county, or from out of the limits of the state shall be punishable by imprisonment in the Penitentiary for not less than five years nor more than seven'.[232]

On 2 July 1829 the Times carried this notice:

ROWLAND STEPHENSON

Whereas ROWLAND STEPHENSON, a partner in the banking house of Messrs. Remington, Stephenson and Co., late of Lombard-street, bankers, and JAMES HARMAN LLOYD, a clerk in the banking house, absconded on or about the 27th of December last, the said Rowland Stephenson being charged with embezzlement and a reward of £300 (subsequently increased to £1,000) for the apprehension of the said Rowland Stephenson, and another of £100 for the apprehension of the said James Harman Lloyd, were advertised to be paid on application to me, the undersigned, Thomas Gates; and whereas the said Rowland Stephenson and James Harman Lloyd have absconded to and arrived in the United States of America, notice is herby given, that the REWARDS so advertised, to be paid for the apprehension of the said Rowland Stephenson and James Harman Lloyd respectively **WILL NOT BE PAID.**

June 26th 1829 THOMAS GATES, 56 Lombard Street

This was reprinted in the American press in July 1829 but by that time Rowland had made up his mind to stay in America. Like John Myers he liked the area around Philadelphia and had seen a farmhouse on the bank of the Neshaminy Creek in Bensalem that the owner, Dr. Shippen, was willing to sell.

Bensalem is a small township, twenty-one square miles in area, in the southern corner of Bucks County, eighteen miles northeast of Philadelphia. It is bounded on the south by the great Delaware River and to the east and west by its tributaries, the Neshaminy and Poquessing creeks. The area known now as the state of Pennsylvania was granted to William Penn in 1681 and by 1682 the area of Bucks County was being settled. Dutch, Swedes and English settled Bensalem, 'an unbroken wilderness'.[233] 1690 saw the initial laying out of the town and township tax records go back to 1693. A very early settler was Dunken Williamson who amongst other things started Dunk's Ferry, an important crossing on the Delaware River, used by George Washington's troops on Christmas Day, 1776, before the Battle of Trenton and immortalized in Emanuel Gottlieb Leutze's famous painting 'Washington crossing the Delaware' despite it being painted in Dusseldorf using German models crossing the Rhine.

The Williamson family had a private burial site on some rising ground above the Neshaminy creek, now known as the Johnson-Williamson Burying Grounds and still to be seen today. The burial site was situated on the estate of the farmhouse that Rowland Stephenson purchased from Dr. Shippen on 22 October 1829. Examination of the deeds reveals that it was not Rowland Stephenson who signed the contract of purchase for the house but his son, Rowland Macdonald Stephenson who had travelled to America in September 1829 and probably brought funds with him to buy the house and support his father. Rowland Macdonald always maintained that his father was penniless in America and lived off money provided by his children. Although Rowland's possessions had been stripped from him, down to the last chamber pot, there was the family fortune from Mary Eliza's side of the Stephensons which was already supporting his children. Rowland renamed his new house Farley to remind him of his wife's childhood home and where they started their married life together. The property was described as 'a splendid brown stone home with an estate of 170 acres'[234] and cost $15,000.

Hearing of Rowland Stephenson's change of fortune, Joseph Parkins wrote a letter to the New York Times in which he accused Rowland Stephenson of having money hidden away in America.[235] Parkins affirmed that he had received four anonymous letters from Savannah informing him that Rowland

Stephenson had sold exchequer bills while he was there. The recipient of the bills was a Mr. Gaston with whom Parkins was now in correspondence. He offered this as proof of the fact that Rowland Stephenson had much money secreted in America. He also stated in the letter to the newspaper that he had visited Rowland Stephenson three times in prison and that his defence was the same as that of the unfortunate Henry Fauntleroy in that he was selling exchequer bills to prop up the failing bank and that this was well known to the other partners. He wrote,

> At the same time I have not the least doubt, from the conversation which I had with Stephenson whilst in goal here, that he brought funds to this country. This conversation took place whilst under the fear of being sent to England and hanged, as he had committed the high crime of forgery. I then inquired what Stephenson had done with mine and other exchequer bills to the amount of about £100,000. He replied that Lloyd had taken them, and that he had also sold or exchanged them and that he had put the proceeds of the said bills in the till of the house to keep up the credit. I soon convinced him from documents I received from London that there was no truth to his statement of putting money in the till of the house. And I am convinced if he had been detained a few days longer in prison, he would have found means to have paid me all the money of which he has defrauded me'.[236]

Back in England the question as to whether the other partners were privy to the abstractions, or negligent in allowing them, was examined in detail during a case that came up at the Vice-Chancellor's Court on 7 August 1832. *Ex Parte Murray in matter of Remington* was a petition to have the £58,000 which was abstracted by Stephenson expunged from the private debts of Rowland Stephenson and transferred to the debts of the banking house. The petition stated, that it was the custom of the banking-house to deposit the cheques, bills and notes, which remained at the close of the day, in a chest, from which various sums of money had from time to time been extracted by Mr. Rowland Stephenson. The monies thus deposited in the chest were entered into a book entitled 'The Copy,' by Mr. Henry Stephenson, and the sum in question was declared by the petitioners to have been abstracted by Rowland Stephenson, with the knowledge of Henry Stephenson who was acting as a partner.

> It was contended by the learned counsel, that Mr. Rowland Stephenson was guilty of this fraud with the consent of the whole of the partnership, and that it was done in prosecution of a course of conduct well known to the firm, and which was permitted by them for the stability of the house, inasmuch as

they well knew the credit of the house depended upon keeping up the credit of Mr. Rowland Stephenson, and that stopping this course would be in effect to stop the payment of the firm.

Mr. Pepys and Mr. Richards appeared in opposition to the petition. No evidence had been adduced by the petitioners to convict the other partners in any knowledge in the fraudulent transactions of which Mr. Rowland Stephenson had been guilty. On the contrary, it was admitted, that Henry Stephenson had known of the abstraction of Stephenson in position of keeper of the copy-book, and that he had filled up fictitious entries, when the money was from time to time abstracted. These transactions having been clearly effected without the knowledge of any of the partners except Henry Stephenson, it was evident this petition could never succeed'.

The Vice-Chancellor said, that the material question for the decision of the Court was, whether all the partners would be considered as having been privy to the manner in which Mr. Rowland Stephenson had dealt with the partnership funds, after the month of April 1826. It appeared upon an examination of the affidavits altogether that some degree of displeasure was expressed by the partners with respect to the transaction of 1826, but it did not very clearly appear in what way that displeasure had been communicated to Rowland Stephenson. He, however, from some reason or other, must have been aware that his conduct was disapproved of by the other partners, because Mr. David Remington distinctly swears that this course of conduct was not proceeded with…. He was therefore of opinion that the £58,000 had been drawn from the banking-house without the privity of the other partners, with the exception of Mr. Henry Stephenson.[237]

The partners were again absolved of blame.

There was another outstanding matter in England that needed resolution. By the beginning of January 1830 a year had passed since Rowland Stephenson had absconded and as far as his parliamentary seat was concerned, a year since he had been declared bankrupt. In the House of Commons on January 19th a letter was read from Mr. J. Bourdillon, who had been appointed solicitor to the estate of Rowland Stephenson. He wrote to confirm that it was now twelve calendar months since Stephenson had been declared bankrupt and none of his creditors had yet been paid. The Act of Parliament passed in the fifty-second year of King George III (Act 32 Geo3 c144) instituted 'An Act to suspend and finally vacate the seats of Members of the House of Commons who shall become bankrupt and who shall not pay their debts in full within twelve calendar months'.[238] It was duly agreed that Rowland Stephenson had forfeited his seat for Leominster and a new Member would be elected in due time. It was noted that Rowland Stephenson had never spoken or voted in the House of Commons.

Only two of the kidnappers ever went to court. On February 18th 1830 George Miller and William Oates pleaded guilty to kidnap and were sentenced by Judge Holt to $1,000 fine and six months imprisonment and $500 and three months imprisonment respectively. The tide of public opinion, however, had turned against the fugitive London banker who now seemed to be doing rather well for himself. On 15 March 1830 at the court in Savannah a resolution of Alderman Owens and seconded by Alderman Cuyler was presented that the kidnappers should be released and the fines annulled because of their exemplary behaviour in custody, their pleading guilty and that they were useful members of society in Savannah, with dependent wives and children. Both men received full pardons.

On 1 September 1830 the estate of Farley in the township of Bensalem formally changed hands from Rowland Macdonald to Rowland Stephenson. The reason for this is unclear but the papers came from London duly signed by Rowland Macdonald. Rowland Stephenson's occupation was recorded as 'Gentleman' and country gentleman he certainly hoped to remain, safely hidden away on his estate in Bensalem for as long as possible, where England was a long way away.

Joseph Parkins was continuing to make a name for himself, much as he had in England.

Despite his great financial loss when Remington's collapsed, Joseph Parkins remained a wealthy man and he was determined to invest his money in land and property in the United States. He first applied to buy land in America in February 1830 and this was referred to the Committee on the Petitions of Aliens but was eventually refused in 1831 since he was not a United States citizen. He now needed an American national to help him. For this he befriended and engaged the services of Abijah Mann who said he was able to help him to invest his money in American land and could also use his influence to detain Rowland Stephenson.

Abijah Mann, Jr. served as member of the New York State Assembly 1828–1830 and then became a Member of Congress in 1832. He gained notoriety by his unjustified and outspoken hostility to the popular Chenango Canal Project in Upstate New York and again when he was asked to investigate the United States Bank; being denied access to the building he simply employed labourers to dig a tunnel in. He was a man with his finger in a number of pies and the sort of person, Parkins thought, might be able to help him. As with so many of Parkins' acquaintances the friendship soured and their personal conflict published, this time by a pamphlet which Parkins produced in 1838.

In 1831 Joseph Parkins began investing money through his new found friend and received a conspiratorial letter; this was to be the first item in the pamphlet:

Fairfield 27 Octr. 1831.

Dear Sir,

I am honoured by the receipt in due course of your kind letter and enclosures of the 22nd current; I have made the copies, one of which is duly executed as you desired and both are enclosed in a separate envelope. Your suggestion as to the form of action is sound and valuable as it will simplify the proceedings to one which is common every day. The interest on your money will be calculated up to the time of recovery. I have not had leisure to test your calculation but will do so soon and prefer to do it myself rather than to trust my clerks as at present I do not wish them to know of my agency in your affairs.

I shall hope to be able about 15th March next year to commence the reconnoitre of **Rowland Stephenson** and unknown and unsuspected my agents will watch his every movements and doings for a time. I do also hope by patient industry and proper firmness of purpose to compel him to at least partial justice.

I am Sir with Sentiments of true Respect,
Your Friend and humble servant

A. Mann. Junr.[239]

A second letter, dated 2 January 1832 from Mann gives Joseph Parkins a history of foreign investment in America and the present more difficult situation that his new friend has already met because of foreign profiteering. But he declared 'it is the Land of Opportunity'. Joseph Parkins might well have asked, 'Whose opportunity?'

More letters follow of little interest until 14 February 1832. The pamphlet prints an order of Joseph Parkins assigning money, mortgages, bonds and policies of insurance over to Abijar Mann in return for securities for $30,000 and this money was to be lent, with interest payable monthly, to eight *upright* associates of Mann in the village Buffalo, west of New York City. The transfer of

Parkins' money is confirmed by Abijar Mann on 22 February 1832 by an order to the Cashier of the Mechanics Exchange Bank explaining the securities to be transferred to his associates in Buffalo, with an additional $4,200.

On 23 February 1832 Abijar Mann wrote a letter of introduction for his friend Joseph Parkins and sent it to one of his cronies, Gilbert Allen of 23 Howard Street New York.

> Let me say that Mr. Parkins is a gentleman of high and honourable feelings and worthy of the esteem and corresponding feelings of honourable men. I have mentioned to you his peculiar situation here and I shall be obliged if you will aid him by being his guarantor if he needs any such aid and moreover will see you fully indemnified in so doing for which Mr. Parkins put abundant means at my disposal. Any advice you may afford him will confer a particular favour on me.

The next few letters reveal the financial arrangement beginning to unravel with failure of the 'associates' in Buffalo to pay the interest on time and on 18 October 1832 Mann wrote to Parkins that he is sorry not to have seen him in New York because of a cholera epidemic ravaging the city.

By 6 February 1833 Abijar Mann was back in favour and wrote a long letter to Parkins about investing in land near Buffalo. First however he told Parkins that he is awaiting a communication from a lawyer called Mr. A. Lenisat Esq. as to how his pursuit of Rowland Stephenson was going. He had high hopes that the lawyer would help Attorney Bronson organise another trial and get Stephenson behind bars as soon as possible. Mann offered to help Parkins buy

> 85,000 acres at 20 cents apiece. I have some knowledge of these lands, having traversed some parts of them and although a wilderness now and accounted poor yet I have little doubt that an investment at that very low price will be, in progress of time, abundantly productive. The timber is abundant and valuable but the minerals, iron, tin and silver which abound in the region are much more valuable.

The above must have ended in tears as Joseph Parkins wrote to his lawyer, Henry A Wise, on October 10th 1835. He referred to Mann as 'that low bred caitiff',[240] asking him to 'belabour the rascal Mann and his Buffalo gang and get them convicted'. He had lost everything he had invested.

It is not known if Rowland Stephenson knew agents of Abijar Mann were watching him in 1832 but he certainly knew Joseph Parkins was still on his trail. On 5 October 1830 the ex-sheriff appeared in court in the nearby town of Doylestown, accused of an assault and battery upon a Constable at Bensalem. There is no record of what this was about but Parkins must have been causing trouble at Farley; he was convicted and fined $20 and sentenced to be imprisoned for 20 days.[241] There was no chance that a short prison sentence would deter Parkins from his regular appearances in court for civil cases of slander and pursuance of debts as well as frequent charges of assault.

Joseph Parkins was in trouble again while visiting Philadelphia in June 1831. At the hotel where he was staying a young man introduced himself as a London acquaintance. Obtaining his confidence the young man traveled with Parkins in his carriage, only to steal his trunk and $100 and then disappeared. To add to the ex-sheriff's discomfiture, the landlord of the hotel sued Parkins for the young man's unpaid bill. Parkins set about the officer who delivered the writ and was sent to prison for another 22 days.[242]

The Times of 15 May 1833 reported that while in New York ex-sheriff Parkins' appearances in court were even more frequent than in London; he had already paid over $5000 to a man from Albany who had sued him for slander regarding the quality of his horses and now he was in the Circuit Court of the United States being sued again.[243] Mrs. Isabella Bard was awarded $6500 damages and costs. The plaintiff was a widow and mother of a large family, who ran a very respectable boarding house in Park Place where Parkins had resided and befriended her. She was not so keen on his management of her affairs and asked someone else to carry out some confidential business for her. Parkins took offence and not only left the lodgings but spread rumours about her 'moral character'. During the trial Parkins was so rude to his counsel that he threatened to resign unless the court ordered Parkins to conduct himself with more propriety. After the testimony was concluded Parkins asked if he could be allowed to argue his own case to the jury; the judge agreed, 'on the ground that he was a foreigner, unacquainted with our institutions, and lest an impression might get abroad unfavourable to the liberality of our courts of justice; this liberty was permitted to him which would have been denied to one of our own citizens'.[244] The judge may have regretted this decision as he had to listen to two and a half hours of Parkins' rambling defense. The heavy damages of $6,500 awarded to Mrs. Bard reflected perhaps the Judge's irritation with the loquacious ex-sheriff rather than the seriousness of the slander. These damages did however stretch his finances and by 27 May he found himself in the City jail in New York, unable or unwilling to pay.

There were now so many cases of slander outstanding that the authorities took the opportunity while Parkins was in prison to have his state of mind

examined in a case of de lunatico inquirendo. The refusal of Parkins to cooperate in any way with the procedure made this impossible and he was therefore
deemed to be perfectly sane.[245]

Parkins' opinion of Abijar Mann was not improved by his giving evidence
against Parkins at this hearing. This was particularly galling, as the loss of his
money in the Buffalo venture had rendered Parkins unable to pay the damages
and because of that, imprisoned.

Abijar Mann did manage to do one thing for Parkins and that was to have
Rowland Stephenson rearrested and returned to prison in New York.

There are no details of the efforts of Mr. A. Lenisat Esq. and Attorney
Bronson, enlisted by Mann, but whatever they were, Rowland Stephenson
returned to prison in New York on Tuesday, 27 August 1833, again under the
writ for a debt, now of $80,000 at the suit of ex-sheriff Parkins. Bail had been set
at $8,000, which he could not pay. The irony was not lost on newspapers both
sides of the Atlantic that he had joined in prison none other than the ex-sheriff;
the first meeting between them was described as 'somewhat peculiar'.[246]

Parkins was also visited in 1833 by an Englishman called George Fibbleton,
who recounted his encounter with him thus,

> They have kept confined here a certain Englishman, on suspicion of debt,
> and fed him on nothing but bread and water. This unfortunate gentleman
> was none other than the celebrated Joseph Parkins, Esq., Ex-Mayor of
> London (sic). He, like myself, being smitten with the love of American insti-
> tutions at a distance, had emigrated to the United States, to find all those
> flattering ideas he had once entertained, vanish into thin air. He had come
> to the country rich; but the Americans, with that dexterity for which they
> are renowned, were contriving every method, which Yankee ingenuity could
> devise, to fleece him of his money. At one time, they would sue him for
> slander; and then, if he discovered so much of a manly spirit as to fall upon
> them, and beat them soundly, they would immediately prosecute him for
> assault and battery. I need not mention on what very trivial grounds various
> suits of both kinds were brought, nor in whose favour they terminated.
> Suffice it to say, that both judge, jury, and plaintiff were Americans, and that
> the defendant was a stranger and an Englishman. Finding that they could not
> get entire possession of his money by means of these suits, the enemies of the
> Ex-Mayor next procured a commission of lunacy; seized upon all his notes,
> mortgages, bonds, and effects; and finally concluded by shutting him up in
> the Bridewell — not, however, until he had knocked down the Sheriff of the
> city, five deputies, and ten constables; for he is a man of mighty strength, and

has a fist that could easily floor an ox. The Ex-Mayor was at length secured, and confined to the dungeons of the Bridewell. In this situation I visited him.

As I entered his cell, taking me no doubt, for one of his persecutors, he seized me by the throat and exclaimed, 'You bloody villain you! Who have you been murdering now? And what the devil do you want of me? Can no place in the world be free from your intrusions? Must you even follow me into my very dungeon, you infernal Yankee scoundrel you?'

'Hold! hold!' I exclaimed, nearly choked to death.

'Hold? Curse you! So I will hold,' he replied, rather tightening than relaxing his grasp.

I should soon have gone for it, for I was now unable by speech to convince him of his mistake, had not the keeper interfered, and rescued me from his grasp. As it was, so severe had been the pressure of his fingers on my throat, that I carried the mark for three weeks. As soon, however, as the Ex-Mayor was made sensible of his error, he rendered a suitable apology for his violence; and understanding that I was an Englishman, he grasped me warmly by the hand, and invited me to take a seat beside him on the cold stone floor of the dungeon.

'And so,' said he, when he had sufficiently recovered from his emotion, 'here we are a couple of English fools together — fools ! did I say ? No, I'm merely a lunatic. At least, so the infernal savages of New York will have it — and they have put me into this cursed dungeon, for a madman. But, damn 'em! they shall find I'm mad to some purpose — the base wretches and conspirators — I'll crush them and their machinations, before I've done — they'll get enough of the Ex – Mayor of London, or I'm mistaken. Here I've been kept for six months in this filthy jail, by the most diabolical conspiracy that ever was hatched in the depths of hell. I, who have saved the lives of innocent people, condemned to death — I have become the victim of a conspiracy in a land of liberty! I came here, with the most enthusiastic feelings for the Americans — as I dare say you have, Mr. Fibbleton — but you're a damned fool — you're a lunatic — you're more crazy than I am. As for these infernal Yankees, the laws protect them in their villainy. There is no more chance here for an Englishman, than there is for a cat in hell, without claws. The whole country is one great nest of lawyers and profligates. Under pretence of defending me from the charge of lunacy, they have laid a plan to prey upon me — to devour me — to eat me up. But I'll defeat the scoundrels yet — the villains, to dare to call themselves my friends ! They are no friends of mine. I need no lawyers to defend me — I can defend myself — DON'T INTERRUPT ME SIR — I won't bear interruption. I'm an English gentleman! a British subject! and these rascally Americans have no right to interfere with my property, even if I was mad. The character of this country, bad as it was before, is disgraced by their conduct to me. I will convict the whole nation of perjury, from the least to the greatest — from the lawyer to the judge — from General Jackson, down to Martin Van Buren.

I like to punish rogues. I was put in jail for having thrashed a tailor — would to heaven I had thrashed him !— Previous to my coming here, I liked this country better than any country in the world — and now, the ungrateful wretches the whole country have conspired against me. The press has libeled me. The courts have held nightly orgies, listening to vile slanders against me. But I'll bring their noses to the grindstone. Ah ! when I was leaving England, the Marquis of Anglesey, and Sir William Curtis, shook me by the hand and said, 'Parkins, why do you leave us? Why do you leave your native country, to go to an imaginary land?' But, madman that I was I came away. But I'm not mad now — I'm in my sober senses.

Ah ! – Since I've been in jail, Rowland Stephenson has been in New York. He would not have dared to come here but he knew that I was shut up in jail, for thumping a tailor, whom I never touched — otherwise he would not have come; lest he should have to disgorge my money, the rascally robber ! The fugitive from justice ! But here he is protected by the dumb-feed lawyers. The country has not energy to punish the numerous rogues that are in it. I have been beset by ruffians in prison — when I wanted the refreshment of a glass of beer, the scoundrel of a jail-keeper, denied me. The devil is said to be ever near, when you are talking about him; and so it happened in this case.' The jailer had appeared, and told the Ex-Sheriff of London to desist from abusing me. At this, Parkins flew into a violent passion, as he had reason to, and would have knocked the jailer down, could he have fairly reached him. But missing the jailer, he made a grab at me; when I dexterously moved myself out of his reach, and wondered he should think of using violence against a subject of His most Gracious Majesty.

'Damn His most Gracious Majesty!' he exclaimed — 'what have I to do with him, I owe him nothing.'

'Pardon me, sir,' said I, ''but methinks you owe him civility, if not allegiance.' Hereupon, he began to rave like a bedlamite, swearing he owed no man, either civility or allegiance. He exclaimed against every kind of government, against every country, and against the whole human race. After he had thus gone the world over, he returned back to me — calling me His Majesty's toadeater; and demanding why I had come from England, if I liked the country so well?

'However,' said he, 'I'm glad you are in prison, but I don't want you in my cell, so clear yourself out, very quick — you're a greater fool than I. Out with you, I say !' Finding the Ex-Mayor in this humour, I pretty soon made my exit. If he was not insane when put in, I am sure it was enough to make any man so, to be confined in that miserable dog-hole ; and I have no doubt, but what the mad starts he exhibited, such as seizing me by the throat, damning His Majesty, and the like, were the effects of the persecutions he had suffered from these vile republicans'.[247]

On 27 August 1833 Parkins was taken from prison to answer yet another charge in the Superior Court for libel which lasted three days.

Mr. PARKINS chose to defend the suit in person, and certainly displayed great vituperative powers, which he exercised alike upon the Court and jury, upon the counsel and witnesses for the prosecution, upon his own witnesses and assistants, and upon the spectators of the amusing scene. His incoherent raving, and the irrelevant matter which he introduced, must have impressed the jury with the absurdity of giving weight to his slanders, and were probably a better defense than the most ingenious counsel could have devised for him.[248]

The plaintiff was awarded six cents damages and six cents costs. The jury felt that 'the words were actionable but the reckless and indiscriminate abuse which the defendant is accustomed to scatter around him is from the estimation in which he is held in the community, altogether impotent and harmless'. It was pointed out that there were countless suits being prepared against him for slander but after this judgment they would be soon abandoned.[249]

Parkins referred to his meetings with Stephenson in prison in the many letters he wrote to William Remington. In a letter dated 20 September 1833 he first complained bitterly about the bank, and was particularly angered by the fact that Remington accepted a large deposit from his French bank when he knew his banking house was failing and about to go under. He told William Remington that he has seen Stephenson in the prison and that he still takes a lot of snuff and lives in fear of being forced to return to England to face the death penalty or transportation.[250]

The same letter also refers to an encounter he had had with Thomas Hornor while Parkins was making yet another appearance in court. Poor Thomas Hornor was ruined by the failure of the bank and he also had fled to America later in 1829, leaving behind many unpaid bills for the construction of the Colosseum. He hoped to make a living in New York by drawing the houses of rich people but he found life hard. In London there was a rumour that he had gone to join Rowland Stephenson but this was untrue. The Times in June 1830 quotes a local witness in Bristol, Pennsylvania, 'Rowland Stephenson, the fugitive London Banker, has been joined at his mansion by Lloyd, his clerk, and Mr. Thomas Hornor, the founder of the Colosseum and that they are living in great splendour, keep many servants and hunting horses'.[251] On 18 June the Times printed a letter from Mr. Thomas Brown of Somers Place London, a friend and admirer of Thomas Hornor who refutes the claim. He had kept up a correspondence with his friend and wrote 'he is living very modestly and spending his time delineating the vast scenery of that country'.[252] He continues that Hornor has written to him and tells him that 'that Rowland Stephenson is living a few hours sail from New York but I shall avoid him most certainly'.[253]

Parkins was in court on this occasion, charged yet again with assaulting a deputy sheriff 'whom I never touched with either stick, fist or foot'.[254] He ranted against the judge, 'virulent prejudice against me', the witnesses, 'hired for the occasion to swear I poked him in the paunch and punched him in the eye---would that I had', and the jurors, 'biased'.[255] Parkins had noticed Thomas Hornor sitting in the public gallery and before he was returned to his prison cell he managed to speak to him. Parkins told William Remington in his next letter how Thomas Hornor 'looked most unwell, shook like an aspen leaf and stank of cheap whiskey'.[256] Parkins advised him to return to England as he would have little to fear and should not have fled in the first place.

Parkins finished the letter saying he had no sympathy for Rowland Stephenson, languishing in prison with him. 'Such is Rowland Stephenson's treatment after robbing me and many others of immense sums of money whilst I who have wronged no one am imprisoned, falsely accused of striking a knavish tailor, slandering an Irish thief who had stolen my gun and horse and cheated by dishonest agents'.[257]

Another letter to William Remington dated 10 October 1833 admits that he seems to be spending rather a lot of time in court but he also says that he has spoken to Rowland Stephenson who is now ready to tell all.[258]

There was always the other side to Joseph Parkins, as illustrated by a man called E.S.Abdy in his book 'A Residence and Tour in the United States of North America.'[259] Abdy was a fellow of Jesus College, Cambridge. He had strong views on slavery and described in graphic detail the horror of the holding pen in the middle of Washington D.C., capital of the 'most free nation in the world'. In New York, Abdy visited the City Jail on 27 Nov 1833 to see some men who had been confined as runaway slaves 'that is they were accused of having committed the heinous crime of stealing their own bodies'. Their stories were sad; the first slave from North Carolina had purchased his freedom three times only to be defrauded by his owner; the second, 'a very decent, good looking man' of about 30 had been living in New York as a free man for four years when he was arrested and had been in prison for a year and the third had run away from the cruelties of a master in Virginia and come to the 'free' state of New York, only to be arrested. They had no means of support and worked for the other prisoners in exchange for small amounts of food. The keeper told Abdy that there was 'no legal provision and no allowance of any kind made for persons under these circumstances'.

While visiting the fugitives Abdy was told that ex-Sheriff Parkins was also in the prison and had been very kind to these men. 'He was imprisoned in a small cell on his own and had been incarcerated for some time for contempt of court for an alleged assault having refused to find bail and thereby acknowledge as he thought that the charge had any foundation' Parkins was receiving rough treatment from the turnkeys who unnecessarily abused and assaulted him and he had been attacked by another prisoner with a hatchet.[260]

Parkins told him that he was in prison because he had lost a lot of money in a land deal which he had made through an intermediary who had robbed him. Parkins had been accused of insanity but Abdy found him sane, if very talkative with some flight of ideas. 'He dealt largely in the parenthesis, – not here and there merely, but one within the other, like an involution of Chinese ivory balls.'

Abdy observes 'Parkins told me he pleaded his own cause in court and I observed whatever sort of client he might have as an advocate, he undoubtedly had not a temperate advocate as a client' He had written countless letters on behalf of himself and other prisoners especially the three slaves. Parkins' lawyer unwisely asked him 'Why do you trouble yourself with these blacks?' Parkins threw him out of his cell.

Abdy was later informed that the three fugitives were all returned to the South and to an uncertain but enslaved future.

On 7 December 1833 the Commercial Advertiser in New York reported that:

> Rowland Stephenson remains confined to prison in New York for a debt of $80,000 at the suit of Ex Sheriff Parkins who is also an inmate of the prison on executions of several large amounts. The banker is dependent upon charity for his food. What strange vicissitudes of fortune![261]

The vicissitudes of fortune were to reverse. Rowland Stephenson remained in the prison from 27 August 1833 until the beginning of the following year when he was released but had to remain within the city limits. On 27 March

1834 he appeared in the New York Superior Court and was finally discharged. New York had moved on and his case now attracted no publicity. He was fortunate that the judiciary had lost all sympathy with Joseph Parkins who was informed that this was the very end of his pursuit of Rowland Stephenson through the courts of the United States.

Rowland returned to the Farley estate by the banks of the Delaware to continue his life as a Gentleman, leaving Joseph Parkins to simmer in the City Jail.

CHAPTER EIGHTEEN

THE ENDS OF THE ROADS

R OWLAND, NOW AGED 54, returned to the Farley estate at Bensalem on 27 March 1834. Further prosecution was very unlikely and he settled down to a quiet country life alone. His name was out of the newspapers and he slipped into obscurity.

Parkins having seen his adversary walk free was to remain in the New York City Jail for a further four years. His natural confrontational manner was getting him into regular brawls with other prisoners but he seems to have found means to protect himself. In August 1834 yet another case concerning him was being heard in his absence at the Superior court. Parkins had possession of certain papers that the magistrate wished to see and Officer Smith was dispatched to the prison with a power of attorney to obtain the papers. Smith entered Parkins' cell and demanded the documents. Parkins denied having them but Smith replied that he knew he had them and if he would not give them up peaceably then he would proceed to search the cell. Parkins dared him to try and produced a three-barrelled pistol. Officer Smith managed to wrench this from his hand but Parkins then pulled out two other pistols hidden in his clothing and a hunting knife and as a last resort he brandished a gun hidden in a walking stick, all of which the heavily built Smith managed to take off him. The firearms were found to be fully charged and primed. The newspapers thought it a wonder that the officer had survived the attack although Parkins probably did not wish to face a death penalty for the sake of a few papers and kept his 'frightful collection of weaponry' for protection against fellow prisoners.[262]

At the beginning of July 1837 Joseph Parkins was released from prison where he had served 'five years in consequence of his irascible temperament but like the man in the Bastille, he knows not where to go and therefore still resides in the goal. He is a man of large fortune'.[263]

Just after this had been published in London, one of the city's police officers was surprised to receive a £5 note sent from the City Jail in New York. The policeman was Inspector Feltham of 'T' division and the reward concerned a man named James Greenacre.[264]

Greenacre was born in 1785 at West Winch, Norfolk and went to London as a young man to start a grocery and tea business in the parish of St George's, Woolwich. He had three wives all of whom died of 'natural causes'. In 1833, after being fined £150 for adding sloe leaves to the tea he was selling, he fled to America where he invented a washing machine. Somehow he landed up in the same prison as Joseph Parkins and there was a disagreement between them such that Greenacre swore to kill him. Parkins survived two savage attacks, the first when five men burst into his cell and he was hit on the head with a hatchet and shortly afterwards he was again savagely attacked by Greenacre and two others.

Greenacre was released from prison and returned to England with visions of producing the Greenacre Patented Labour Saving Washing Machine. He proposed marriage to a woman called Hannah Brown who herself was a wash-erwoman but also had enough money to finance Greenacre's invention. He, however, murdered her before the marriage and cut up the body, leaving parts around London; her left arm was found in St. John's Wood and her head in a ditch in Stepney. Inspector Feltham tracked him down, along with his mistress, Sarah Gale. They were both found guilty of murder and sentenced to death. Sarah Gale's sentence was reduced to transportation for life and she died 51 years later in New South Wales. Greenacre, now known as the 'Edgeware Road Murderer', was hanged at Newgate and his death mask was exhibited at Madame Tussauds. When Parkins heard of the execution he sent the five £5 to Inspector Feltham 'so that he could buy himself a medal'.[265]

Parkins finally left the prison in 1838. He had already been involved in over a hundred lawsuits in America alone. His first task was to publish his pamphlet, reproducing the correspondence with Abijar Mann.[266] The introduction was signed 'The Publishers' but was undoubtedly written by the hand of Joseph Parkins referring to himself as 'him'.

He began by declaring his unconditional freedom after 5 years, incarcer-ated in a filthy dungeon in order to 'starve him into the consent of rendering up his property to individual plunder. . . . . . he has been compelled to depend for subsistence upon the crumbs which fell from the alms house table during the whole period of his confinement'.[267] He complained bitterly of how he was attacked by a policeman and robbed of important documents. To lay the matter in the public domain, Parkins published 21 letters, 19 from Abijar Mann to Joseph Parkins and two replies of Parkins.

'When the reader has glanced over the letters, affidavits etc. contained in this pamphlet, he will be ready to acknowledge that Mr. Parkins is the most victimised man he ever read of.' Parkins accused Abijar Mann of ingratiating himself by the most servile flattery before turning around and 'stinging him like an adder'. He also accused Mann of showing 'a most flatulent pretention of knowledge and the utmost contempt for grammar (considering that the writer is a member of Congress)'. He lambasted him for his servitude, having used such expressions as 'Dear Sir' and signing himself 'your obedient servant' but his greatest crime was to give evidence at the hearing to prove Parkins to be mad,

> Touching the idea of the insanity of Mr. Parkins is all nonsense. Indeed he has given evidence of possessing more than an average of sound sense, for had he not been a man of uncommonly strong and well regulated mind he must either have sunk under the mountain of injuries that have been heaped on him or else have actually gone mad, the anticipation of one of which results first, induced his tormentors to incarcerate him in a filthy prison.

Joseph Parkins was 63 in 1838 and his health was beginning to fail. He had lost much of his fortune but he still had some fight left in him. In September 1839, Parkins, now for some reason referred to in the American press as the 'double X-Sheriff',[268] appeared as a defendant in a suit in the Marine Court in New York. During the hearing two sheriffs' officers entered the court and tried to arrest him under a Recorder's warrant. Parkins resisted and was joined by his friends who were appearing in his defence at the hearing. Not wishing to miss a fight but not knowing quite what it was about, the friends of his opponent at law joined in on the side of the officers. The judge tried to call order above the shouts,

'Give it to him
That's the ticket
You've torn my coat
Pox on officers
Huzza for Parkins
Down with the Bums'[269]

The fight lasted ten minutes and Parkins was taken off to the police headquarters where they added to his troubles with a charge of assault and battery for which he was held on bail of $200 and discharged. Judge Kent spared him another custodial sentence because of his poor health and he was eventually taken into the house of a hatter in New Jersey called George Best whose grandfather, Dr Jameson, had been a close childhood friend of Parkins in Carlisle.

On 12 April 1840 Joseph Wilfred Parkins died in Newark, New Jersey.

> 'In his last illness he was as irritable as ever. He was at the house of Mr Best, hatter, in Newark, and Dr D'Arcy attended him. One day he refused to take some medicine, and the next day he denied doing this. Dr. Darcy said 'I can prove you did'
>
> 'Prove!' said the sheriff, 'Prove, you can prove anything in this damn fool country.'
>
> He died at half past five on Sunday morning and was sensible and talking to the end. He told those around him to send is body back to Carlisle to be buried in the churchyard alongside his parents because he did not wish to be buried 'in this bloody country'.[270]

His death was reported in the Times, 'With all his foibles, and they were many, Joseph Wilfred PARKINS was not without his merits; he went out to India a poor boy, he returned a wealthy man, and, with all his whimsicalities, he was not unmindful of the interests of the poor.'[271]

Parkins wrote his will on 6 March 1840, leaving his entire estate to Mr. George Best. The estate was worth £25,000 with a small freehold estate in Workington in Cumberland as well as unspecified property in France. In 1842 his family in Carlisle contested the will but after much consideration the decision of the judge went against them.[272]

There is no record that his body ever returned to Carlisle.

Thomas Hornor's health and finances did not improve after his encounter with Parkins nor did he ever visit Rowland Stephenson. He died by the roadside in New York on 14 March 1844 and was buried in the Friend's burial ground in the city. Thomas Hornor is forgotten now but there has been some interest in the work he performed in Wales before returning to London and his ill fated London Panorama. His biographer summed him up as 'a supreme example of misdirected genius'.[273]

The Colosseum was finally finished in 1831 and visitors could enjoy to the full the sight of his panorama as well as the other 'delights' on offer. The building changed hands and was refurbished frequently but proprietors failed to make it pay and the building and its contents were auctioned in 1868. There were no bidders for the panorama and it was sent to America for display on Broadway but was soon discarded and lost. The Colosseum was demolished in 1875, less than 50 years after it was built, and the site was eventually replaced by the Royal College of Physicians.

The builder of the Colosseum, Henry Peto, died on 15 September 1830. The court case to recover his £28,738 from Remington's was continued in his name by his nephews, Thomas Grissell and Samuel Morton Peto and a little money was recovered from the estate of Rowland Stephenson. They also inherited the building business which was renamed Grissell and Peto and became well known for their work in London throughout the nineteenth century.

Decimus Burtonn whose extravagant design for the Colosseum was the undoing of the enterprise, prospered of course. Amongst many projects all over England and Ireland he designed Hyde Park, a number of triumphal arches, the giraffe house at London Zoo, and the layout of Kew Gardens which included the largest greenhouse in the world, 363 feet long, 100 feet wide and 66 feet high. He died, unmarried, on 14 December 1881 in St. Leonard's-on-Sea where he had designed the layout of the town. He left £63,000.

Thomas Welch was never pursued by the authorities for his part in the escape of Rowland Stephenson. He continued to manage the Argyle rooms until 5 February 1832 when fire broke out in the auditorium and the rooms were burnt to the ground.[274] After this he gave up the idea of a concert hall and instead erected six shops, which were later, replaced by the premises of Messrs. Dickens and Jones. Thomas Welch died in 1848 at the age of 67.

Ruin came fast and furiously upon the builder Robert Wright. Bankruptcy was announced on 6 January 1829 and, by March, Mr. Shuttleworth had sold his premises and all his possessions. Wright paid dearly for the promissory notes with which he had furnished his good friend.[275]

The remaining partners at the bank had been declared bankrupt but all their estates paid 20 shillings in the pound. William Remington rounded up the administration of the bank and continued to put up with caustic letters from Joseph Parkins. David Remington lived in Montague Square with his wife Martha and five children. His occupation is recorded as 'Gentleman' in the 1841 census and 'Stockbroker' in 1851. He died in 1854, aged 71.

Joseph Toulmin never recovered his health after the collapse of the bank and had to sell his house on Clapham Common and move to a small house in Clapham High Street where he died in 1839. His cause of death is recorded simply as 'Brain Disease'.

Henry Stephenson who had been severely criticised by the Commission, lost his home above the bank and went to live at the family house at Farley Hill. His wife died in 1835 and the 1841 census reveals him living with his only child, Henry James, aged 14, and his occupation recorded as 'farmer'. He died in March the following year, aged 42.

William Walter Stephenson, who had nearly caught up with Rowland at Clovelly, rose to the rank of Major in the British army, had six children and died in 1874, aged 81.

Rowland Stephenson, the cousin of the dapper little banker and younger brother of Mary Eliza, played little part in the story. In 1834 to satisfy the conditions of a will of which he was the beneficiary he took the surname and arms of Standish and was now known as Orlando Standish rather than the more notorious Rowland Stephenson. Orlando Standish went to Florence and was not heard of in this country until the Times announced his death on 14 April 1843.[276]

Ellis Reeve continued trading as a stockbroker and also lived in Montague Square where he is recorded as residing in 1841. He died in 1871 aged 79.

Kitty Stephens continued to perform all the leading roles in London and the provinces until her voice became weakened and she wisely retired in 1835, aged 41. Having been described in the press as a 'meritorious spinster' she surprised everyone on 14 April 1838 by marrying George Capel-Conningsby, 5th Earl of Essex.[277] He was eighty and had lost his wife three months earlier. He died the following year and as Lady Catherine Capel-Coningsbury, Countess of Essex, she continued to live quietly at 9, Belgrave Square, the house in which she had been married by special license. She died of bronchitis on 22 February 1882, leaving an estate valued at more than £70,000.

The London Life Assurance Company survived the loss of its exchequer bills. In 1831 it moved to new offices at 81 King William Street, and stayed there for 130 years and adopted the logo of Dick Whittington and his cat. The company grew steadily and in 1918 took over the Clergy Mutual Assurance and in 1928 the Metropolitan Life Assurance. In 1981 it relocated to Bristol and merged with the AMP Group in 1989.

Saint Bartholomew's Hospital of course survived the loss of its exchequer bills. It also kept the money that had been hastily withdrawn on the Saturday morning.

In November 1963, knowing nothing of the events of 1828, I entered the medical school of Saint Bartholomew's Hospital. Their errant treasurer, Rowland Stephenson, my mother's grandfather's grandfather, was long forgotten.

The Gloucester Hotel in Bristol was demolished 1887 but the Lamplighters Hotel still stands and remains a public house at the water's edge in Shirehampton. Pill lost its trade when the ferry to Shirehampton closed with the coming of the Avon Bridge and mud swallowed up many of the slipways.

The Kings Arms, Clovelly is long gone.

Tybee Island, off Savannah, where Rowland was unceremoniously tossed into the bottom of the sailing boat to be taken to New York, was made famous in 1958 when a U.S. Air Force B-47 jettisoned a Mark 15 hydrogen bomb off the coast. It was never found but the Air Force claimed the 'Tybee bomb' lacked a nuclear warhead and posed no threat, as they might.

The estate lands of Marshalls were sold in 1924 for new homes and the house itself pulled down in 1960. It was described by the local paper, at the time as 'not of historical or architectural value'.[278] All that remains of the days of Rowland Stephenson is the small lake that lies just to the north of the A118, east of Romford centre.

The house at Farley Hill in Berkshire remains as handsome as it ever was, now known as Farley Hall.

The family house at 41 Queen Square fared less well. In 1836

> This once handsome mansion is now literally a dangerous ruin. In the front there is not a single sound square of glass; even some portion of the window frames is mouldering away; the ironwork of a handsome flight of steps has been carried away piecemeal, the stone work having been completely torn up in the effort. A long succession of winters has rendered the roof so pervious to the weather that the floors from top to bottom are saturated with rain-water, and the splendid ceilings are fast dropping away. Into what hands the property may ultimately fall it must be pulled down and rebuilt. The father of Rowland Stephenson, the banker, was the last occupant.[279]

Rebuilt it was and became the Italian Hospital that still stands in the corner of Queen Square.

Dilapidated Marshalls being demolished, 1960

Captain John Myers remained at sea for many years and captained a ship named the Grace Brown, which took immigrants from Europe to America, sailing out of Baltimore.[280] He was in Liverpool on 3 May 3rd at a meeting of American sea captains to commemorate the sudden death of the American President General Harrison whose presidential inauguration speech was very long but his presidency very short, 30 days, 12 hours and 32 minutes.[281]

Rowland Macdonald Stephenson recovered from the trauma of Christmas 1828 and without formal training he began a second career as an engineer and entrepreneur. The Stephenson family in the past had prospered in India so that is where he went and he too did well. In 1840 he married Marianne Hederstelt, daughter of Lieutenant Edward Hedersterdt of the Royal Navy. In the same year he became secretary of the short-lived rival to the P&O Company, the East Indian Steam Navigation Company but his heart was in railways. He conceived it possible to 'girdle the world with an iron chain, to connect Europe and Asia from their furthest extremities by one colossal Railway and to connect so much of the two continents as should enable a locomotive to travel from Calcutta to London with but two breaks, one at the Straits of Dover, and one at the Dardanelles'.[282] He was the founder and managing director of the East India Railway Company and was described as the 'outstanding pioneer of Indian Railways'.[283] His vision in India was from the start not just a single line between the two great cities of Calcutta and Delhi but he outlined six major lines comprising a network of five thousand miles of track. In 1851 the construction of the first railway line began between Calcutta and Raniganj which eventually reached Delhi and was opened in early 1855. In 1867 he was knighted by Queen Victoria for services to Indian Railways. He also found time to patent machinery for shifting stage scenery.

Rowland Macdonald returned to America once more in 1837, to replenish his father's dwindling resources and brought him some of the family portraits and mementoes of his mother. He later retired to Tunbridge Wells and died there on 20 November 1895, aged 87.

A little is known of Rowland's other six children. Frank Hall was a civil servant and died in 1868 at St. James, Westminster and James Owen died in 1886 in Staffordshire while Cecil Mackintosh who worked for East India Railway Company with Rowland Macdonald, died in 1875 in India. Nothing is known of Edward John or Robert Musgrave, but it is assumed they too went to India. His last-born and only daughter, Emma Louise, married on 15 March 1851 Siegerich Christopher Kreeft – Consul for the Grand Duke of Mecklenburgh Schwerin.[284]

The marriage of Rowland Macdonald to Marianne Hederstelt produced nine children, six girls and three boys. The eldest son was Rowland Macdonald who was born in Madras in 1847 and, like his father, worked in India. His oldest son was Rowland as was this Rowland's son who too had a son born in 1969 and that was the end of the line of Rowland Stephensons.

James Harman Lloyd, left behind at the house of Dr. Garbutt in Effingham County, returned to Savannah where his evidence convicted two of the kidnappers. From there he found his way to the town of Clarke, Georgia, where he appears on the census in 1830. On 12 January 1833 he married Julia Tanner (born 1813 in Clarke County). Nothing more is to be found of the enigmatic James Harman Lloyd or his descendants. It is not known whether Rowland and James ever met again. They almost certainly did not.

And what happened to Rowland Stephenson himself? He never returned to England nor did he ever see his other children again. After his release from New York City Jail in 1834 he returned to his quiet life at Farley. On 18 March 1844 he applied for American citizenship through the Pennsylvania Supreme Declaration of Intent Court and took the Oath of Allegiance on Friday, 8 September 1848.[285]

Paul Bangay at the grave of Rowland Stephenson in Bristol PA — after some excavation to find the inscription.

Shortly after this he began to extend the estate of Farley by buying strips of land to the north and west. He bought eight separate small lots from his neighbours, costing in all about $3,000. Why he bought more land is unknown but perhaps it was out of habit.[286]

The census of September 1850 reveals that Rowland, now aged 72, was living at Farley and at the same address was Rosanna Conily, aged 45, who is recorded as born in Pennsylvania. Rowland certainly never married again and this lady was probably his housekeeper since he left her nothing in his will.

The Bucks County Intelligencer on 4 July 1856 contained this notice:

DEATHS

In Bristol, on Wednesday evening, the 2nd instant Rowland Stephenson, aged about 76 years. The deceased was formerly an English banker. He removed to this country a long time since and settled at Bristol, in this county. He was universally esteemed for his benevolence and kindness to the poor and distressed.[287]

It was indeed a long time since he had removed to America and in England the only notice of his death was his name hidden amongst the list of deceased at the Court of Probate two years later on 18 May 1858.[288] The records of St. James Episcopal Church in Bristol reveal that he was a member of the church and is buried in the churchyard. Three years later his American home of Farley was destroyed by fire.[289]

His will was recorded on 25 April 1856 in Bucks County Will Book 14, page 95. He instructed his executors to sell the household goods and settle his debts and the remaining money he left to his son Rowland Macdonald 'and I further direct my executors to send to my said son the portraits, pictures, scrap books, card boxes, painted by my mother, painted screens and guns. If Rowland Macdonald should die before me, the property is to be as near as can be equally divided among my remaining children'.[290]

The will was proved 16 July 1856 and an inventory of his goods, chattels, rights and credits was made. His household contents were valued at $13,689.94. There was no Elegant and Valuable Household Furniture as sold by Mr. Shuttleworth but items such as 'a kitchen table valued at $12, iron bedstead $5, and towel rail $1.50'.[291] The bulk of the value was stock in the Camden and Amboy Railroad Co. of New Jersey, amounting to $11,300.

His final expenses revealed that he was attended by two doctors, Dr Phillips who was paid $207 and Dr. Smith $50. Reverent William Perkins held the service, $5; William Scott dug the grave, $5, and John Horn made the coffin, $20. Another doctor, Dr. Malone's medical bill was $100 but included 'provision of tombstone'.

Such were the paltry sums for a man who was accustomed to shuffle thousands before breakfast.

EPILOGUE

O N SATURDAY 24 DECEMBER 1892 Sir Rowland Macdonald
Stephenson, son of Rowland Stephenson, and now 84 years old, walked
into the office of Holmfield, Rusthall & Co. Solicitors in Tunbridge Wells. He
handed over a letter addressed to one of the partners, Mr Morton Latham.
Why the letter was delivered 64 years after the events and ten months after it
was written is unclear. With the letter was a package of correspondence to be
kept for safe keeping,

Dear Morton

The enclosed copies of letters from J.H. Lloyd to Lady Owen, then Miss
Mary Frances Stephenson, my mother's sister, were copied by her and sent
to me in 1829. Remembering Mr. Lloyd and the implicit confidence placed
in him I believe that his statement is strictly correct but that it would be
unavailing to remove the impression entertained at the time.

On the night of their leaving London my father was scarcely in his right
mind, and bewildered. He had no money or clothes except the few we
packed hastily for him as Mr Lloyd said it was imperative that they must
leave. My father was unable to do anything or to give any assistance or
information. He was taken away by Mr. Lloyd. M. Hornor was the artist
who painted the Panorama of London from the top of St Paul's for the
Colosseum. My father assisted him greatly but Mr Lloyd appears to have
made heavy advances without my father's knowledge. My father lived very
quietly in the country without any extravagant tastes, always at his post,
and had no idea or apprehension of the bank failure until Lloyd made his
communication. The bank had prospered for 100 years 1728–1828. He
had no London House but one was provided for him at St. Bartholomew's
Hospital of which he was treasurer. My father had no money when he was
taken away and was supported until his death by his children.

Signed R.M.Stephenson, February 16th 1892

The package of papers reads thus:

Clovelly January 2nd 1829

To Miss Mary Stephenson

Queens Square, London

Dear Miss Stephenson

Seeing a paragraph in the Barnstaple newspaper today I feel called upon to
make the following declaration. I herby declare that the imputations against
Mr Rowland Stephenson relative to his having left England with a large sum
of money are utterly false and further I declare that his having withdrawn
Exchequer Bills from the house is equally untrue, the apparent deficiency
of money is fully explained in as much that there were various cheques left
for the amount and had only to be debited the respective accounts. I further
declare that Rowland Stephenson has not withdrawn nor has he possession
of any exchequer bill or other security whatever of any description.

   The above I assert from my own Knowledge. I have had Mr. Stephenson
confidence many years and in exchange and custody of various Exchequer
Bills my speculations have obliged me to have recourse to the temporary
use of some of these and moreover I am confident that had no run taken
place on the firm that in one fortnight from Christmas all would have been
reinstated. I further declare that Rowland Stephenson was not privy to any
set of defalcation or alteration until Friday morning December 26th 1828.

J.H. Lloyd

* * *

At Sea 21st January 1829

To Miss Mary Stephenson

Queen Square, London

Madam

From the moment of leaving the English shore I have endeavoured to
bring my mind into a more quiet state and will to the utmost of my power
explain every circumstance that has taken place from the time of my having
Rowland Stephenson's confidence and I think trust and hope that the
explanation will satisfy any unprejudiced mind that Mr Stephenson ought

not to be a sufferer, nor should he, as he did by my advice, have left his own country. The circumstances as nearly as my recollection goes are thus-

Whenever Mr. Stephenson made a purchase of foreign or any other security they were either put into my name or handed over to me according to the nature of them and payment was accordingly made for him by me. I had always sent to him a statement of the Balances and whatever was at the bank every evening either in Town or Country and sometimes when he thought the balance low he would give me a blank book cheque to fill up previous to his being in Town on the following morning and when he has gone out for a day on his shooting or other amusements he would leave several blank bank cheques with me which were to be used as occasion required. Mr. Stephenson was almost without exception gainer by his purchases indeed in almost everything that he embarked in although never to any great amount. As trustee he never mixed up the Exchequer Bills or India Bonds with those of the general customers but kept them apart giving me the charge of them for exchanging, receiving the interest etc. Finding Mr. Stephenson so fortunate and knowing the broker he employed and having frequently taken down orders to him from Mr. Stephenson I was induced to try a little for myself knowing that the broker could not know but the instructions were from and on account of Mr Stephenson. Unluckily for me at one period I had invested between £16,000 and £20,000 and the result of the speculation was just the reverse of what I calculated upon. This first instance obliged me to have resource to the floating securities with which I had been entrusted and from that time continually have I had to apply to the same means of straightening the accounts all the time of the pressure for Bank notes being still short and finding great difficulties of borrowing on securities (English or Foreign) in the Stock Exchange to make up what was supposed to be at the bank I was obliged to have resource to the expedient of asking Mr. Stephenson to raise money on Exchequer Bills among private friends and that he did on Sunday or Monday following the run on the House at the same time not knowing until Friday morning that they were the property of Individual customers of the house.

It may be said how could Mr. Stephenson say there was no money at the bank a few days previous to Christmas. The answer is this; I had filled up the cheques and he did not know any otherwise than what I told him. I solemnly swear that Mr. Stephenson never while in England was aware of the advances not a tenth part that had been made to Mr. Hornor and when I told him the foreign funds of his friend Mr J.A. Fauntleroy had been sunk in the speculations his distress and dismay may be more easily imagined than described. The interest had always been regularly credited to his account at the usual period of its becoming due and he had given me the key of Mr. F's box for the purpose of receiving the interest quarterly. In making this declaration I feel that I have only done an act of justice to my best of friends and shall have woefully for his sake as well as my own to lament that he ever made me an object of his confidence.

Had it been otherwise he might have still been in the midst of his family and I in a situation to have lived and enjoyed what I believe I always had the good opinion of my employers generally in Lombard Street.

J.H. Lloyd

As Rowland Stephenson said to Joseph Parkins when they met in the debtors prison in March 1829:

'Hear my story – don't condemn me yet. I solemnly declare I am not the guilty man you suppose me.'

ENDNOTES

CHAPTER 1

1   National Archives, Kew.
     T1/546/153–158 and T/543/13–
     16

CHAPTER 2

2   Cecil D., *The Young Melbourne.*
     Constable and Company 1939

3   Ibid

4   Dirks, Nicholas. *The Hollow Crown:*
     Ethnohistory of an Indian Kingdom.
     University of Michigan Press, 1993.

5   White, W. Notes and Queries.
     Oxford University Press 1905

6   National Archives Currency
     converter

7   Roger Ekirch, A. *Bound for*
     America: The Transportation of British
     Convicts to The Colonies 1718–1775.
     Clarendon Press, Oxford. 1987

8   *The Times Newspaper* 13th April 1790

9   Kassler, Michael. *The English Bach*
     Awakening. Ashgate 2004

10   Ibid

11   Ibid

12   Horn, Charles Edward. *Charles*
     Edward Horn's memoirs of his father and
     himself. Ashgate Publishing Ltd.,
     2003. Horn's memoirs

13   Ibid

14   Ibid

15   Pevsner, Nicholaus. *The Buildings*
     of England: Essex. Harmondsworth:
     Penguin Books 1954

16   *The Saturday Review, 16 (1863)*

17   Lennox, William Pitt. *Fifty Years of*
     Biographical Reminiscences. Hurst and
     Blackett, 1864

CHAPTER 3

18   *The Times Newspaper* 7th January
     1829

19   Hansard, T.C. *House of Commons List*
     of M.P.s

20   *Royal Cornwall Gazette* 29th March
     1823

21   *The West Briton Newspaper (Truro)* 21st
     March 1823

22   *John Bull* J, 31st March 1823

23   Robbins, Alfred Farthing.
     Launceston, past and present: A
     Historical and Descriptive Sketch.
     Weighell, 1888

24   Ibid

25   *The Essex Herald* 23rd January 1829

26   *The Times Newspaper* 13th May 1823

27   *The Essex Herald* 26th June 1823

Chapter 4

28 Private correspondence from
    Archivist St. Bartholomew's
    Hospital, 1969

29 Ibid

30 *Biography of the British Stage.*
    Sherwood Jones and Co 1824)

31 *Quarterly Musical Magazine, 3.* 1821

32 Ibid

33 Ibid

34 *The Edinburgh Advertiser* 16th
    February 1824

35 *The Edinburgh Advertiser* 23rd
    February 1824

36 Ibid

37 *The Edinburgh Advertiser* 9th January
    1829

38 Marsh, Charles. *The Clubs of London:
    With Anecdotes of Their Members,
    Sketches of Character, and Conversation.*
    H. Colbur, 1828.

39 Ibid

40 Joseph Davey, Proceedings of the
    Old Bailey Ref: t17831210-140

41 Bleachley, Horace. *Some
    Distinguished Victims of the Scaffold*
    (London 1905), 189

42 Joseph Hunton, Proceedings of the
    Old Bailey: Ref: t18281023-269

Chapter 5

43 *The Times Newspaper* 9th January
    1829

44 R. N. Hyde, 'Thomas Hornor:
    Pictural Land Surveyor', *Imago
    Mundi*, 29 (1977)

45 National Archive, Kew, Ref
    B3.4342-B3.4349, Friday 4th March
    1831 Evidence of Edward Gardner
    At the Court of Commissioners of
    Bankrupts

46 Ibid

Chapter 6

All dialogue and quotes from proceedings
of court of bankruptcy, unless otherwise
cited, are from The National Archives,
Kew. Ref: B3.4342-B3.4349

47 *The Times Newspaper* 23rd September
    1829

48 *The Morning Chronicle* 29th
    December 1828

49 *The Times Newspaper* 4th January
    1829

50 *The Courier Newspaper* 10th January
    1829

51 Ibid

52 Ibid

Chapter 7

All dialogue and quotes from proceedings
of court of bankruptcy, unless otherwise
cited, are from The National Archives,
Kew. Ref: B3.4342-B3.4349

53 William John. *The History of
    Banking,* 1850

54 *Cobbett's Weekly Political Register* 3rd
    January 1829.

Chapter 8

All dialogue and quotes from proceedings of court of bankruptcy, unless
otherwise cited, are from The National
Archives, Kew. Ref: B3.4342-B3.4349

55 *The English Chronicle Newspaper* 14th
    January 1829

56 Hilton Price, Frederick George,
    *Handbook of London Bankers; with some
    account of their* predecessors 1876

57 *The Times Newspaper* 1st January
    1829.

58 Lennox, William Pitt. *Fifty Years of
    Biographical Reminiscences.* Hurst and
    Blackett, 1864

59 *The West Briton (Truro)* 21st March 1823

CHAPTER 9

All dialogue and quotes from proceedings of court of bankruptcy, unless otherwise cited, are from The National Archives, Kew. Ref: B3.4342-B3.4349

60 *The English Chronicle* 10th January 1829

61 National Archives Currency converter

62 *The Times Newspaper* 23rd October 1829

CHAPTER 10

All dialogue and quotes from proceedings of court of bankruptcy, unless otherwise cited, are from The National Archives, Kew. Ref: B3.4342-B3.4349

63 *The Times Newspaper* 3rd August 1829

64 Ibid

65 *TheMorning Chronicle* 3rd June 1829

66 National Archives Currency converter

67 *The Times Newspaper* 30th December 1828

CHAPTER 11

68 Briggs, Vernon. *Cabot Genealogy*, Boston 1927

69 F.Jollie, F. *A Political history of the city of Carlisle*. Jollie 1820

70 Ferguson, Richard Saul. *Cumberland and Westmorland M.P.s from the Restoration to the Reform Bill of 1867*. Bell & Daldy, 1871

71 Ibid

72 *The Times Newspaper* 25th June 1819.

73 *The Times Newspaper* 29th September1819

74 *The Times Newspaper* 30th September 1819

75 Hunt, Henry. *Memoirs of Henry Hunt, Esq., written by himself in his majesty's jail at Ilchester,* 3 vols. Chivers, 1822

76 *The Times Newspaper* 30th September 1819

77 *The Times Newspaper* 15th October 1819

78 *The Times Newspaper* 22nd October 1819

79 *The Times Newspaper* 29th October 1819

80 Ibid

81 *The Times Newspaper* 20th January 1820.

82 Captain Hayes, *Points of the Horse*. W. Thacker & Co., 1897

83 *The Times Newspaper* 7th February 1820.

84 *The Times Newspaper,* 28th April 1820

85 *The Times Newspaper* 21st October 1820

86 Papers of Thomas Serres reproduced in Anecdotes of Impudence. 1827

87 *The Times Newspaper* 14th March *1822*

88 *The Times Newspaper* 15th August 1823

89 *The Times Newspaper* 3rd August 1822

90 Ibid

91 Richardson, Thomas. *Churchyard gleanings, or, collection of epitaphs and monumental inscriptions*. Richardson 1838.

92 Bean, W. W. *The Parliamentary Representation of the Six Northern Counties of England*. Barnwell, 1896

93 Bleackley, Horace. *Some Distinguished Victims of the Scaffold*. London 1905

CHAPTER 12

94   *The Courier* 9th January 1829
95   *The Times Newspaper* 30th December 1828
96   *The English Chronicle* 8th January 1829
97   *The Courier* 9th January 1829
98   *The Morning Herald* 7th January 1829.
99   *The English Chronicle* 20th January 1829
100   *The North Devon Journal* 1st January 1829
101   Ibid

CHAPTER 13

102   *The English Chronicle Newspaper* 11th January 1829
103   Griffiths, Arthur. M*ysteries of Police and Crime; a general survey of wrongdoing.* London 1899
104   *The Times Newspaper* 7th January 1829
105   *The English Chronicle Newspaper* 9th January 1829
106   *The Times Newspaper* 7th January 1829
107   *The English Chronicle Newspaper* 9th January 1829
108   *The English Chronicle Newspaper* 11th January 1829
109   Ibid
110   *The Times Newspaper* 30th December 1829
111   *The English Chronicle Newspaper* 30th December 1828
112   *The Morning Herald* 5th January 1829
113   *The Times Newspaper* 1st January 1829
114   *The Times Newspaper* 7th January 1829
115   *The Morning Herald* 5th January 1829
116   *The Times Newspaper* 30th December 1828

117   *The Edinburgh Advertiser* 23rd January 1829.
118   *The Times Newspaper* 2nd January 1829
119   *The Times Newspaper* 5th January 1829
120   Ibid
121   *The Times Newspaper* 3rd January 1829
122   The National Archives, Kew. Ref: B3.4342-B3.4349
123   Ibid
124   *The Times Newspaper* 3rd January 1829
125   Ibid
126   *The Times Newspaper,* 5th January 1829
127   *The Morning Herald* 7th January 1829
128   The National Archives, Kew. Ref: B3.4342-B3.4349
129   *The English Chronicle* 11th January 1829
130   *Woolmer's Exeter and Plymouth Gazette* 7th January 1829
131   *The English Chronicle* 9th January 1829
132   Ibid
133   The National Archives, Kew. Ref: B3.4342-B3.4349
134   Ibid
135   Ibid
136   Ibid
137   *The Exeter Flying Post* 15th January 1829
138   *The English Chronicle* 20th January 1829
139   Ibid
140   Ibid
141   *The Times Newspaper* 20th January 1829
142   The National Archives, Kew. Ref: B3.4342-B3.4349

CHAPTER 14

143 *The Times Newspaper* 10th January 1829

144 *The Times Newspaper* 9th January 1829

145 *The Times Newspaper* 4th January 1829

146 *The English Chronicle* 10th January 1829

147 Ibid

148 *The Times Newspaper* 31st December 1828.

149 *The Times Newspaper* 14th January 1829

150 *The London Literary Gazette* 9th January 1829

151 *The Times newspaper* 8th August 1829

152 *The New York American* 4th June 1829

153 *The English Chronicle* 10th January1829

154 *The Times Newspaper* 21st January 1829

155 Proceedings of the Old Bailey Ref: t18290115-143

156 *The English Chronicle* 17th January 1829

157 *The Morning Herald* 17th January 1829

158 *The Times Newspaper* 17th January 1829

159 Ibid

160 Ibid

161 *The Times Newspaper* 19th January 1829

162 *The Times Newspaper* 14th February 1829

163 Ibid

164 *The Times Newspaper* 20th June 1829

165 *The Times Newspaper* 10 February 1829

166 Ibid

167 *The English Courier* 10th February 1829

168 *The Morning Herald* 1st February1829

169 *The Morning Herald* 30th January 1829

170 *The Times Newspaper* 20th January 1829

171 *The Times Newspaper* 5th February 1829

172 *The English Chronicle* 9th January 1829

173 *The Times Newspaper* 9th February 1829

174 *The Times Newspaper* 10th February 1829

175 Ibid

176 *The Times Newspaper* 26th March 1829

177 *The English Chronicle* 11th March 1829

178 *The Times Newspaper* 19th March 1829

179 *The Times Newspaper* 23rd June 1829

180 *The Times Newspaper* 30th June 1829

CHAPTER 15

181 *The Times Newspaper* 14th April 1829

182 Fennimore Cooper, James. *Letter XIX :A Residence in France.* 1829

183 *The Times Newspaper* 14th April 1829

184 *The Daily Georgian* 3rd March 1829

185 *The Daily Georgian* 4th March 1829

186 Ibid

187 *An Abridged Correspondance between J.W. Parkins and his late bankers Messrs. Remington, Stephenson & Co.* 1835

188 *The Observer Newspaper* 12th April 1829

189 *The Richmond Enquirer* 24th March 1829

190 Ibid

191 The National Archives. A letter from Consular general to the Earl of Aberdeen

Chapter 16

192 *The New York Times* 10th January 1892

193 *The New York Journal* of Commerce 20th March 1829

194 *The New York Gazette* 18th March 1829

195 *The Times Newspaper* 22nd April 1829

196 Ibid

197 *The Baltimore Patriot* 21st March 1829

198 *The Connecticut Mirror* 28th March 1829

199 *The Times Newspaper* 29th April 1829

200 *The New York Enquirer* 18th March 1829

201 *The New York Gazette* 18th March 1829

202 *The New York Enquirer* 18th March 1829

203 *The Eastern Argos* 24th March 1829

204 *The New York Gazette* 18th March 1829

205 *The New York Herald* 18th March 1829

206 *The Times Newspaper* 10th April 1829

207 *The New York Herald* 18th March 1829

208 *The New York Journal of Commerce* 18th March 1829

209 *The New York Herald* 18th March 1829

210 *The New York Herald* 20th March 1829

211 Ibid

212 *The New York Herald* 20th March 1829

213 Ibid

214 *The Richmond Enquirer* 24th March 1829

215 *The New York Herald* 20th March 1829

216 *An Abridged Correspondance between J.W. Parkins and his late bankers Messrs. Remington, Stephenson & Co.* Publisher S N 1835

217 *The Engish Chronicle* 11th April 1829

218 *The English Chronicle* 23rd April 1829

219 *An Abridged Correspondance between J.W. Parkins and his late bankers Messrs. Remington, Stephenson & Co.* Publisher S N 1835

220 *The Richmond Enquirer* 31st March 1829

221 *The New York Herald* 31st March 1829

Chapter 17

222 Myers, John. *The Life, Voyages and Travels of Capt. John Myers*: Longman, Hurst, Rees and Co. and John Bolster, Cork, 1817

223 Gifford, Edward. *Deeds of Naval Daring or Anecdotes of the British Navy.* John Murray 1867

224 Ibid

225 Myers, John. *The Life, Voyages and Travels of Capt. John Myers*: Longman, Hurst, Rees and Co. and John Bolster, Cork, 1817

226 *An Abridged Correspondance between J.W. Parkins and his late bankers Messrs. Remington, Stephenson & Co.* Publisher S N 1835

227 The Proceedings of the Old Bailey Ref: t18190217-6

228 *The Dublin Patriot* 24th May 1820

229 *The Times Newspaper* 4th September 1824

230 Ibid

231 Ibid

232 Blunt, Joseph, *The American Annual Register* 23rd November 1829

233 Travelling through Bensalem 1692–1984 compiled by the Historical society of the Bensalem Township History Book Committee (1984)

234 *Bucks County Deed Book* 54 Vol 1 Page 272

235 *The New York Times* 18th June 1829

236 Ibid

237 *House of Commons Journal 4th February 1830 and Hansard's Parliamentary debates of the House of Commons.*

238 King George III (Act 32 Geo3 c144)

239 *Original letters and Correspondance Of Abijar Mann and others to J.W.Parkins, Ex-sheriff of London* Published 1938 Stanley and Monk, New York

240 Ibid

241 Bucks County Criminal Docket 1810–1836, September Sessions 1830, p.435

242 *The Times Newspaper* 17th June 1831 citing Baltimore Patriot

243 *The Times Newspaper* 15th May 1833

244 Ibid

245 Extraordinary Proceedings at the City Hall New York, commenced May 21st and continued, by adjournments to June 17th 1833

246 *The New York Herald* 17th August 1833

247 Fibberton, George. *Travels in America.* Green 1833

248 *The New York Herald* 28th August 1833

249 Ibid

250 *An Abridged Correspondence between J.W. Parkins and his late bankers Messrs. Remington, Stephenson & Co.* Publisher S N 1835

251 *The Times Newspaper* 17th June 1833

252 *An Abridged Correspondence between J.W. Parkins and his late bankers Messrs. Remington, Stephenson & Co.* Publisher S N 1835

253 *The Times Newspaper* 18th June 1834

254 Fibberton, George. Travels in America. Green 1833

255 Ibid

256 *An Abridged Correspondence between J.W. Parkins and his late bankers Messrs. Remington, Stephenson & Co.* Publisher S N 1835

257 Ibid

258 Ibid

259 Abdy, E. S. A *Residence and Tour in The United States of North America.* John Murray London 1935

260 Ibid

261 *The Commercial Advertise New York.* 7th December 1833

CHAPTER 18

262 *The New York Times* 18th August 1834

263 *The Times Newspaper* 14th August 1837

264 *The Times Newspaper* 18th August 1837

265 Ibid

266 *Original letters and Correspondance Of Abijar Mann and others to J.W.Parkins, Ex-sheriff of London* Published 1938 Stanley and Monk, New York

267 *Abridged Correspondence between J.W. Parkins and his late bankers Messrs. Remington, Stephenson & Co.* Publisher S N 1835

268 *The Newport Mercury* 5th May 1836

269 *The Times Newspaper* 17th October 1839

270 *The Gentleman's Magazine* November 1840

271 *The Times Newspaper* 23th May1840

272 *The Times Newspaper* 4th December 1843

273 Hyde, R. N. *Thomas Hornor: Pictorial Land Surveyor'*, Imago Mundi 1977

274 *The Morning Herald* 5th February 1832

275 *London Gazette* 6th January 1829

276 *The Times Newspaper* 17th April 1843

277 *The English Gazette* 15th April 1838

278 *The Romford Times* 23rd June1960

279 *The Times Newspaper* 13th October 1836

280 Immigrant ships Transcribers Guild 18th September 1846

281 *The Times Newspapers*, 3rd May 1841

282 *The Calcutta Review* 1856

283 Thorner, Daniel. *Investment in Empire*, Chicago 1977

284 *The Times Newspaper* 15th March 1851

285 United States, Work Projects Administration. *Index to records of Aliens' Declarations of intentions and / or Oaths of Allegiance*, (1789–1880)

286 Bucks County Land Registry, Borough of Bristol P.A.

287 *The Bucks County Intelligence* 4th July 1856

288 *The Times Newspaper* 18th May 1858.

289 *The Bucks County Intelligence* 23rd April 1859

290 *Will Book, Bristol PA*. Book Number 14 Page 95

291 Inventory of Goods and chattels of Rowland Stephenson, late of the borough of Bristol, PA Register No. 4 Page 264

EPILOGUE

All letters in private collection

INDEX